W9-APU-785

TRIUMPH
B O O K S

NICKLAS LIDSTROM

THE PURSUIT of PERFECTION

Nicklas Lidstrom
with Gunnar Nordstrom and Bob Duff

TRIUMPH
BOOKS

Copyright © 2019 by Nicklas Lidstrom, Gunnar Nordstrom, and Bob Duff

First Triumph Books paperback edition 2020

No part of this publication may be reproduced, stored in a retrieval system, or transmitted in any form by any means, electronic, mechanical, photocopying, or otherwise, without the prior written permission of the publisher, Triumph Books LLC, 814 North Franklin Street, Chicago, Illinois 60610.

The Library of Congress has catlogued the hardcover version as follows:

Names: Lidstrom, Nicklas, 1970- author. | Nordström, Gunnar, 1953– author.
  | Duff, Bob, author.
Title: Nicklas Lidstrom : the pursuit of perfection / Nicklas Lidstrom with
  Gunnar Nordstrom and Bob Duff.
Identifiers: LCCN 2019018751 | ISBN 9781629375359
Subjects: LCSH: Lidstrom, Nicklas, 1970– | Detroit Red Wings (Hockey team)
  | Hockey players—Sweden—Biography.
Classification: LCC GV848.5.L55 A3 2020 | DDC 796.962092 [B]—dc23
LC record available at https://lccn.loc.gov/2019018751

This book is available in quantity at special discounts for your group or organization. For further information, contact:
Triumph Books LLC
814 North Franklin Street
Chicago, Illinois 60610
(312) 337-0747
www.triumphbooks.com

Printed in U.S.A.
ISBN: 978-1-62937-839-8
Design by Patricia Frey
Title page photo courtesy of Getty Images
Photos courtesy of Nicklas Lidstrom unless otherwise indicated

CONTENTS

Author's Note   vii

1. The Perfect Human   3

2. The Best Draft of Them All   23

3. Heartbreak in Hockeytown   45

4. The Cup Finally Arrives   65

5. Norris Nick   97

6. A Generational Talent   117

7. The Greatest Team   141

8. The Golden Goal   165

9. A Historic Captaincy   191

10. One More Cup   211

11. Soaring to the Finish   229

12. The Ultimate Honor   249

Appendix: Nick by the Numbers   273

Acknowledgments   277

AUTHOR'S NOTE

Writing a book about my life and hockey career was an intriguing idea when it was presented to me by a Swedish publishing company a couple of years ago.

There were a lot of stories to be told and I wanted to incorporate the thoughts and memories from teammates, coaches, friends, and opponents. I was curious to hear how they saw me and the way I played my game. That called for a co-writer, and I immediately had one person in mind: Swedish hockey journalist Gunnar Nordstrom. He had followed my whole journey, from playing for the Swedish national team in the 1991 Canada Cup to Detroit and all the Stanley Cup runs with the Red Wings. Based in Los Angeles for more than 20 years, Gunnar had access to everybody from Scotty Bowman to Wayne Gretzky to Sidney Crosby, among many others.

I trusted Gunnar and longtime NHL writer Bob Duff, who also followed much of my career, to faithfully tell my story, and I have been very involved all along the way. I couldn't be more pleased with the result.

—Nicklas Lidstrom

NICKLAS LIDSTROM

1
THE PERFECT HUMAN

THE PERFECT HUMAN. ON THE SURFACE, IT SEEMS SUCH AN ABSURD IDEA.

No one is perfect.

Not even Nicklas Lidstrom, although those who know him best will swear that he is the closest thing to perfection that they've ever encountered.

It's why in the midst of his Hall of Fame career with the Detroit Red Wings, teammates Kris Draper and Chris Osgood hung the handle on Lidstrom.

The Perfect Human.

It's a nickname that makes Lidstrom smile, even though he's certain that it's entirely misplaced.

"I took a lot of pride in being prepared for games and practices and trying to play at a high level all of the time," Lidstrom said. "When I first heard it, it was through [teammates] Kris Draper and Chris Osgood, who were joking about it, and that's when it first came out and that's how it grew. But that nickname is kind of something that I just chuckle about."

Lidstrom is certain that there is someone in his life who could refute this notion that he's the picture of perfection: his wife, Annika.

"She could have killed that story real quick," Lidstrom said with a laugh. "She could have on many occasions, but she didn't."

In general, athletes are not the most imaginative bunch. Across professional sports, the vast majority of nicknames are nothing more than derivatives of a player's surname. That's how Draper came to be known as Drapes, and Osgood was christened Ozzie.

In the Detroit dressing room, there were occasional bouts of creativity that bubbled to the surface. "We were able to throw some nicknames on some guys that stuck," Draper explained. "Some came out in the media, and some weren't allowed to come out in the media."

Igor Larionov was known as the Professor due to his cerebral approach to the game. Slava Fetisov, patriarch of the mighty Russian hockey powerhouse, was Papa Bear. Gallows humor sometimes entered into the nickname dropping. After undergoing a surgical procedure to correct a congenital heart defect, backup goalie Kevin Hodson was known thereafter as Ticker.

In Lidstrom's case, his moniker wasn't so much a nickname as it was an apt description of who he sought to be and how he sought to carry himself, both as a hockey player and as a man.

Lidstrom was an inspiration to all around him, a sensational performer who made playing the most difficult position on the ice seem easy. Off the ice, Lidstrom carried himself with similar poise.

"He was one of the few guys in the league ever that can make the game look easy at this level," Osgood said. "That's when you know a guy is a superstar and Hall of Fame player, when he's playing with the best of the best and still makes it look easy."

Between the boards, Lidstrom was a one-of-a-kind talent. Even the Internet says so. If you Google "Lidstrom synonyms," the answer you get back is that there are none.

Go through his résumé and Lidstrom ticks every box required in order to qualify for elite superstardom. By the time he hung up his skates for good in 2012, he'd won seven Norris Trophies—only Bobby Orr won more (eight)—and was the first European-trained NHLer to win the Conn Smythe Trophy and captain a Stanley Cup winner. He also scored the gold-medal-winning goal for Sweden in the 2006 Winter Olympics and was a first-ballot inductee into the Hockey Hall of Fame.

But that's only part of what defined Lidstrom as the Perfect Human in the eyes of his teammates.

Few athletes walking this planet can ever hope to equal Lidstrom's unique combination of high performance and low maintenance.

"He was almost like a machine that tuned itself," former Detroit coach Dave Lewis said. "You didn't have to change the oil or anything. He was like a Swedish-built Volvo."

To understand what made Lidstrom tick, there are a lot of places you can look and a number of people you could contact, but a good place to start would have been Lidstrom's stall in the Detroit dressing room.

It was immaculate, a picture of perfection. All the pads were hung up in their appropriate area. The helmet was situated dead center on the shelf, each skate dangling from its designated hanger.

A place for everything and everything in its place.

"He'd do that all himself," Osgood said. "It was perfect, for a perfect player."

There's an axiom that says you can judge a person's character by the manner in which they treat those who can do nothing for him. Lidstrom was the same down-to-earth person when he was mingling with the parents at one of his kids' hockey games as he was in the midst of all the elite hockey talent that populated the Red Wings dressing room.

"Yes, Nick was a professional hockey player, but he always had time for people," said Bob Tripi, who served as an executive of the Novi Youth Hockey Association in Michigan and whose children played alongside Lidstrom's children. "I actually remember one time when we had our annual hockey day and he volunteered to sit at a table and sign autographs all day for free. Nick's support for youth hockey was unbelievable, from helping coach on the ice to donating his jerseys to raise money."

On the ice, when the game was on the line, Lidstrom was the voice of reason, the settling force who eased the tension and calmed the mood.

"Just the way Nick played, the composure he had when we went out in a game," Draper said. "You know when you're playing in a big game that momentum is going to go back and forth, and Nick always seemed to be that calming influence when he'd go on out on the ice and settle things down for us."

Lidstrom didn't bring the lift-you-out-of-your-seat dynamic explosiveness of Orr to the ice. He wasn't one to deliver a punishing payload of shock and awe between the boards like Scott Stevens did.

His was an understated brilliance.

"He was smart," said Wayne Gretzky, the NHL's all-time scoring leader, who opposed Lidstrom on the ice for eight seasons, including an epic 1996 Western Conference semifinals when the Great One's St. Louis Blues fell to the Perfect Human's Red Wings in a set decided via double overtime in Game 7. "He might have been the smartest defenseman in the game. He didn't ever have to overcompensate. He was always in the right position. His angles were as good or better than anyone who ever played the game."

Just as Gretzky compiled an unmatched 894 goals and 2,857 points during his NHL career through his uncanny ability to anticipate where the puck was going to go next, Lidstrom displayed an equally prophetic intuition in his knack to foretell how the play was going to unfold from the defensive side of the puck, and was able to position himself correctly to thwart such attacks before they could develop into a dangerous threat.

"He was not the fastest," former NHLer and longtime NHL television broadcast analyst Bill Clement said. "He didn't have an overpowering shot. He was not the most physical. But he was a composite of everything you need to be an incredible player.

"His hockey IQ was off the charts. His anticipation of what was happening on the ice was flawless. His execution was almost always without a mistake. When you put all of those components together, I consider him the greatest defensive defenseman of all time."

He maintained that same calm, steadfast demeanor off the ice. Lidstrom never got rattled. He didn't lose his cool.

Had Steppenwolf penned their signature hit song after watching Lidstrom in action on the ice and interacting with others for a few days, it would have been entitled "Born to Be Mild."

Toronto Maple Leafs coach Mike Babcock, who coached the Wings from 2005 to 2015, including a Stanley Cup win in

2007–08 with Lidstrom as team captain, remembered that it was well into January of his first season behind the Detroit bench before he was able to go up to Lidstrom and point out an error he'd made on the ice.

"He's the best player I've ever coached, by far," Babcock said. "He was absolutely beyond professional. How can you do everything right, all the time? I've never seen anything, anyone like him.

"Nick drove the bus. In my mind, his steadying force was instrumental. Never mind his skill level—just who he is as a man.

"Obviously, he was a gifted, gifted athlete who read the game as good as anybody and played in all situations. He was really important for us, and when your best defensive defenseman is your best offensive defenseman, I think it helps, because you get the puck going.

"His everyday professionalism and the modeling he did for the rest of us and how he carried himself, how well he played, how hard he practiced, how good of a fitness level he maintained, was an example to everybody."

Lidstrom didn't make the play of the day. He made the plays that paid off day after day, shift after shift, game after game, season after season, all at a level of consistent excellence.

"I didn't realize how good he was until I started playing with him, and I'm a Swede," said former teammate Henrik Zetterberg, who succeeded Lidstrom as Detroit captain in 2012. "To me, he was the best, night in and night out. It was just awesome to be able to play with him."

Spend a few minutes watching hockey highlights on YouTube and you are bound to come across video vignettes of Orr's catapult rushes, leaving defenders grasping at air as he spun past them. You'll find frightening packages of the punishing hits of Stevens, who left opponents a quivering pile of flesh, laying on the ice in the fetal position.

If you were to put together a highlight reel of Lidstrom, it would be like watching footage of Albert Einstein as he developed the theory of relativity. A genius at work in each instance, but hardly the stuff that created footage with an abundance of sex appeal.

"I don't think people realize, still, how good he really was," longtime Detroit teammate Niklas Kronwall said. "There's no one like him, and there probably never will be another guy like him."

Believe it or not, this wasn't always the way it was in Lidstrom's life. Like all babies, he cried from time to time. Like many young boys, there was rambunctiousness in his personality.

Like so many NHL stars, Lidstrom started his career on the driveway where he grew up. In Lidstrom's case, that was a small Swedish town named Hogbo on the outskirts of Avesta, an area with a population of less than 12,000 situated in the middle of Sweden.

This is where Lidstrom spent his early childhood years in an apartment with his mother, Gerd; father, Jan-Erik; and his sisters, Ann-Sofie, Eva-Lena, and Petra.

His dad worked for the Swedish Road Administration, while his mother had a job in a local school kitchen cafeteria.

Before his middle-class family moved to their own house in Hogbo, they lived in an apartment in Krylbo. There the young Nicklas could prove to be quite the handful at times.

"He was an active child and used to chase his two older sisters around the apartment with a bandy stick in his hand," Jan-Erik recalled. "And he always had a ball of some kind with him. He really liked them."

Then something happened. Nicklas mellowed. He steadily evolved into a more calm, cerebral child.

To hear his father tell it, Hogbo, a town known for its quaint peacefulness, was where a tiny perfect human began to take shape.

"Nicklas was four years old when we moved to Hogbo," Jan-Erik said. "When we moved to the house in Hogbo, he cooled down. It was like turning a page. But he was no saint. Like every other kid, he ran around doing stuff, like stealing apples from the neighbors and things like that."

Being so close to nature, Hogbo was a setting that offered numerous outdoor sporting opportunities, from cross-country skiing, to mountain biking, to water sports such as kayaking and canoeing. But those early days of chasing his sisters with that bandy stick had established a trend. Lidstrom became passionate about pursuing pucks.

"I was seven years old when I started playing street hockey with my friends, classmates, and my cousin Tomas where we lived," Lidstrom said. "That's how I got interested in the sport. It was just for fun, but it got me to sign up for more organized games in a club called Skogsbo SK in Avesta."

When Lidstrom skated for the first time and took part in his first hockey practices, it was on an outdoor rink. He and his teammates had to shovel snow off the ice after every practice so the homemade Zamboni—a barrel on rails—could be brought out to make new ice.

"To be able to travel down to Avesta later and practice indoors in their arena was a luxury when I grew up," Lidstrom said.

"Almost all of my classmates belonged to the same team, so we played hockey in the winter and soccer in the summer. I played soccer until I was 15."

Jan-Erik remembers his son as a good student and a natural learner to whom new concepts came easily.

"Yes, he was doing well in school," Jan-Erik said. "He didn't say much, but he got things done and went through high school without a problem. Learning came easy to him.

"I remember when he borrowed a bike from an older friend to learn how to ride. Nicklas didn't need any practice. He got on and just biked away. He had a natural way of learning new things. He never backed away from challenges."

Lidstrom stayed with Skogsbo SK until he was 14, before moving on to Avesta BK. He stayed there as a member of the club's midget team for two seasons. However, he still loved hockey in its unorganized forms.

"What I remember from that period is that if you didn't take part in a team practice, you just took your skates and hockey stick and found a friend to go skating with outdoors," Lidstrom remembered. "There were no hockey rinks with boards and all that, but the town had a couple of places where they made ice on soccer fields, or other open spaces, so we kids could skate. The winters were long and cold, so after a couple of hours you headed home with frozen hands and feet."

Already, Lidstrom dreamed of becoming a professional hockey player. His idol was a Swedish NHL star whom he would later call a teammate. And it will no doubt come as a surprise to Red Wings fans to learn that one of their favorite sons favored a member of the Toronto Maple Leafs as a youngster.

"Borje Salming became my idol early on," Lidstrom said. "Borje Salming was my big hero growing up."

A star on the Swedish national team, Salming wasn't the first European to play in the NHL; fellow Swedes Ulf Sterner, Juha Widing, and Thommie Bergman beat him to that. But Salming would develop into the NHL's first European superstar.

During a 17-season career—16 seasons for the Leafs from 1973–74 through 1988–89, and his final NHL campaign for the Red Wings in 1989–90, two seasons prior to Lidstrom's arrival in Detroit—Salming performed at an All-Star level, contended for the Norris Trophy, and broke down the barriers that suggested European players couldn't cut it in the rugged NHL. He became the first European-born-and-trained NHLer to be inducted into the Hockey Hall of Fame.

He was selected to the NHL Second All-Star Team in 1974–75, his second NHL season, launching a string of six consecutive seasons in which Salming was either a First or Second Team choice. Salming was also picked to the Second Team in 1975–76, 1977–78, 1978–79, and 1979–80. He was a First All-Star Team choice in 1976–77 and finished second to Larry Robinson of the Montreal Canadiens in the Norris Trophy balloting. Salming was also second in Norris voting to Robinson in 1979–80 and finished in the top five on four other occasions, including a fifth-place showing as a rookie in 1973–74.

Salming holds Leafs franchise career records for assists (620) and plus-minus (plus-155), and for goals (148), assists, and points (768) by a defenseman. His 66 assists in 1976–77 stand as the club's single-season mark for a defenseman, and Salming is also the NHL record holder for the most points by a defenseman who wasn't selected in the NHL entry draft. He and Russia's Viacheslav Fetisov were named the defensemen on the IIHF all-time team in 2008.

Imagine Lidstrom's level of excitement during the 1991 Canada Cup when he was paired with Salming on the Swedish defense.

"I had a chance to partner up with him, and that was a big thrill for me," Lidstrom remembered.

The first great Swedish defenseman in NHL history skating in tandem with the player who'd go on to become the greatest Swedish defenseman to play in the NHL.

The admiration was mutual.

"That was nice to play with him, too," Salming said. "You could see how much talent he had. He was just a young kid and you knew that not only was he going there [to Detroit], he was going to stay there a long time.

"When he went to Detroit, I knew he was going to make it really good. He was such a talented guy and he had a fantastic career. Amazing player and a nice guy, too."

European players like Lidstrom will never forget what Salming's success in the NHL meant to them. Salming was the template for what Lidstrom would become, but before Lidstrom could position himself as Salming's heir, he first needed to learn how to play Salming's position.

When Lidstrom started playing street hockey in the fall every year, and then later when he signed up for youth teams in his hometown, he didn't know what position he wanted to play. He wasn't sure if he wanted to be a goalie, defenseman, or forward.

"It took a while for me to decide that I wanted to be a defense-man full time," Lidstrom recalled. "I tried different positions, but it was the most fun to play defense. So, I decided to stick to that. Nobody told me that it suited me best or anything. I just enjoyed being a defenseman.

"What I liked about it was how you could see the play develop in front of you. And that you could still contribute to the offense. It was the most fun thing to do."

It also mattered that Salming was a defenseman.

"I didn't know much about Salming then, not more than he was a defenseman and that he was one of first Swedish players that had succeeded in the NHL," Lidstrom said.

In his day, unearthing news about the exploits of Sweden's NHL pioneers was a far greater challenge than being the last defender back trying to thwart a two-on-one break. Coverage was spotty and news reports were few and far between.

"They didn't show any games at all on TV," Lidstrom remembered. "There were no NHL games on TV in Sweden at that time, so you had to wait for the Sunday evening sports TV magazine and hope that they would show some highlights.

"I read about Borje and other Swedish hockey players who had gone to the NHL in the beginning of the 1980s. I tried to follow them in the newspapers. They had their stats in there all the time. I watched Mats Naslund, Hakan Loob, Thomas Steen, Bengt Gustafsson, and guys that played in the later '80s like Ulf Samuelsson and Tomas Sandstrom. There were a lot of players that I followed."

Eventually, as Lidstrom grew older, the opportunities to see his boyhood idols in action came with more frequency.

"The only games that they showed on TV were the Stanley Cup Finals, especially if there was a Swede involved," Lidstrom said. "It got better when the Edmonton Oilers started winning Stanley Cups in the middle of the '80s. Hockey was a big part of my life already then. I tried to watch as much as I could on TV.

"Now, with the Internet, which we didn't have back in the '80s, all the kids, all the people back in Sweden are paying attention, and they're good at it."

As Lidstrom's hockey career evolved through his teenage years, it was becoming apparent that he was also good at it, and people in important places in the hockey world were paying attention and taking notice.

Just as Salming was the man for him as a youngster, there were countless young defenders who grew up adoring Lidstrom and imagined that they were him.

"He's not the same type of player that I am, but at least defensively I've always idolized him and the way he shut down guys when he was playing," said Arizona Coyotes defenseman Niklas Hjalmarsson. "Lidstrom always had a good gap, and never was a stick length away from his guy."

"Growing up in Sweden, he was the guy everybody looked up to as a role model," added Kronwall.

There was a large membership in the Lidstrom admiration society, and not all of them were Swedes.

"He's why I wear the No. 5. It's kind of who I've idolized my whole life as a hockey player," said Florida Panthers defenseman Aaron Ekblad, the 2014–15 Calder Memorial Trophy winner. Ekblad grew up in Belle River, Ontario, minutes from the Detroit-Windsor border, affording him many opportunities to go to Joe Louis Arena and watch his hero perform.

"I admired his ability to play good, strong, reliable, responsible defense and have confidence put in him as a good defender, as well as to be able to jump up in the rush, play good power play minutes and good penalty kill minutes, kind of a well-rounded, two-way game.

"That's kind of what I always looked at, the ability he had to play so well on both sides of the puck and be such a good player. He was fun to watch and an inspiration to me."

In Michigan, every young defenseman dreamed of becoming the next Lidstrom.

"He was always my favorite player growing up," said Red Wings defenseman Danny DeKeyser, who was born in the Detroit suburb of Macomb Township. "He was just so smooth, so smooth with the puck. He made great decisions all the time. It just seemed like he always made the right play out there."

Wanting to play like Lidstrom was the dream, but the reality was that few could.

"I think a lot of kids probably tried to do that, but it's kind of hard to do," DeKeyser said. "The way he skated, it was just kind of effortless. He played a lot of minutes because he was able to not exert a lot of energy when he didn't need to."

Lidstrom can relate to these stories. On the ice as a kid, Lidstrom wanted to be just like Salming, the NHL's original Swedish superstar.

"Of course, the NHL was a dream for me, like everybody else," Lidstrom said. "I skated around on the ice and pretended that I was playing in the NHL, that I was Borje Salming, and that I was going on the rush from the defensive zone up the ice with the puck to score a goal. That fantasy was on my mind all the time.

"It was a happy time in my life. To have all those dreams at that age."

It took a number of years before Lidstrom understood that those dreams could actually come true one day.

"I guess I had reached junior age before I thought it was a possibility," Lidstrom said. "When I was 16, I moved to Vasteras to study at the local hockey high school. That's when it all really started to happen for me."

But before that, Lidstrom had been chosen for the nation-wide tournament TV-pucken, where he played for the county of Dalarna.

To be picked to represent your county in the TV-pucken tournament is the highest honor that can be bestowed on a teenage Swedish hockey prospect. The national event was the brainchild of Sven "Tumba" Johansson, the first legendary Swedish hockey star, and is contested by district teams of 15-year-old players. It draws its name from the fact that when it began, all of the tournament's games were broadcast on national television.

"The first time I was picked for a spot on a real team was as a 13-year-old when I was picked for a tournament called the Folksam Cup," Lidstrom said. "It was a tournament that you played two years before TV-pucken. It was a big deal for me coming from Skogsbo SK, which was a really small club."

When Lidstrom played for Dalarna as a 15-year-old in TV-pucken, he had Tony Rickardsson as a teammate. Lidstrom and motorcycle speedway champion Rickardsson are the most famous people from their part of Sweden. Rickardsson went on to be a superstar in speedway, winning a number of world championships.

"We played together for two seasons in Avesta BK," Lidstrom said. "Tony was a talented forward; he did everything at full speed already then. But he decided to put all his focus on motorcycling and became very successful in that sport."

Rickardsson, considered the most successful speedway rider of his era, won six world titles. Lidstrom, considered the finest defenseman of his generation, won seven Norris Trophies.

Coincidence, or was there something about the fresh air in Hogbo that produced athletes who would have no peers in their chosen sport?

Ronnie Sundin, who would play in the NHL with the New York Rangers in 1997–98, was another of Lidstrom's teammates on that TV-pucken team in 1985. Sundin represented Sweden in six IIHF World Championships and teamed with Lidstrom again on the Swedish national squad that won the 2006 Olympic gold medal at the 2006 Winter Games in Torino, Italy.

"We had a pretty good team that year, and Ronnie also became an NHL player. It was really special that we could win an Olympic gold medal together in Torino 2006," Lidstrom said.

Lidstrom played on two teams during his years in Avesta, the older midget team and the B-junior team.

"It was during my time there that I decided to apply for the hockey high school in Vasteras," Lidstrom recalled. "I was supposed to attend the school in Leksand, but they didn't have the education I wanted, a four-year engineering course, so I applied for Vasteras instead and was accepted there."

In Vasteras, Lidstrom would be schooled by a Swedish hockey icon. Par Marts had played for Vasteras in the Hockeyettan, the Swedish third division, and the Allsvenskan, the Swedish second division. Marts also played for AIK Stockholm in the Elitserien, Sweden's top division, winning a silver medal with them in 1978. But it was as a coach that Marts became a household name in his homeland.

His playing days concluded with Vasteras following the 1984–85 season, and Marts turned to coaching in 1986. By 1992, Marts was involved with the Swedish national team as an assistant coach, winning a gold medal in 1992, silver medals in 1993 and 1995, and a bronze medal in 1994 at the World Championships. Marts also earned an Olympic gold medal at the Winter Games in Lillehammer, Norway, in 1994.

Gaining the opportunity to work as a head coach in the Swedish national team program, Marts guided the Swedes to silver medals at the 2008 and 2009 World Junior Championships, as well as a bronze medal in 2010. Moving up to take charge of the senior national team, Marts led his country to an IIHF world tournament title in 2013, a silver medal in 2011, and a bronze medal in 2014. He also won a silver medal at the 2014 Olympic Winter Games in Sochi, Russia. At the club level, Marts led HV71 to the league title in 2003–04 and was named Elitserien coach of the year. This was the brilliant hockey mind who would hone Lidstrom's game during his formative teenage years of development.

There were also a number of players ahead of him in the Vasteras junior program who would serve as mentors to Lidstrom. He was energized by the older students at the school, like Peter Popovic and Leif Rohlin, and driven to follow in their footsteps as he saw them make it to play for the Vasteras senior-level team.

Popovic would later play 485 games in the NHL, mainly for the Montreal Canadiens. He also skated with the Swedish national team in the 1993 World Championships and the 1996 World Cup of Hockey. Rohlin also won an Olympic gold medal at the Winter Games in 1994. He was part of Swedish teams at one World Junior Tournament and two World Championships, as well as spending two seasons in the NHL with the Vancouver Canucks.

The Vasteras program when Lidstrom arrived was deep in talented prospects. Patrik Juhlin and Stefan Hellkvist were also in Lidstrom's age group. One other very promising player, Fredrik Nilsson, was one year younger than Lidstrom.

Although none would go on to be Hockey Hall of Famers like Lidstrom, all would make their mark on the game. Juhlin was another member of Sweden's 1994 Olympic gold-medal club at the Winter Games in Lillehammer. He would represent his country in World Junior, World Championships, and World Cup of Hockey games, and he'd play in the NHL with the Philadelphia Flyers, who selected him 34th overall in the 1989 NHL entry draft, 19 picks before the Red Wings selected Lidstrom.

Hellkvist launched his pro career with Vasteras in 1988 and finished it with the team in 2010 at the age of 40, retiring from the game just two years prior to Lidstrom. Nilsson played with the Swedes in two World Junior tourneys and the World Cup of Hockey. He was drafted by the San Jose Sharks.

"We had a number of very good young players and won the national championship for J-18 [under-18] that year, 1989," Lidstrom recalled. "We beat Modo in sudden death. Patrik Zetterberg scored the winning goal."

Lidstrom was just 16 years old when he came to Vasteras. He rented a basement apartment from an older couple and learned how to take care of himself.

In what some might see as a diversion, Lidstrom is one of few Swedish hockey stars of the modern era who served a year in the military. He was 20 at the time.

"I spent a couple of months at S1 in Enkoping to get my basic training, but after that was assigned to a local unit in Vasteras, where me and another soldier drove a truck around the county delivering equipment," Lidstrom said. "It wasn't that hard, to be honest. They gave me time to practice with my hockey team in the afternoon, so I did not have a problem combining my military service with my hockey career."

By this time, Lidstrom was a regular player on the main team in Vasteras and had a chance to play a couple of games with the national team.

"During my first three months in the military, I learned how to march, handle an automatic weapon, and drive an all-terrain vehicle," Lidstrom said. "I got the basic training, so to speak."

When it came to hockey, he got his basic training in Vasteras. The national championship he won with their junior team in 1989 was his first championship title.

There would be more to come. Soon, Lidstrom would get his marching orders to skate in hockey's greatest league, the NHL.

2

THE BEST DRAFT OF THEM ALL

ONE OF THE PURPOSES OF YOUTH SPORTS IS TO HELP YOUNGSTERS develop and build character, and certainly, hockey enabled Lidstrom to stand on his own two feet earlier than most. He was only 16 years old when he left home to attend a more hockey-focused high school an hour away in Vasteras. He rented his own small apartment in the basement of the house of an older couple and settled in.

"It was an adjustment to live on my own at that young age," Lidstrom said. "The first months were tough. I had my own entrance and my own small kitchen, so it was like living alone even if there was a family upstairs."

Lidstrom didn't even have a driver's license during his first couple of years away from home, so he had to bike to school and to hockey practice.

"It taught me how to take care of myself and learn how to cook," Lidstrom said. "My mom used to bring baskets of food when my parents came to see me. I always hoped that the food they brought would last the whole week, but of course that wasn't always the case."

His career took off during these years in Vasteras, as he established himself as a player in Sweden's top league. He made his senior-level debut with Vasteras at the age of 17 while the club was still situated in the Allsvenskan, the Swedish second division.

Lidstrom played three games for Vasteras that season and was eligible to have been selected in the NHL entry draft in the summer of 1988, but he wasn't picked. The rules of the NHL draft were different back then, so he needed to be drafted in one of the first three rounds to be eligible because he hadn't played enough games with Vasteras. But the club would earn a promotion to Sweden's top league that winter, and so would its blossoming teenage defenseman.

Lidstrom made his debut in the Elitserien as an 18-year-old during the 1988–89 season. He made a splash in an exhibition game against Stockholm-based Elite League regulars AIK Solna when he skated through the entire opposing team and scored a spectacular backhanded goal on goaltender Ake Lilljebjorn.

"[Vasteras coach] Par Marts gave four junior players a chance on the team and I was one of them," Lidstrom said. "We were a new team in the Elite League and played Farjestad, one of the top teams, in the season opener, which was nerve-wracking. I adjusted fine and was pretty happy with what I accomplished, but we were relegated after Christmas to the lower division. We had to play a qualification round to stay in that league in the spring but made it after beating Frolunda in the fifth and deciding game."

Wearing sweater No. 9, Lidstrom produced a goal and six assists in 34 games for Vasteras in 1988–89, a team that included former NHL forward Roland Eriksson and future NHL defenseman Peter Popovic on its roster.

Soon, the NHL would also be in Lidstrom's future. The Detroit Red Wings had the talented Vasteras blueliner on their radar but, believing they had unearthed a rare gem skating for an unfashionable Swedish squad, they were doing their utmost to keep their interest quiet.

"Christer Rockstrom deserves most of the credit," suggested Neil Smith, Detroit's director of amateur scouting in 1989. "He was the team's European scout and he's the guy who really pushed for Lidstrom."

That the Wings were watching might have come as a surprise to other NHL teams, but Lidstrom's unique hockey instincts told him that something was up with Detroit.

"I knew that Detroit had their eyes on me," Lidstrom said. "Their Swedish scout, Christer Rockstrom, came to Vasteras a couple of times during the 1988–89 season to scout me."

Rockstrom, who now works for the Montreal Canadiens, spent a lot of time trying to figure out how good Lidstrom really was, and that proved to be a challenging task.

"It wasn't that easy, because Nicklas wasn't a regular in the lineup," Rockstrom recalled. "For that reason, I traveled to Vasteras from Stockholm off and on to follow the team's practices, just to get a chance to see him in action. I also knew one of the other players on the team, a forward named Jorgen Holmberg, so he tipped me off when Nicklas was going to play and it was worth a trip there to catch a game."

There was one single incident that convinced Rockstrom that Lidstrom had potential, that he was an elite talent.

"It was a road game in Stockholm against AIK and Nicklas had been on the ice for a least a minute and a half killing a penalty, when he saw his teammate come back on the ice from the penalty box," Rockstrom said. "But instead of clearing the puck out off the boards to get himself a chance to change, he delivered a perfect pass up the ice, so his teammate got a breakaway.

"To be that tired and still be so focused was really impressive in my mind. That is still one of my best scouting memories I have during a long career in the stands. I thought, 'This guy must be special.' To be able to make that pass under those circumstances made me understand his extraordinary playmaking skills."

Lidstrom clearly was green in terms of development, but it was also abundantly clear that there were qualities in his game, raw materials that displayed the potential to be refined into a jewel of a specimen.

"Nicklas was tall and thin at the time—he couldn't have been more than 170 pounds—but you could see he had something special," Rockstrom said. "And that's what you do as a scout; you have a lot of pieces and then you try to put the puzzle together. With young players you have to weigh how they perform both during games and practices, what kind of personality they have, and what the development curve can be.

"Of course, there was no way I could predict that he would be that good and win four Stanley Cups and seven Norris Trophies. He has done it all on his own, of course. But I must say that I saw some qualities early on that made me keep a close eye on him in Vasteras before the draft in 1989."

He wasn't the only hockey person out there searching for budding talent whose eye was caught by Lidstrom's potential. Once when Rockstrom was sitting in the stands in Vasteras, he was approached by Canadian super agent Don Meehan.

"He already represented Patrik Juhlin and Peter Popovic on the Vasteras team and started to ask me questions about Nicklas Lidstrom," said Rockstrom, who remembered trying his utmost to throw Meehan off Lidstrom's scent. "I kind of lied to him that I didn't know much about Nick.

"Donnie and I have become good friends and we joke about that meeting off and on. I did not want one of the NHL's biggest agents to go back to North America and brag about how good this kid was. At this time, Nicklas wasn't that well known outside of Vasteras, and I didn't want him to be on everybody's scouting list before the draft."

Meehan, who ultimately represented Lidstrom, remembers being puzzled by Rockstrom's odd behavior.

"The purpose for my visit was to see Leif Rohlin, who was one of my clients then," Meehan recalled. "I noticed a young defenseman in the first period and tried to get a grip on who he was. Somebody told me his name was Nicklas Lidstrom and that he was only 17. During the second period it became more clear to me that this guy had exceptional talent. I kept my eyes on him and in the third period he was even more noticeable, so I said to Rockstrom, 'Are you missing something here?'"

The answer Meehan got from Rockstrom was a suggestion that perhaps Lidstrom was just having a good day, but Meehan was intrigued and determined to find out more about this budding talent.

"I told [Rockstrom] that I was not going to drive back to Stockholm together with him, as we had arranged," Meehan remembered. "I wanted to stay after the game and give Lidstrom my credentials. The next morning, I had a chance to meet

Lidstrom's parents and he retained me as his agent. That's how I signed Nicklas."

Meehan received a phone call from Smith after he got back to Toronto. "Neil called me and was curious how my trip to Sweden had been and I told him that I had seen an exceptional talent in Vasteras named Nicklas Lidstrom," remembered Meehan, who recalled Smith's attempt to play coy about Detroit's familiarity with Lidstrom's work.

"Oh, really," Smith said. "That's interesting."

"Stop the b.s., Neil," Meehan countered. "I know you know who he is."

At that point, Smith altered his tactics from pleading ignorance to pleading with Meehan to stay mum about his impressions of Lidstrom.

The Red Wings did not invite Lidstrom to attend the draft, which was held in Bloomington, Minnesota, in June of that year. Team management was afraid that another team might pick him. There was a lot of hush-hush as Detroit realized it had unearthed a diamond in the rough.

Lidstrom was at his parents' house when the phone call came that the Wings had selected him with the 53rd overall pick.

"It was Christer who called to tell me that Detroit had drafted me, and then he handed over the phone to their assistant general manager, Nick Polano," Lidstrom recalled. "It was a big moment for me. I felt that I had taken a huge step closer to the NHL. To be drafted was evidence that you had succeeded in some way."

Though he'd become a household name in Hockeytown, on the day he was drafted, Lidstrom would have been hard-pressed to name many Red Wings.

"My favorite team in the league at that time was the Toronto Maple Leafs because Borje Salming was playing there," Lidstrom said. "I also followed the Edmonton Oilers, because they were so good. The only thing I knew about the Red Wings was that Steve Yzerman played there and was their superstar and face of the franchise."

Detroit's 1989 draft crop is often referenced as the greatest in the history of the league. It was the building block that would make the Red Wings a top team in the NHL for the next two decades.

After Lidstrom, Detroit selected Sergei Fedorov 74th overall. Fedorov would win the Hart Trophy in 1993–94 and team with Lidstrom on three Stanley Cup winners in Detroit. In 2015, Lidstrom and Fedorov were inducted into the Hockey Hall of Fame together.

Forward Dallas Drake, selected 116th overall, joined Lidstrom on Detroit's 2007–08 Stanley Cup winner and played in 1,009 NHL games. Defenseman Vladimir Konstantinov (221st overall) was an NHL All-Star and Lidstrom's Stanley Cup teammate in 1996–97. His career was tragically cut short by debilitating closed-head injuries suffered in a limousine accident just days following that Cup triumph.

"Two of those players are Hall of Famers, and Konstantinov was on that path before the tragic post-Cup accident in 1997," *Sports Illustrated* writer Michael Farber said.

Forward Mike Sillinger, Detroit's first-round pick, played for the Wings from 1990–95 and appeared in 1,049 NHL games. Although he never played for the Wings, defenseman Bob Boughner, Detroit's second-round choice, skated in 630 NHL games.

While predicting how an 18-year-old talent will develop is an inexact science, it is mind-boggling in retrospect to study the list of the 52 players who were drafted ahead of Lidstrom in 1989.

Nine players chosen before him never played a single NHL game. Only one of those who heard his name called prior to Lidstrom's—fellow Swede Mats Sundin, taken first overall by the Quebec Nordiques—has joined Lidstrom in the Hockey Hall of Fame. Of all the players taken in that draft, just Sundin (1,349) and Fedorov (1,179) accumulated more points in their NHL careers than Lidstrom (1,142). Lidstrom collected 722 more points than Patrice Brisebois, the second-highest-scoring defenseman selected in the 1989 draft. And no player drafted in 1989 won more Stanley Cups than the four won by Lidstrom.

There were 19 defensemen picked ahead of Lidstrom, who turned out to be arguably the best player ever at the position since the legendary Bobby Orr. Some of the defensive prospects that NHL scouts deemed a better bet than Lidstrom on draft day included Jason Herter, Jason Soules, Dan Ratushny, and Bob Kellogg.

Back home, the news that Lidstrom had been drafted by the Red Wings did not make any huge headlines in Sweden.

"No, remember that this was the year that Mats Sundin went No. 1 in the draft and that had never happened before, that a European player had gone first," Lidstrom. "It was huge."

Lidstrom had met Sundin on the national junior team during the World Championships in Finland 1989. Sweden finished fifth in a close tournament, where only two points separated the winning team from the fifth-place team.

"Mats was our leader and best player," Lidstrom remembered. "He was the one that everybody noticed. I can't say that we became close friends immediately. We got to know each other more as teammates."

The Wings opted to keep Lidstrom in Sweden as he continued to grow both physically and as a player. He skated for Vasteras again in 1989–90 and also played for Sweden once more in the World Junior tournament. He collected 3–3–6 totals in seven games as the Swedes finished fifth, but just like at the NHL entry draft the spring before, Lidstrom would be overlooked on the all-tournament team. Two other future NHL rearguards—Russia's Alexander Godynyuk and Czech Jiri Slegr—were named to the squad. Years later in 2001–02, Slegr and Lidstrom would team on Detroit's Stanley Cup–winning defense.

Lidstrom got a chance to play for the Swedish national B team that winter. The coaches had finally discovered how talented this young defenseman from Vasteras was. He had one year left at the hockey high school he attended there, and his ice time increased with Vasteras IK.

"Par Marts showed me more and more confidence," Lidstrom said. "He meant a lot to me in my development as a player. I was not a big-and-strong guy, so I had to rely on my skills."

Lidstrom's big breakthrough came during the 1990–91 season. He played 38 games in the Swedish top league and his offensive talent started to show in the form of four goals and 19 assists. He was now on the radar for the team managers and coaches of Sweden's national team, known as Tre Kronor.

"I made my first appearance on Tre Kronor in the fall of 1990," Lidstrom said. "I played the Deutschland Cup and the Izvestia

Tournament in Moscow right before Christmas. And then I did qualify for the yearly February tournament at the Globe Arena in Stockholm."

Conny Evensson was the coach for the national team at that time. "I had Curre Lundmark as my assistant coach and he came from Vasteras, so he knew about Nicklas and convinced me how good he was," Evensson said. "It didn't take long for me to figure out what extraordinary talent he had."

Lidstrom's first big test was the World Championships in Finland in the spring of 1991. It was there that Evensson knew that he had an up-and-coming superstar in the lineup.

"When you were able to see Nicklas on the ice with the big boys, the established players in the world, you knew what kind of talent he had," Evensson said. "He was so calm and created time and space for himself and his teammates.

"The reason was that he was so quick to predict what was happening and what was the next step. He showed what a smart player he was. Nobody else had that hockey sense. His skating was technically complete. I don't think I had ever seen a defenseman shift from skating backward to going forward and vice versa that quick and smooth."

The World Championships in Finland became a big success for both Sweden and Lidstrom. They went through the tournament undefeated and won the gold after a 2–1 win over the Soviet Union in the finals. The winning goal by Mats Sundin was a highlight-reel number where he went around legendary Soviet defender Viacheslav Fetisov and scored.

Lidstrom posted 3–3–6 numbers in 10 games. "It was a fantastic tournament, but let's not forget that we actually tied two games," Lidstrom recalled. "We were down 4–2 against Finland before we came back and got a 4–4 tie."

Thomas Rundqvist was the captain of that Swedish team, and he remembers the coming-out party for the young Lidstrom.

"This was the international tournament where Nicklas had his big breakthrough," Rundqvist said. "He had been playing well in the Elite League, but there were people who thought it was too early for him to be picked for the national team that year. But he showed everybody that he was ready for the big stage. He acted very mature in every situation on the ice. Nothing rattled him."

Because Lidstrom made his presence known on the ice, he had no need to be seen outside the rink. "No, you hardly noticed him off the ice," Rundqvist said. "He was quiet in the dressing room. He was so humble from the beginning and Conny Evensson gave Nicklas a lot of confidence by letting him play in all different situations."

What impressed his teammates most was Lidstrom's calmness on the ice. "He was so smart using his energy and never overdid anything," Rundqvist said. "No unnecessary hits and he never missed any assignments covering opponents. He just kept playing his game and was always in the right position.

"I was immediately impressed with him, as everybody else on our team was. He had an exceptional ability to read the play, he skated very well, and was equipped with a hard shot. You could see that he was an up-and-coming superstar on our team. It was no surprise that he was on the roster for the Swedish Canada Cup team a couple of months later."

To come home from his first World Championships with a gold medal was a big boost for the young Lidstrom, and he wasn't the only one emboldened by his performance on the world stage. The Red Wings wanted him on their team for the 1991–92 NHL season.

Originally, the thought process among the team's brain trust was that another year in Sweden might do wonders for Lidstrom. After watching him in action at the worlds, they came to believe that Lidstrom could do a world of good in Detroit.

"They didn't know whether to bring him to North America or not," recalled Bryan Murray, Detroit's GM at the time. "I went over to the World Championships to see him. He scored a goal on his first shot and I said, 'Yeah, I think this guy can play.' He was without a doubt the best defenseman on the Swedish national team. Without a doubt. You watched him, and you knew there was something good you liked about him.

"He was definitely a key player for Sweden, anchoring the power play—a very good, young offensive talent. I called Don Meehan and we got a deal done."

Lidstrom signed an NHL contract with Detroit on May 12, 1991. He traveled to Detroit at the end of May to get to know the city and club better. "I had a year left on my contract with Vasteras, but there was a deadline at the end of April to get out of it," Lidstrom said. "So that was what I did during the World Championships in Finland."

Lidstrom arrived in Detroit in the early summer of 1991, his first trip to the United States. "My first thought was, 'Wow, everything is so huge here,'" Lidstrom recalled. "I stayed with the Red Wings assistant general manager, Nick Polano, and was shown around town with a special stop at Joe Louis Arena."

That move did not go down well with Lidstrom's Swedish team and its management; Vasteras IK demanded $1 million to release Lidstrom. "The team was having financial problems and saw a chance to make some money off me," Lidstrom said. "This made me feel uneasy. I didn't know if I was going to be suspended or what would happen."

The Swedish Hockey Federation took Vasteras' side and told Lidstrom that he was obligated to play the 1991–92 season in Sweden. At the same time, the Red Wings contacted the NHL and got approval for Lidstrom to play in North America if he signed the contract they were offering him.

"I had already decided to move to Detroit and give the NHL a shot," Lidstrom said. "There was nothing that could change my mind."

It would take another year and a half before the issue was settled. According to Swedish media at the time, Detroit paid less than $100,000 to get Lidstrom released from his contract.

But before Lidstrom could move to Detroit, there was another exciting hockey tournament waiting for him around the corner. He was picked for Sweden's Canada Cup team that would play in the late summer tournament of the same year.

"It was almost unreal to be named to the Canada Cup team," Lidstrom said. "I had never played on the smaller rinks in North America and now I was going to play against the biggest stars in the world. I had a hard time believing it was true."

The teammates who populated the roster read like a who's-who of the Swedish hockey elite. Tommy Soderstrom was in goal, and the defense included Lidstrom's idol Salming, the king of Swedish hockey, as well as Calle Johansson and the Samuelssons,

Ulf and Kjell. Sundin, Thomas Steen, Tomas Sandstrom, Mats Naslund, and Ulf Dahlen were among the forwards.

Lidstrom started the tournament as Sweden's seventh defenseman, but after Tommy Albelin was injured in the opening game, he was put into the lineup and paired with Salming.

"What can you say? It was fantastic and a dream come true," Lidstrom said. "I had only met Borje and said 'Hi' to him during our training camp back in Sweden, which took place in Sunne and Stockholm, before we departed for Canada. I remember how nervous I was the first time I met him."

Suddenly, Lidstrom was Salming's defensive partner. "It was such a great feeling to be on the ice together with Borje," Lidstrom said. "We quickly developed a good chemistry. He was a veteran who blocked shots and delivered hits, and I liked to join the rush. We complemented each other so well."

When it was time for the game against Canada in Toronto, the organizers played a dirty trick on Sweden by scrapping the starting lineup presentation before the puck drop. They wanted to prevent a standing ovation for Salming from his old home crowd at the Maple Leaf Gardens, similar to the one he received at the 1976 Canada Cup. But the Swedish coach, Conny Evensson, came up with a smart move to counter the change.

He named Salming the captain for that game, which gave Borje the assignment to skate to center ice and exchange pennants with Canada's Wayne Gretzky. That gave the fans a chance to celebrate their beloved Salming one more time.

"It was magical for me to see how respected and loved Borje was in Toronto," Lidstrom said. "We lost 4–1 to Canada, and then one more time in the semifinals with a 4–0 defeat in a tight game.

In the end, we couldn't keep up. Canada was too good, but we all learned one thing—Borje was an icon in Toronto."

When Lidstrom later became teammates with Brendan Shanahan in Detroit, the Canadian told him a funny story from the 1991 Canada Cup. "Shanahan told me that he had hit Salming pretty hard on the ice and both of them ended up with penalties," Lidstrom explained. "When they were sitting in the penalty box, Salming shouted across to Brendan, 'Kid, do you know who I am?' Shanahan shouted back, 'Yes, you're Borje Salming.'"

Dahlen, who had a long career in the NHL with the New York Rangers, Minnesota North Stars, Dallas Stars, San Jose Sharks, Chicago Blackhawks, and Washington Capitals, met Lidstrom for the first time during this tournament.

"What I remember from the Canada Cup was that we had a really good game against Canada in the semis, but Wayne Gretzky scored at the end of the second period," Dahlen said. "We were not able to come back after that.

"Nicklas was a new acquaintance for me. He was somebody you noticed right away. We would go on to play many international tournaments together on the national team. It was always a pleasure to have him on the team."

Johansson had been a late addition to Tre Kronor at the World Championships in Finland in the spring of 1991 after the Washington Capitals got knocked out of the Stanley Cup playoffs in the second round against Pittsburgh. He noticed the young defenseman from Vasteras immediately.

"Gosh, this kid was so calm and poised," Johansson remembered. "He never looked stressed in any situation. That was my first thought. Nicklas had a way of getting the puck out of our own end without breaking a sweat. He played a simple, effective game, which really impressed me."

Johansson was an established and successful NHL player after many years in Washington. He could judge talent and knew Lidstrom would make it in North America.

"Nicklas didn't have to change the way he played when he moved from the bigger ice surface in Europe to the smaller rinks," Johansson said. "The Canada Cup was a big test for him, and he passed with flying colors."

Lidstrom wore No. 4 and finished the 1991 Canada Cup with a goal and an assist in six games. His goal came on a power play against Finland in a game that Sweden lost 3–1. Sweden won two games, beating the Soviet Union 3–2 and Czechoslovakia 5–2. Tre Kronor also lost 6–3 against the U.S., besides the loss to Finland and the two setbacks handed to them by Canada.

Salming was pleasantly surprised by his young partner on the national team. "I was the oldest player on the team, Nicklas was the youngest," Salming said. "But he was the one who carried me and not the other way around. I remember how easy he was to play with, and I knew right away that he would turn into a remarkable player. He was very serious about his hockey; he wasn't there just to have fun.

"We were roommates during the tournament, so I got to know him, and even if he didn't say much, he was a very likeable guy. You enjoyed being in his presence. The 1991 Canada Cup was the beginning of a long friendship with Nicklas. We still see each other off and on here in Sweden, and I have never seen him angry. I like those kind of guys, the ones that are kind and humble."

There was one teammate on the Canada Cup team that would be extra important to Lidstrom after the tournament. Forward Johan Garpenlov had just finished his rookie season with the Red Wings. He would be the one who helped Lidstrom adjust to life in Detroit and the NHL.

"There was no time to go home to Sweden after the Canada Cup, so Johan and I flew from Toronto to Detroit where the Red Wings already had opened their training camp before the 1991–92 season," Lidstrom said.

He stayed at a hotel in a suburb of Detroit with Garpenlov and some other players. Garpenlov did what other teammates had done for him a year earlier, acting as a guide and chauffeur for Lidstrom to get him around and adjusted.

"I didn't know much about Nicklas before we met on the Canada Cup team," Garpenlov said. "It didn't take long for me to be aware of his potential. I think the tournament was a good experience before the adventure that awaited him in Detroit. Being the only other Swede on the Red Wings at that time, it was a given that I would take care of him."

When Lidstrom and Garpenlov arrived, the camp had been going on for a week and the first cuts had been made. "There were still around 40 players there, and I immediately felt, 'This is for real,'" Lidstrom remembered. "Everybody was fighting for a job, nobody held back. I had never experienced a training camp like that. There were some teammates at camp that did not hesitate to hit you as soon as they had the chance."

Detroit had a tough team at this time. The roster included one of the league's most feared fighters, Bob Probert. "Probert was a friendly and nice guy off the ice," Lidstrom said. "He turned on the meanness when it was game time. But there were others who wanted to test me. Somebody like Stu Grimson, who came to us a couple of years later, would run you over at practice and then excuse himself by saying, 'Oh, sorry, sorry.' He turned into a different person when he was on the ice. During my first year in Detroit we also had Dennis Vial, a huge defenseman, who loved to hit people whenever he could."

Lidstrom was paired with Brad McCrimmon early on during his first training camp. This big and strong veteran defenseman was nicknamed Beast by his teammates. "McCrimmon took me to the side and showed me some tricks, like how to grab the other guy's jersey if you ended up in a fight," Lidstrom said. "He stood up for me from the first day, which was nice to know when the exhibition games started."

Garpenlov also gave him some advice. "There is no reason for a Swede to keep getting into fights," Garpenlov said. "It was also something that our tough guys pointed out to us. 'We'll take care of that,' they said.

"At the same time, you could not show that you were scared. You had to stand your ground, and I think Nicklas did that from the beginning. He understood the level he should be at and started right there. He didn't try to make those long opening passes out of his own end right away."

The first preseason game was played against Philadelphia Flyers. It was quite an experience for the 21-year-old Lidstrom.

"For some reason the game was played in Orlando, Florida," Lidstrom said. "When one of our players skated by their goalie, Ron Hextall, he lifted his stick and hit it with full force into the chest of my teammate. My first reaction was, 'How did I end up here? What's going on?' Every preseason game had four or five fights. Many opponents wanted to test me and see how much abuse a Swedish rookie could take. I was a deer in the headlights."

Lidstrom was often comforted by assistant coach Dave Lewis, who was responsible for the defensemen on the Red Wings. "He was a brilliant man when it came to communicating with his players," Lidstrom said. "He took us to the side before every game and told us how to act in detail against every player on the opposite team. He prepared us in a detailed way. There should be no surprises."

It didn't take long into training camp for Lidstrom to make an impression. He knew then that management thought he was good enough to play in the NHL. After a week at camp, he and Garpenlov were both called into coach/GM Bryan Murray's office and told to look for an apartment. They had made the team. He wouldn't have to go down to the American Hockey League to get adjusted to the style of play in North America, something that often happened to European players who had just come over.

"It was a relief to know that I was staying with the Red Wings and starting the season in the NHL," Lidstrom said. "Playing in the Canada Cup definitely helped me get used to the smaller rinks, but I knew I was going to have to make quicker decisions on the ice."

He would also need to get acclimatized to the North American way of life, and Lidstrom leaned heavily on Garpenlov for guidance.

"I had lived in the suburb of St. Clair Shores during my first year in Detroit, but now both Nicklas and I got an apartment in

Northville, on the other side of the city," Garpenlov said. "Many of our teammates were already living there, so it sounded like the place to be."

Lidstrom had a number of things to take care of during his first week in Detroit. As with any other team in the league, the Red Wings required their players to be dressed in suits on game days, so Lidstrom brought Garpenlov with him on a shopping spree.

"I felt I was more of a chauffeur than a dress consultant," Garpenlov said. "We did find a good store not far from where we lived. The staff there helped him pick out some suits that looked good on him."

Lidstrom's big adventure had just started. "It was an exciting time, and I felt that I was ready for the NHL after going up against the best Canadians, Russians, and Americans during the Canada Cup tournament," Lidstrom said. "The odds that I would make it in the NHL felt pretty good."

3

HEARTBREAK IN HOCKEYTOWN

IT ALL STARTED FOR LIDSTROM IN THE WINDY CITY. DETROIT TRAVELED to Chicago for the 1991–92 NHL regular season opener. The Blackhawks weren't your ordinary opponent. The rivalry between the teams has always been intense and extends back to 1926. Both teams are part of the Original Six, the six clubs that were in place when the league doubled in size to 12 teams in 1967, so there is always a lot of prestige at stake when they meet.

"And on top of that, Chicago had a really good team at this time with players like Chris Chelios, Steve Larmer, and Jeremy Roenick, to name a few," Lidstrom remembered. "I was pretty nervous the days before the premiere, as we were playing them at their dreaded Chicago Stadium."

Lidstrom and Brad McCrimmon were the Red Wings' first defensive pair. The second pairing had Vladimir Konstantinov and Brad Marsh, with a number of guys fighting for a spot on the third unit. Among them were Yves Racine, Bobby Dollas, Steve Chiasson, and Doug Crossman.

"I was honored to be rewarded a spot on the first pairing with McCrimmon, and the coaches had me playing in all situations,"

Lidstrom said. "We were on the ice for around 20 minutes every game."

The home crowd at Chicago Stadium was famous for being loud. The arena had a special atmosphere, and for Lidstrom it was the most challenging debut he could have in the NHL.

"It was impossible to even hear the national anthem, and to just make it up that stairway from the dressing room to the rink was quite an experience," Lidstrom recalled. "McCrimmon told me it was 18 steps. He knew that by heart. The pressure inside that little arena was enormous and something I never had been through before. The fans were seated so close to the ice that you felt you couldn't get away from them."

Lidstrom was in the starting lineup together with McCrimmon, Sergei Fedorov, Paul Ysebaert, and Shawn Burr. Chicago tough guy Mike Peluso tried to get Lidstrom off his game early, sidling up next to the rookie during the first or second shift of the game.

"He stared at me and said, 'Fuck you,'" Lidstrom said. "And then he looked at the back of my jersey and continued, 'Lidstrom.'

"It ended up being a very physical game. Our goalie, Tim Cheveldae, wasn't that good with playing the puck behind the net, so Chicago kept dumping it in to get to him. That meant that we defensemen had to help him out by skating down there and getting the puck at the end boards. And of course, they hit us hard as soon as we got there. The Blackhawks had a number of good forecheckers and a coach in Mike Keenan who was on them all the time to be aggressive."

Detroit came away with a 3–3 tie. Lidstrom did not get a point in his first NHL game, but he was plus-two.

And he was still alive.

"I played an okay game," Lidstrom said. "Most importantly, my first game was over, and we got a tie."

Lidstrom had shown management, coaches, teammates, and perhaps most significantly one of the toughest opponents in the league that he belonged in the NHL.

"The unwritten rule at this time was that you had to prove yourself before anybody took you under their wing, before they were willing to stand up for you and protect you," Lidstrom said. "I didn't have to wait long before I felt that I was accepted among my teammates. My defense partner, Brad McCrimmon, was always there when things got heated, and Bob Probert came to my side to grab anybody who tried to run me over or engage me in a fight. It felt good to have the tough guys on my side. It didn't take long for me to feel that I was part of the team."

Lidstrom wasn't the only one in his circle for whom life was changing at a whirlwind pace. When management told Lidstrom that he had made the final cut and gave him the go-ahead to get an apartment, he called his girlfriend, Annika Eriksson, back in Sweden.

They had met at Stadshotell in Avesta during a Christmas party in 1990. As a tradition in towns all over the country, there were gatherings for young people who had left town and had come back for the holidays.

Annika lived and worked an hour away in Stockholm, and she and Nicklas had met through mutual friends. After they became a couple, she visited Vasteras every weekend to see him. With his busy hockey schedule and games every Sunday, it was difficult for him to get to Stockholm to see her.

"We had only dated for six months when I asked her if she wanted to move to Detroit with me," Lidstrom remembered. "I did it after I had been to Detroit in May to sign my first contract."

He looked at the move to Detroit as an adventure that would last a couple of years. Nothing more. "My thinking was in the line of, 'Well, I'll play a couple of years there and then we'll move home again.' My initial deal with the Red Wings was for two years with an extra option year. I had no further plans than that."

Annika left her job in Stockholm and moved to Detroit to live with Nicklas in the apartment for which he had just signed a lease. "I had no idea what that would mean, how it would affect me and how long we were going to be gone," Annika recalled. "It wasn't a given that I would move with him, but I didn't hesitate too long. I was in love and I did let that be the deciding point. Love conquers."

Both just 21 years old, Nicklas and Annika rented a furnished two-bedroom apartment in the same Northville neighborhood where teammates Johan Garpenlov, Kevin Miller, and McCrimmon lived. This made it easy to commute together to practices and games.

"It was exciting and fun, all the new people we got to meet and got to know both on and off the ice," Annika said. "We got our own apartment and learned how things worked in the U.S. after hardly knowing how they did in Sweden. The hockey part was also fascinating. We both got an insight on how an NHL club was built from the ground up."

As Nicklas assimilated into the team concept with the Wings, so did Annika. She soon learned how to socialize with the other players' wives and girlfriends.

"We all quickly became good friends, no matter the age," Annika said. "The Red Wings were good in taking care of us, so we bonded easily and did a lot of things together. Living in Detroit felt like an adventure for me and a chance to experience a new city and a new country. What I missed from Sweden was family and friends. Other than that, it would be things like Swedish candy and food products. Plus, nature and the clean air back home."

For Lidstrom, life was surrounded by hockey, including all the rituals that come with playing in the NHL. Dressing up for the games and life on the road soon became part of his everyday routine.

"I had learned to get the knot on my tie right back home in Sweden, so that wasn't a problem," Lidstrom said. "A bigger issue was to be able to sleep a couple of hours in the afternoon on game days. That was hard in the beginning. I was used to laying down and reading the newspaper for a little while after lunch on game days, but never actually sleeping for two hours. I had never done that before."

As a rookie, he was sharing a room with a veteran player on the road. For Lidstrom that meant having McCrimmon as his roommate and instructor on the ways of the NHL. "'Listen, kid, this is how it works,' he told me," Lidstrom remembered.

Lessons in napping weren't the only part of the learning curve, as Lidstrom would soon discover. McCrimmon liked to lower the thermostat in the room when he was taking his power nap between 2:00 and 4:00 PM. "He wanted it really cold," Lidstrom explained. "Same thing during the night. One time in Edmonton, when he had opened a window in the evening before we went to bed, I woke up early the next morning with snow in the room. It had started to snow during the night and part of our hotel room was covered in white."

Lidstrom was shivering under his blanket but quiet as a mouse, not daring to say anything. It was part of the ritualistic life as a rookie. You had to go along with how the veterans wanted things done.

There were other things that made him pay attention. Every other week, he got an envelope in his mailbox at the rink with a check.

"I think the first check I got paid was $15,000," Lidstrom said. "That was unreal. I couldn't grasp it. After a number of weeks, I went out and bought myself a new car, a Nissan 300. I wrote a check for the first time in my life. I had looked at a car like that back in Sweden but felt that it was too much money to spend. As a 21-year-old professional hockey player in Detroit, I couldn't resist the car. My rookie contract paid me an annual salary of $275,000, including a signing bonus of $125,000. The bonus money was put into an account that the Red Wings had opened in my name. That also was a special moment for me. I had no clue they could do that."

Lidstrom didn't have any problems adjusting to the game on the smaller rinks in North America. "He's a good, solid player in every aspect," McCrimmon said of his defense partner in an interview during Lidstrom's rookie NHL campaign. "He's good offensively and he's good defensively. He's got good composure and he works hard. He's a great skater. You can't say that he has one dominating quality."

McCrimmon felt that Lidstrom's international opportunities in the World Championships and Canada Cup had served as a sort of finishing school to enable him to smoothly make the transition from Swedish hockey to the NHL.

"With Nick, I think having been exposed to the World Championships, the Canada Cup, and five years of the Swedish Elite League, he's had good experience," McCrimmon explained. "It's the same with Vladdy [fellow Detroit rookie defenseman Vladimir Konstantinov]. They're rookies in the NHL, but they're not rookies in experience."

Lidstrom credits McCrimmon's influence and steadying presence for enabling his relatively seamless transition to the NHL. "He was more of a stay-at-home defenseman, and that gave me a chance to be part of the offense," Lidstrom recalled. "He was my partner for every game my first year. He was that steady defenseman who stayed home all the time. He would protect me in situations when things got heated. He was a great partner and I learned a lot from him that first year."

Off the ice, since the two lived in the same area, they carpooled to games. Their wives also developed a friendship. "He was always happy, always looking at things the positive way," Lidstrom said of McCrimmon, who died tragically in 2011 when the plane carrying the Lokomotiv Yaroslavl team, of which McCrimmon was the coach, crashed. "He was always trying to encourage players when things weren't going their way. He helped me out a lot my first year in the league."

Lidstrom gained a reputation on the ice for intuitively anticipating what would happen next on a play. Off the ice, he did his best to prepare for his next hockey step into the NHL.

"When I played in the World Championships in the spring, I asked Tomas Jonsson, Hakan Loob, Bengt Gustafsson, former NHL players that were playing back in Sweden, how it was over here," Lidstrom said. "I talked to Borje Salming during the Canada Cup. I just tried to talk to as many players as I could. I just wanted to know how it is, how the cities are, the food…well, everything."

Once he arrived in Detroit, his tutelage was taken over by Swedish teammate Garpenlov. "When I first came over here, I didn't know anything," Lidstrom said. "How to order a phone, find an apartment—things like that. Johan, he helped me. He was great."

Lidstrom discovered that things on this side of the Atlantic weren't measurably different than back home. "There was a little difference, but not much," he said. "Back in Sweden everything was not as spread out as it is here. I had to drive a half hour in my car to get to the arena. I spent a lot more time in my car. The cities in Sweden are a couple hundred thousand people. Here, cities are a million.

"The food was almost the same. There were a lot more fast food places. We had some fast food—McDonald's, Pizza Hut—but we didn't have Little Caesars."

He smiles at that memory. "I thought maybe I should eat that now," Lidstrom said with a laugh. Little Caesars Pizza is owned by the Ilitch family, who signed Lidstrom's paychecks as owners of the Red Wings.

Steve Yzerman was the team captain when Lidstrom arrived in Detroit. Yzerman was one of the league's best forwards, often chasing only Wayne Gretzky and Mario Lemieux in the scoring race.

"Before you were accepted and had earned a regular spot on the team, he treated everybody the same," Lidstrom recalled. "Stevie wasn't as outgoing as McCrimmon, but you could see how hard he worked every day. Both on and off the ice. He was highly respected for the person and leader he was."

Lidstrom's rookie season was a big success. He played all 80 regular season games and produced 60 points (11 goals and 49 assists). But what impressed his coaches and teammates the most was his plus/minus rating of plus-36, which led all rookies and was third in the NHL behind only teammates Paul Ysebaert (plus-44) and McCrimmon (plus-39).

Yzerman was immediately impressed with the rookie Swedish defenseman. "From the day Nick arrived in Detroit, he clearly belonged in the NHL," Yzerman said. "Initially, the thing that stood out the most was how poised he was in his play. Nick showed no panic ever when he was on the ice."

Yzerman did not see Lidstrom having to clear any big hurdles during his first season in Detroit. "I believe Nick adjusted very well both on and off the ice," Yzerman said. "He was a mature young man, intelligent, very professional in his approach to hockey. No one, including myself, ever had to do anything to help him out."

Lidstrom was proud to have started off well in the NHL without any complications. "I had a very good first year in the league and was nominated for the Calder Trophy together with Pavel Bure and Tony Amonte," Lidstrom said. Bure, who scored 34 goals, won the award given to the league's best rookie;

Lidstrom finished second in the voting. Lidstrom and teammate Konstantinov were named the defensemen on the NHL All-Rookie Team, and future Detroit teammate Dominik Hasek was the netminder selected to the squad.

Detroit was an extremely offensive club in the beginning of the 1990s and that suited Lidstrom's style of play. "The team they had was on the rise, so Nicklas couldn't have ended up on a better club," said Calle Johansson, at that time a star defenseman on the Washington Capitals. "They had speedy forwards and he liked to join the attack. It looked like he fit right in. He stepped into what was a dream team in my opinion."

Originally, Lidstrom had built his reputation around his offensive skills. "That's how they pictured me," Lidstrom said. "Somebody who could run a power play, but what happened was that I also got a lot of ice time as a penalty killer. But the power play was my thing. That's where I thought I could contribute from the get-go."

Lidstrom wasn't the only young talent the Red Wings made room for at this time. Other players who gave the team a spark and were in the early stages of their careers included Konstantinov; forwards Fedorov, Slava Kozlov, Keith Primeau, and Darren McCarty; and goalie Chris Osgood.

"When me and Konstantinov became regulars in the lineup, it was an overhaul of the defense corps," Lidstrom said. "Detroit let some older blueliners leave and the coaching staff gave us more ice time. I thought we deserved the increasing ice time we got."

Lidstrom was rapidly earning the respect of his NHL peers as well. Brian Hayward, today a TV analyst for FOX Sports West, had been a goalie in the NHL since the 1982–83 season. "I was there really early in Nick's career and it's funny because no one really knew anything about him when he came over," Hayward said. "He wasn't a high draft pick but it was evident right off the bat that his decision-making was on another level. And that is what I always think about him, that he seemed to make the right play all the time whenever he had the puck. He had such an unbelievable poise and his panic threshold was so high. He always seemed to know where to put the puck. He put it in the right spot and he had a surprisingly good shot."

Lidstrom got a chance to experience the atmosphere in the playoffs during his first season in the NHL. The Red Wings rallied from a 3–1 series deficit to beat the Minnesota North Stars in the first round and reach the Norris Division final, but then fell to Chicago in four straight games. Lidstrom had three points (one goal and two assists) in 11 playoff games in his first year in the league.

The playoff heartbreak that the Wings endured in the spring of 1992 would become a recurring theme in Hockeytown. Detroit scored the most goals of any team in the league the next two years but could not make it past the first round of postseason play. The Wings lost against Toronto in a seven-game series in 1993 and to San Jose in another seven-game set in 1994.

The loss to the Maple Leafs gnaws away particularly at Lidstrom, because it was his man who netted the Game 7 winner in overtime. Lidstrom might struggle to remember Nikolai Borschevsky's name, but he's never been able to erase the memory of the moment.

"If I look back at my career in Detroit, there was a goal by a Toronto player in the early rounds one year that knocked us out of the playoffs that still haunts me," Lidstrom said. "We lost against the Maple Leafs at home and the player that scored the game-winning goal in Game 7 was my guy. I didn't cover him the way I should have, and he was able to redirect the puck into our net after a shot from one of his teammates. I had his stick, but not enough of it. I think it was one of their Russian players. A smaller guy, pretty thin."

Lidstrom recalls those early playoff setbacks as building blocks along the learning curve that would eventually turn the Wings into Stanley Cup champions. Detroit led the NHL in goals in both 1992–93 (369) and 1993–94 (356). The 1992–93 Wings scored 113 power play goals. In NHL history, only the 1988–89 Pittsburgh Penguins (119) tallied more often with the man advantage. But keeping the puck out of its own net proved a real issue for Detroit.

"The year we lost against Toronto, we weren't a good enough team to make it to the finals and win the Stanley Cup," Lidstrom said. "We had some growing to do. We scored a lot of goals but we let even more in."

Studying that 1993 division semifinal series confirms Lidstrom's assessment. The Wings surrendered 24 goals in seven games, an average of more than 3.4 goals per game. Particularly galling was Game 5; playing at home at Joe Louis Arena, Detroit frittered away a 4–1 second-period lead and lost 5–4 in overtime.

Lidstrom had one goal and was a minus-2 in the seven-game series. That was his second season in the NHL. For him, though, that didn't change anything. He was the one who didn't stop Borschevsky from scoring the winner for Toronto in overtime and that was all that mattered to him.

As the eighth-seeded Sharks stunned No. 1 seed Detroit in 1994, one of San Jose's heroes was Russian hockey legend Igor Larionov. But even in victory, Larionov sang the praises of the slick Swede on Detroit's blueline.

The Russian star had noticed Lidstrom performing against him for a number of years before coming to Detroit. "I played an exhibition game with the national team in Vasteras before the World Championships in Stockholm in 1989 and heard a Russian player, who was a friend of mine, mentioning this local young defenseman," Larionov said. "We were told that he was an extraordinary talent.

"I wasn't picked for the Canada Cup tournament in 1991 because of a conflict with [coach Viktor] Tikhonov, so I did not have a chance to play against Nick there. I must have played against him once or twice during my years with Vancouver, but it took until my time with the San Jose Sharks before I really noticed him."

Larionov was reunited with his old CSKA linemate Sergei Makarov in San Jose, and Detroit often matched Lidstrom against the Russians. "Nick was either paired with Paul Coffey or Mark Howe, so he was surrounded by good defensemen that made him comfortable," Larionov said. "Nick had time to adjust to the NHL style of play and that helped him big time. He was not flashy, but very smart and efficient. Nick was hard to beat, because he was so slick. He was not physical and we played Soviet-style hockey, but we still had a hard time scoring against him.

"His style was different than the North American defensemen in the league and you could see a young and upcoming superstar.

It was a nightmare for me, the way he patrolled the blueline without giving up any breakaways for us."

The future Hall of Famer observed how easily Lidstrom started a breakout with a nice pass up the middle. This was something Larionov would benefit from later when he and Lidstrom became teammates in Detroit following a 1995 trade.

Murray was fired as Detroit coach after the 1992–93 season and replaced by Scotty Bowman, who had coached the Pittsburgh Penguins to a Stanley Cup two years earlier. It didn't take long for Bowman to identify the cornerstone player he had in Lidstrom.

"When I came to Detroit in 1993 I had no opinion on Nick as a player with the Red Wings, but I soon found out how smart and efficient he was," Bowman said. "Especially how he enjoyed practices."

The legendary coach with championship titles from Montreal and Pittsburgh emboldened Lidstrom to develop his game further. "I encouraged him to go on the offensive when he felt he could, as he was so good defensively," Bowman said. "What stood out in my mind with Lidstrom was his effortless passing and skating style. He very rarely took low-percentage chances in moving the puck out of his end."

Bowman brought with him his assistant coach from Pittsburgh, Barry Smith, and together with Dave Lewis, they put in place the famous left-wing lock-checking system. "We felt forced to change the style of play the team had been using," Smith said. "Scotty and I inherited a team that was totally focused on the offensive part of the game and some of the older players did not work that hard defensively."

One reason the new coaching staff was able to change the system was the presence of Lidstrom and Coffey as defensemen on the left side. "You could say that we didn't need a third left defender," Smith said. "Nick and Coffey never got tired, they were such good skaters and could cover most of the ice. We also had another young blueliner in Vladimir Konstantinov and I'm convinced he would have gone on to win a Norris Trophy if he hadn't been injured in that tragic car accident after the Stanley Cup victory in 1997."

Changes were afoot in Lidstrom's family life as well. Nicklas and Annika bought a condo during their third year in Detroit, where they stayed for another three years. That's where they lived when they had their first son, Kevin, in 1994. They bought their first house in Detroit in 1996 when their second son, Adam, was born. The house was located in Novi, and they stayed there until 2005. That's when Nicklas and Annika found their dream house in Northville, where they stayed for seven years before they moved back to Sweden in the summer of 2012.

Oddly, the addition to their family brought out surprising feelings in Annika. For the first time since leaving Sweden, she felt homesick. "I was longing for my family back home more when I became a mother," explained Annika, who sought out other interests to help alleviate the feeling. "I had taken some classes in photography, computer science, and interior design during my first years in Detroit, when the kids were young. Later on, when Adam was born, I spent a lot of time taking him and Kevin to different activities, like music, gymnastics, tennis, swimming, skating, and soccer that were available for young children where we lived."

The 1994–95 season took Lidstrom and Detroit within one step of winning the Stanley Cup. But it would prove to be a giant step. Bowman had finally convinced his players to buy into his defensive system, and the result was the Wings finished first overall in the regular season standings and improved in goals against from 16th in 1993–94 to second.

"This was a lockout season, so the regular season didn't start until January and only included 48 games," Lidstrom said. The Wings were an impressive 33–11–4 during the regular season, losing back-to-back games just once and finishing third in the NHL with 80 goals scored. "We were surfing on a positive wave and just kept winning. Everything was so easy, and we never looked back."

In postseason play, that positivity kept on flowing. "We made it to the finals after a strong performance throughout the playoffs where we only lost two games," Lidstrom said. The Wings blasted their way to the Stanley Cup Final for the first time since 1966, falling only twice in their first 14 playoff games.

In the process, Lidstrom made a little Red Wings postseason history. Game 1 of Detroit's Western Conference Final series with the archrival Blackhawks at Joe Louis Arena was tied 1–1 after regulation. The extra session was barely underway when Lidstrom's low-point shot beat Chicago goalie Ed Belfour at 1:01 to give Detroit the 2–1 victory.

It was Detroit's first playoff OT win in its own building since Gerry Melnyk's goal gave the Wings a 2–1 triumph over the Maple Leafs in Game 4 of the semifinals at Olympia Stadium on March 29, 1960. The Red Wings had waited for a home-ice playoff overtime victory almost as long as they had been waiting to lift the Stanley Cup, something the team had most recently done in 1955.

The historic marker caught Lidstrom completely off guard. "Thirty-five years?" Lidstrom asked at the time. "Really? I didn't know that."

Thanks to Lidstrom, the wait was over.

Gerry Melynk?

The name drew a blank stare from most Red Wings. "No, I can't say that I'd ever heard of him," Lidstrom said.

Since that time, Detroit had been 0–10 in home playoff OT contests, the most recent loss coming when Toronto's Borschevsky ended Detroit's season in Game 7 of the opening round of the 1993 playoffs, the goal that haunted Lidstrom's dreams.

This time, the right Nick dented the twine.

Keith Primeau won the draw to the left of Belfour. With Burr in front of the net, Lidstrom's shot skipped past Belfour's out-stretched left pad.

"I think I screened him," Burr said.

Asked if he saw the puck, Belfour said, "Yeah. When it was in the net."

Chicago was dispatched in five games, three of them Detroit overtime victories. The Wings were going to the Stanley Cup Final for the first time in 29 seasons.

This was the hope of all NHLers. Everybody in the room had a Stanley Cup story to tell. Some told them with emotion, some were more stoic, and some, like Lidstrom, simply wore their heart on their sleeve—or to be more exact, on the T-shirt he'd been given to commemorate the occasion. Consider the following words, which appeared next to Lord Stanley's Cup on the back of a T-shirt worn by the Wings defenseman at a pre-Final practice:

Best Of Seven. Cracked Ribs. Fresh Stitches. Black Eyes. Broken Bones. This Is No Beauty Contest. It's About The Dream.

The mood in Detroit was festive. And then in an instant, it was fractured.

"We ended up with New Jersey in the Stanley Cup finals and they were bigger and stronger than us," Lidstrom said. "We had a harder time creating scoring chances. We lost four straight games to the Devils, but we learned what it took to go all the way, something that would be useful for us in the playoffs the next couple of years."

There were still lessons that required learning before Lidstrom and his teammates would prove worthy of calling themselves champions. Further storms would be weathered, including being hit by an Avalanche.

4

THE CUP FINALLY ARRIVES

AS THE 1995–96 NHL SEASON GOT UNDERWAY, LITTLE DID NICKLAS Lidstrom and the rest of the Red Wings realize that their biggest win of the season would ultimately lead to their greatest heartbreak of the campaign.

The Quebec Nordiques had moved to Denver and been rechristened the Colorado Avalanche before the 1995–96 season. The Wings provided the opposition in the Avalanche home opener on October 6, 1995, and lost 3–2. But that was merely an appetizer of what would become hockey's most savored rivalry by the end of the season.

A dozen games into the season, the defending Western Conference champion Wings weren't wowing anybody, idling along at 5–5–2. But then they took the NHL by storm, going 22–2 the remainder of the calendar year.

One of those triumphs was an 11–1 rout of the Montreal Canadiens on December 2 that would forever change the landscape of the NHL.

The drubbing led to an incident between Canadiens Vezina Trophy–winning goalie Patrick Roy and Montreal coach Mario Tremblay. There was bad blood between the two stemming back to when they were teammates with the Habs, and it spilled over into a verbal altercation on the Montreal bench after Tremblay left his No. 1 netminder between the posts to absorb nine of the 11 Detroit goals.

As Roy left the ice, he told Canadiens team president Ron Corey, who was sitting right behind the home team bench at the Montreal Forum, that he had played his last game for the Canadiens. Later that week, on December 6, Roy was traded to Colorado in a blockbuster multiplayer transaction, a move that shook the hockey world and forever altered the landscape in the NHL's Western Conference.

As great a goalie as Roy was, his arrival in the Mile High City didn't seem to have any immediate impact in games between the Avalanche and the Red Wings. Detroit won all three regular season contests against Colorado after Roy arrived, including a 7–0 whitewash on March 22, 1996, in which Roy was chased to the bench after surrendering five goals.

The Wings set an NHL record, winning 62 games. It looked as though nothing could stop them in their quest to end the city's Stanley Cup drought, which extended back to 1955.

Then the playoffs began.

It took the Wings six games to dispatch the pesky Winnipeg Jets in the opening round. Up next was a longtime divisional rival, the St. Louis Blues. The Blues had made a bold trade to land Wayne Gretzky, but no one in Hockeytown seemed too worried about the Great One after Detroit opened the series with a pair of home-ice wins. But the tide suddenly turned. The Blues won three straight and were headed home to the Kiel Center with a chance to eliminate the winningest team in NHL history.

Lidstrom remembers a story Red Wings general manager Ken Holland told him about that game. Holland, then the team's assistant GM, ran into Scotty Bowman in the hotel lobby on game day afternoon and wanted to check in and see if everything was okay. Bowman told Holland that if St. Louis was going to start the game with the Gretzky line, he would counter with this line, and then the next line would be this one, and so on. Bowman had the first seven or eight shifts figured out hours before the game.

"Scotty was so focused and well-prepared hours before the puck would drop," Lidstrom said. "This was in the second round of the playoffs and we were down 3–2 in games, so we had an important game in front of us. But the story says a lot about Scotty's attitude and how professional he was. He had imagined the first 10 minutes of the game in his mind and knew exactly how he would coach our team."

The Wings dug deep and staved off elimination with a solid 4–2 road win in Game 6. Lidstrom assisted on Dino Ciccarelli's game-winner and scored the vital insurance goal. It was back to Detroit for a winner-take-all Game 7, and what a game it was.

The contest remained scoreless for 81 minutes and 14 seconds. Finally, Detroit captain Steve Yzerman stepped over the blueline and into a powerful, high slapshot that eluded St. Louis goaltender Jon Casey and ended the series.

The Red Wings got only two days' rest before the Western Conference Final against Colorado. It was not enough time to regroup. "We were tired and couldn't handle Colorado, it was as simple as that," Lidstrom said.

The Avs jumped on the weary Wings quickly, winning the first two games of the series at Joe Louis Arena. The Wings gained a split in Denver and after a solid 5–2 home-ice victory in Game 5, held to a semblance of hope that they could survive again just as they had against St. Louis. But it was not to be. The Wings fell 4–1 in Game 6 at McNichols Arena.

Another magical season had ended in heartbreak for the Wings, but this time, it also ended with broken bones and bloodshed that would ignite one of the most fiery and bitter rivalries that hockey has ever seen.

Early in Game 6, Avalanche forward Claude Lemieux hit Detroit center Kris Draper with a forceful check from behind that sent Draper crashing into the boards face-first in front of the Detroit bench. Draper suffered a broken cheekbone, a fractured jaw, a broken nose, and several broken teeth, as well as a concussion. Lemieux was assessed a major penalty and thrown out of the game, while Draper ended up in the hospital and needed 30 stitches to close the facial cuts. His jaw had to be wired shut for weeks and he underwent plastic surgery to repair some of the other damage.

Lemieux had been involved in earlier incidents and scrums during the series; he had punched Slava Kozlov after the Detroit forward had slammed Avalanche defenseman Adam Foote face-first into the glass in Game 3. Foote was bleeding hard, but none of the officials saw the hit and no penalty was called. Lemieux skated up to Kozlov and sucker punched him in the mouth.

Lemieux was suspended for one game after a review of the incident by the league. That suspension caused Colorado coach Marc Crawford to accuse Bowman of manipulating the media, referees, and league officials. This was only the beginning of a heated rivalry; over the next several years, Lidstrom and his teammates would endure many wild and brutal battles with the Avalanche.

Heading into the next season, there was a feeling that things could escalate quickly between the two teams. Detroit wanted revenge for the hit Lemieux had placed on Draper the season before. Draper's bloody and broken face was something his teammates would not forget. At least not his close friend on the team, Darren McCarty.

The next chapter in this bloody war came on March 26, 1997, exactly 301 days after Lemieux's hit on Draper. The scene was Joe Louis Arena in Detroit. It started with a scrum between Colorado's Peter Forsberg and Detroit's Igor Larionov. The two European players engaged in a wrestling match next to the Detroit bench. It didn't look like much from the start, but the two skilled stars ignited a brawl that would spread all over the ice.

When Forsberg looks back at that night, he is still confused about how it turned so ugly. "I have seen it on video afterward and it's kind of funny to watch," Forsberg said. "We were two guys that had never been in a fight, and then we start this chaos. I did talk to Lemieux afterward and told him that I had no idea that him and McCarty were on the ice at the same time."

It was McCarty who escalated things. He blindsided Lemieux and started punching him. Lemieux took to the turtle position, down on all fours to try to protect himself, and did not hit back.

Then Roy came storming out of his crease and skated to the middle of the ice to fight Detroit goalie Mike Vernon. Brendan Shanahan intercepted Roy, and they both went flying. It was mayhem.

"Lemieux used to joke with me and blame me for starting the whole thing," Forsberg said. "We both laughed about it later on. My first thought on the ice was, 'Oh, this is escalating into something really bad. Yikes.' But I think it would have happened anyway. Maybe it would have come at the end of the game. Looking back, I think it was good to get it over with early. We were two really good teams who both wanted to win so badly. And we did not like each other."

Lidstrom was not involved in any of the rumbles on the ice when things got out of control. Keith Jones, today a color analyst with NBC Sports, was a member of the Avalanche at that time. He offered a simple explanation as to why Lidstrom didn't get involved.

"He never backed off, but he was always above the fray," Jones said. "You could never draw him into whatever type of chaos was going on around him. He just played his game, and I give him credit for that, because there was a lot of chaos going on in those games."

Jones' conclusion is that Lidstrom was so cool that it was impossible to get him off his game, something Lidstrom agrees with.

"That's right," Lidstrom said. "First of all, my style of play wasn't that physical, and I also had the ability to control myself. Things were going on all the time out there on the ice, including slashes and yelling expletives. It happened after every stop in the play, but I stayed out of it."

This blood feud carried over off the ice as well. Fraternization between Colorado and Detroit players simply wasn't acceptable. Forsberg recalls the tension between him and his friend Lidstrom during this time.

"There was absolutely no contact between me and Nicklas during those intense years," Forsberg said. "To talk to him was totally taboo. I remember a situation when we had been in

Detroit, and my linemate Valeri Kamensky chatted with another Russian player outside the dressing room after a regular season game. He got an earful from Claude Lemieux on the team bus when we left Joe Louis Arena. I was pretty new on the team then, and thought, 'Hmm, I better not speak to any of their Swedes.'"

"We didn't trash talk between us on the ice, but we did not hold back with the physical play," Lidstrom said. "Peter was one of Colorado's best players, and we needed to keep an eye on him all the time. We were ordered to not give him any space, so as soon as he had the puck, we tried to hit him or interfere with him. He was not allowed to have any time with the puck and set up a play. He was so dangerous.

"I remember how tense the relationship was between us. Even at the All-Star Game, we couldn't put it aside and act like friends. Once, when the All-Star Game was in Denver and we were on the same team from the Western Conference, I was booed so badly during the introduction it felt like the fans hated me then as much as they did at a playoff game."

The Red Wings were down by two goals when things got out of hand that infamous March night at the Joe. They turned the game around and won 6–5 on an overtime tally by McCarty. As the Wings moved into the playoffs, they hoped this outcome would be a stepping stone on their path to becoming Stanley Cup champions.

The loss against Colorado in the Western Conference Final in 1996 made Red Wings management aware of the team's weaknesses. They thought their team had to become tougher and stronger. They knew they needed bigger bodies in the lineup and a better presence in front of the net.

At the start of the 1996–97 season, Detroit got Shanahan from the Hartford Whalers, a big, strong winger and goal-scorer, and sent defenseman Paul Coffey, forward Keith Primeau, and a first-round draft pick to Hartford.

Shanahan had established himself as a power forward after years in the league with the New Jersey Devils, St. Louis Blues, and Whalers. He had racked up points everywhere he'd been and reached 52 goals and 102 points with the Blues in 81 games during the 1993–94 season.

Detroit's plan was to get a more balanced team on the ice by adding Shanahan's skill and toughness. They already had the Russian Five and a blooming Swedish defenseman in Lidstrom.

Going into the season in the fall of 1996, the Avalanche were the defending Stanley Cup champions and the team to beat. They started the season strong, and it looked like they would be back-to-back champions after finishing first in the regular season with 107 points. Detroit finished third in the Western Conference and fifth in the league with a roster that included players from Canada, the U.S., Russia, and Sweden.

Bowman's love for international hockey and European influences made him the perfect coach to get this mix of talent to work well together. Larionov had been trying to play his successful Russian style of hockey in Vancouver and San Jose but didn't feel at home until he ended up in Detroit in October of 1995 under Bowman's leadership.

"Scotty Bowman orchestrated everything," Larionov said. "He was a big fan of the legendary Soviet coach Anatoly Tarasov. Scotty's biggest asset was his ability to see every player's skill level and use that to put the puzzle together. He could spot details in everybody's play and didn't care what passport you had or what language you spoke. It was all about putting 20 guys on the same page with no restrictions. He respected European hockey and the background of every player. Scotty's mix was built on chemistry, commitment, respect, and unity. It worked so well."

When Shanahan had arrived in the Motor City in October of 1996, he had played against Lidstrom for years in the league. But he still was surprised by what he saw. "He was even better than I realized," Shanahan said. "You had to see Nick every day to appreciate how good he was. Not just in games, but in practice."

The 6-foot-3, 220-pound Canadian could check, fight, and score, and Shanahan became a fan favorite on his first shift at Joe Louis Arena when he fought Edmonton's Greg de Vries.

Lidstrom and his teammates knew right away that Shanahan had arrived and that the Red Wings' image had changed. They were not a soft team any longer; they had more bite than previous years. The early exits in the first round in 1993 and 1994, the four straight losses to New Jersey in the Final in 1995, and the heartbreaking loss in the Western Conference Final against Colorado a few months earlier had formed a dark cloud over Detroit. Things had to change. Shanahan was the superstar they needed.

Lidstrom had a stellar regular season in 1996–97 with 57 points (15 goals and 42 assists) in 79 games. He was fourth on the team in scoring, behind only Shanahan (87 points), Yzerman (85), and Sergei Fedorov (63).

The playoffs started ominously when St. Louis beat Detroit 2–0 in Game 1 of the Western Conference quarterfinals, but the Red Wings won four of the next five games to beat St. Louis in six games and then breezed through Anaheim with four straight victories in the conference semifinals.

Next up was Colorado, and it was time for revenge. The Western Conference Final started on May 15 and the hype was huge after what had happened a year earlier.

Lidstrom's assignment was to stop countryman Peter "Foppa" Forsberg. "Scotty wanted us to be as close to Foppa as possible," Lidstrom recalled. "He was a key player, so to eliminate his line with Kamensky and Lemieux, you had to stop him. We tried to get under his skin and had Kris Draper and Kirk Maltby irritating him to get him off his game.

"I knew that Peter would hit me hard if he got the chance. He was a competitor and never gave up. We both wanted to win so badly, and the friendship was put on hold."

Colorado won the first game 2–1 at McNichols Arena in Denver, but Detroit came back and tied the series with a 4–2 win. The series moved to Joe Louis Arena for the next two games and a 2–1 win in Game 3 gave the Red Wings a lead in the series for the first time. Roy tried to boost his team with some tough talk before Game 4 and challenged the Detroit players by asking if they had what it would take to beat the defending champions.

Roy's pep talk fell flat. Detroit crushed Colorado with a 6–0 win, and now had a 3–1 lead in the series. At the end of Game 4, Colorado coach Marc Crawford launched into an angry tirade at Bowman between the benches that led to the league fining him $10,000.

Lidstrom enjoyed a bird's-eye view of the shouting match. "Scotty and Marc Crawford had some heated discussions between the benches when we played Colorado and the rivalry was at its peak," Lidstrom said. "They often stood and screamed at each other on the bench. Crawford at one time was hanging over into our bench and just lost it. Scotty shouted back, 'I know your father and he would not be very proud of you right now.' That made Crawford totally lose it."

The next day Crawford issued an apology, saying, "You have a responsibility as a head coach in a prestigious league like the NHL to carry yourself with a lot more dignity than I did. For that, I am sorry. I embarrassed the league, and more important, I embarrassed my team with my actions. There is no way you can justify anything like that."

The heat was back on between Detroit and Colorado. Crawford's actions showed that his team was not going away peacefully. And they didn't. Colorado returned the favor in Game 5 in Denver, winning by the same 6–0 score. Lemieux had two goals and told the media afterward that he believed the Avs could turn the series around.

But that didn't happen. Detroit closed out the series with a 3–1 win in Game 6 at home. Forsberg came back after missing Game 5 because of a severe charley horse that made it impossible for him to skate. Once more, he was kept under close watch by Lidstrom and his defensive partners on the Red Wings.

"Nick was one of the hardest guys to play against," Forsberg said. "Not physically. I didn't have any problems with that part of his game. It was more his ability to read the game and his reach. Anytime you thought you had gained some space away from him with the puck, he was there and closed it. He did not give you an inch.

"He also was a master at bringing the puck down in the air with his stick. I have never seen anybody else with that eye-hand coordination. Add to all his skills that he played 25 minutes per game, and it felt that you never could get rid of him."

Detroit was back in the Stanley Cup Final two years after losing in four straight to New Jersey. This time they were up against the Philadelphia Flyers, powered by the imposing top line of Eric Lindros, Mikael Renberg, and John LeClair, nicknamed the Legion of Doom.

Everybody expected Bowman to have the defensive pairing of Vladimir Konstantinov and Viacheslav Fetisov on the ice against the Flyers' top line. Bowman had another idea, much to Lidstrom's surprise. He knew the strength of the Flyers' dominating, physical line lay in their ability to get the puck down low in the other team's zone and create chances off the cycle, and the best way to combat that tactic was to keep the puck out of Detroit's end of the ice. So, Bowman opted to counter Philly's brawn with brains.

"Konstantinov and Fetisov were big, strong, and hard-hitting defenders, but Scotty decided to put me and Larry Murphy against the Legion of Doom," Lidstrom said. "We were not the same physical players as the Russians, but Scotty masterminded a game plan where he wanted us to go down into our own end, pick up the puck, and deliver a quick pass up the ice. Scotty did not want us to spend much time in our own end. He did not want the Flyers to have the chance to hit us time and again."

The Wings had acquired Murphy, who'd won two Stanley Cups with the Pittsburgh Penguins—one with Bowman as his coach—from the Toronto Maple Leafs at the NHL trade deadline.

Detroit assistant coach Dave Lewis described the Lidstrom-Murphy pairing as "a veteran with an older veteran." He wasn't the least bit surprised when Bowman's ingenious plan worked to perfection.

"There was a caveat there," Lewis said of the symbiotic relationship between Murphy and Lidstrom. "They were the best pair to play against the other team's best forwards. Not some of the time. Always."

Murphy marveled at the way Lidstrom could dominate on the ice. "He made your game a lot easier," Murphy said. "He liked to play the control game and liked to make the play with the puck."

Lidstrom found that Murphy's game meshed immediately and effectively with his own. "I think our styles were pretty similar and that's why we played so well together," Lidstrom said. "I think it clicked right away when we were put together. It was easy to play with Murph. He was always there for a pass and to help you out."

The Red Wings had their engine running at full speed when the Final started after a tough six-game series against Colorado. "I always thought it took a while to get going in the playoffs," Lidstrom said. "The intensity hit another level, and it took some time to adjust from the tempo of the regular season. We had won a hard-fought series against St. Louis in the first round in 1997, and after knocking out Anaheim and Colorado, we were ready for Philadelphia.

"I think their top line got very frustrated by Scotty's tactics. The Flyers liked to forecheck hard and hit the opponents as often as they could to make them tired. It had worked so well for them in the earlier rounds, but now they couldn't get to us. Scotty outsmarted their coaching staff and we won the first two games on the road in Philadelphia, both 4–2."

Back in Detroit, Lidstrom felt that this could be the year when he would finally fulfill his dream of winning the Stanley Cup. The team was strong and they had taken command of the series. Now they were coming home with all the advantage of having the crowd at Joe Louis Arena behind them.

"We were well aware of what a good position we had put ourselves in, but already when we landed back in Detroit, our captain, Steve Yzerman, took us aside and told us that we hadn't achieved anything yet," Lidstrom remembered. "That state of mind was the key for us winning it, in my mind."

Detroit won its third straight game in the series, this time by the score of 6–1. Philadelphia seemed to be incapable of creating much offense and appeared to be in a state of disarray. "They changed goalies all the time between Garth Snow and Ron Hextall," Lidstrom said. "We felt we had the upper hand. It seemed that they were struggling in all aspects of the game."

The fourth game was a more even contest, but the Red Wings came away with a 2–1 win to complete the sweep. Lidstrom opened the scoring, blasting a shot from the point past Hextall late in the first period. He was also on the ice when McCarty tallied a spectacular breakaway goal for the eventual Cup winner at 13:02 of the second period. The long wait was over. The Stanley Cup was back in Detroit for the first time since 1955.

"It was an amazing feeling," Lidstrom said. "Unreal, in a way. This was something I had been dreaming about since I was a kid playing street hockey back home in Sweden. To win your first Stanley Cup was very special. I was well aware of the fact that Detroit hadn't won it in 42 years.

"I remember the buzz in the city the day before Game 4. We stayed at a hotel downtown the night before the game, and even if it wasn't more than a five-minute drive to the arena, you could feel the buzz in the air. The expectations were high. Something special was about to happen. I knew it."

There was a moment on the ice that Lidstrom still recalls warmly. It came when team captain Yzerman handed over the Stanley Cup to Red Wings owner Mike Ilitch. "It was just fantastic to see how happy he was," Lidstrom said. "Mr. Ilitch had worked so hard for this, we all knew that. You could tell by looking at his eyes how overwhelmed he was. I will never forget that moment. It said it all."

The parade down Woodward Avenue to Hart Plaza three days later displayed to Lidstrom and his teammates how much the fans loved their Red Wings. An estimated 1 million people showed up on this sunny day in June to cheer their champions.

"We didn't really know what to expect, but with the sea of fans out along the victory parade route I got very emotional," Lidstrom said. "They talked about a million people. For me, a guy from a small town in Sweden, it was crazy. I couldn't believe it. An older man in his 70s came up to me with tears in his eyes to personally thank us for bringing the Stanley Cup back to Detroit."

Bowman's mix of tough Canadian and American players with a touch of European skill from the Russian Five and the Swedish trio of Nicklas Lidstrom, Tomas Holmstrom, and Tomas Sandstrom had paid dividends. The new model was based on a speedy passing game and puck control. The opponents did not have the tools to stop Bowman and his Red Wings. But as skilled as they were, as they'd shown the Avalanche, that Wings team could also play rough when necessary.

"Of all the Wings teams that won Cups, I thought our team in 1997 was maybe the most difficult to play against," Shanahan said. "We were skilled but also very physical. We could play the game any way you wanted to."

Sadly, the joy would be short-lived. Six days after the Stanley Cup win, the Red Wings' celebration turned into tragedy in Detroit. The driver of a limousine with Russian stars Fetisov and Konstantinov and team massage therapist Sergei Mnatsakanov fell asleep behind the wheel when taking them from a golf event outside Detroit to a team party with family and friends. The car crossed three lanes, jumped the curb, and slammed into a tree. The two Russians did not play golf, so they had decided to leave the country club a little earlier while their teammates finished off their rounds on the course.

"They had been cheering us on, being driven around in a golf cart together with our Russian massage therapist," Lidstrom recalled. "When the event was nearing the end, Vlad, Slava, and Sergei got in the limousine so they could go ahead and greet us at the restaurant in the suburb of Birmingham, where we all would have dinner. A number of vehicles had been rented, so nobody would have to drive. We were trying to be responsible."

The accident occurred less than half a mile from the Birmingham exit. Konstantinov, Fetisov, and Mnatsakanov were taken by ambulance to the nearby Beaumont Hospital in Royal Oak. Konstantinov and Mnatsakanov were seriously injured.

Yzerman got a phone call about the accident just before the rest of the players were about to leave the golf course. "We all understood how serious it was," Lidstrom said. "At that point we didn't know if they would survive or not. It was terrible. We were very worried."

Many players rushed to the hospital, and others gathered at goaltender Chris Osgood's house. "Konstantinov was in a coma for weeks and never regained his health," Lidstrom said. "It was devastating, and we all knew it could have been any of us in that limousine."

Konstantinov was partially paralyzed and suffered damage to his brain; he would never play another game. For Konstantinov's teammates, it was an upsetting and sad end to all the satisfaction that came after winning the team's first Stanley Cup in 42 years. Konstantinov had risen from being an unknown Russian defenseman taken in the 11th round of the 1989 NHL entry draft to be a key player in Detroit. Together with Lidstrom, he was the future of the Red Wings defensive corps.

"I think having Konstantinov around overshadowed Lidstrom in his early years," *Sports Illustrated*'s Michael Farber said. "Konstantinov was a more visceral defenseman, a physical force who played more of an old-school game. Lidstrom was more subtle, the perfect man for an evolving game, especially in the next decade. He was the master of body and stick position, flicking passes out of the air, swiping pucks in the corner without having to wallpaper an opponent. There was rare nuance in Lidstrom's game, while Konstantinov was a T-Bone, medium rare."

Farber viewed the Cup win as a coming-out party for Lidstrom. "I think appreciation grew for Lidstrom with his play in the 1997

Stanley Cup Final against the Flyers," Farber said. "I had assumed Scotty Bowman would match Konstantinov and Slava Fetisov, smart and physical defensemen, against Eric Lindros and the fellow Legion of Doom. Instead, Bowman matched the Legion of Doom with Lidstrom and Larry Murphy, who would end up in the Hall of Fame because of his offensive prowess. They were both skilled puck-movers.

"Combined with the Red Wings' ability to support the puck, to always provide an outlet for a defenseman, the big-bodied Flyers rarely were able to get in on the forecheck against the pair and turn over pucks in the offensive zone. The Flyers had spotty goaltending, but Lidstrom and Murphy played a major role in the Red Wings' unexpected sweep."

To be recognized as a star in the NHL, a player has to be able to play well against the best. Lidstrom was well aware of that, and with the confidence Bowman had shown in him during the 1997 Final, he was now entering superstardom. The coaching staff gave him more difficult assignments, and he always seemed to rise to the occasion.

The limousine accident cast a dark shadow over the Cup win and the celebrations in Detroit. Lidstrom's stall was next to Konstantinov's in the dressing room, and they had become good friends.

They were both drafted the same year and both made it into the NHL for the 1991–92 season. Konstantinov was three years older than Lidstrom and had played seven seasons with CSKA Moscow in Russia before moving to Detroit.

The parallels continued. They both enjoyed stellar rookie seasons. Konstantinov collected 34 points (eight goals and 26 assists) in 79 games and piled up 172 penalty minutes. He was plus-25. Lidstrom played all 80 games and had 60 points (11 goals and 49 assists) with only 22 penalty minutes. His plus/minus rating was an impressive plus-36.

When Detroit won the Stanley Cup in the spring of 1997, they were both seasoned blueliners on a very solid defensive unit. At 30 years of age, Konstantinov had posted a career-high 38 points and was the runner-up for the Norris Trophy as the NHL's best defenseman in 1996–97 behind Brian Leetch of the New York Rangers.

Known as the Vladinator, on the ice Konstantinov asked no quarter and gave none. "He was a fierce competitor and in the prime of his career," Lidstrom said. "He never backed away and didn't care who you were. He used his body to deliver hits all over the ice."

The driver of the limousine, Richard Gnida, told the police that he had blacked out. His license had been suspended at the time for drunk driving. The accident happened on June 13, less than a week after the championship-clinching game at Joe Louis Arena. "It changed everything," Lidstrom said. "It put things in perspective. We got a reminder of how fragile life is."

Fetisov would continue his NHL career the next season after his broken ribs and punctured lung had healed. Mnatsakanov, who like Konstantinov spent some time in coma, was paralyzed from the waist down after the accident. Both suffered brain damage from closed-head injuries.

Back in Sweden for his vacation later in the summer, Lidstrom was excited to host the trophy for a day during its European tour. "I had it on display at the city square in Vasteras, so everybody could see it," Lidstrom said. "We had a good crowd, and I remember how impressed people were of its size. I also took it to the hockey arena and had Phil Pritchard, who is the guardian of the Stanley Cup from the Hockey Hall of Fame, talk about its history to the players from my old home team."

The trophy then was put on a boat and taken on the Dalalven River up to Lidstrom's hometown of Avesta, where he had invited 120 guests to a private party. "It was an outdoor party on a beautiful summer night," Lidstrom said. "For me, it was an evening never to be forgotten. To have your family and closest friends there celebrating with you felt so special. Truly a magic moment."

Thanks to moves made by the Wings during the 1996–97 NHL season, Lidstrom was able to share his Stanley Cup success with a couple of fellow Swedes.

Johan Garpenlov, who'd helped Lidstrom settle into the North American way of life, was traded by Detroit to the San Jose Sharks during Lidstrom's inaugural NHL campaign, late in the 1991–92 season, leaving Lidstrom as the only Swede on the Red Wings roster for the next four seasons.

On the one hand, that gave him a chance to make new acquaintances. Among the teammates he started spending time with were Yves Racine, Mike Sillinger, Bob Rouse, and Mike Ramsey.

Lidstrom had to wait until the fall of 1996 before he got a countryman in the lineup again. That player was Tomas Holmstrom, who had been drafted in the 10th round as the 257th choice in the entry draft of 1994.

"I didn't know much about Homer when he came to us in the late summer of 1996," Lidstrom said. "Both of us had played on the Swedish national team in the World Cup right before the

NHL season began. We flew together to Detroit after the tournament, where we had lost against Canada in the semifinals in Philadelphia."

Holmstrom was known as a rugged player in the Swedish top league, where he had played for Lulea. He earned his nickname, Demolition Man, for his tough and self-sacrificing play. "I had heard that they called him that, but I didn't really know who he was or what he had done in the Swedish League," Lidstrom said.

Personally, the two Swedes made an instant connection. "I liked him immediately," Lidstrom said. "He was very funny and easy to get along with. Not much seemed to bother him. I tried to help him adjust to life in Detroit and do what Johan Garpenlov had done for me a couple of years earlier.

"One thing I noticed about Tomas was that he was very focused and serious as soon as he got his skates on; it didn't matter if it was practice or a game. He always gave everything, and I think that Scotty Bowman liked that."

Holmstrom went through plenty of nicknames that first season in Detroit. The Demolition Man was dubbed Sandstrom due to similarities between his game and rugged Swedish NHLer Tomas Sandstrom, but that became problematic when the Wings traded for Sandstrom later that season. Holmstrom soon got the nickname Homer in Detroit.

Originally, Holmstrom wore No. 15, but when Detroit dealt for veteran defenseman Dmitri Mironov in 1998, he asked Holmstrom for that number. Holmstrom obliged, switching to No. 96 to mark the year he'd arrived in the NHL. Bowman jokingly suggested to

Holmstrom that he should have taken No. 98, because that was the year he'd be heading back to Sweden.

Bowman could test his younger players with challenging comments about their play. "He did it with Tomas Holmstrom just to tease him and see what reaction he would get," Lidstrom said. "Scotty never played that game with me. It was rare that he approached me and asked me something or had an opinion about the way I played. I took that as a good sign. He played me a lot and my ice time was often around 28 or 30 minutes, so I had no complaints."

In truth, the man called Homer and the No. 96 would reside in Detroit for many years to come. Holmstrom didn't make the team out of training camp. He was sent to the Red Wings' farm team in the American Hockey League, the Adirondack Red Wings. There he played six games and scored three goals before he was called up to Detroit. Holmstrom was mad about being sent down to the AHL and came back to Detroit with a vengeance.

"He didn't get much ice time," Lidstrom said. "In the beginning, he was placed on the fourth line, but Homer soon found his niche, especially on the power play, where he parked himself in front of the opponent's goal and took a lot of beating to have a chance to score. He was extremely brave. Nobody could scare him off."

NHL officiating was different in the mid-1990s. For a young forward like Holmstrom, it was more or less a suicide mission to take up space in front of the net. "As a defenseman, you were allowed to do a lot more to stop forwards in front of your own net than you are today," Lidstrom said. "The referees told players like

Homer, 'You can only blame yourself if you are getting beaten up there.'

"If it wasn't the defensemen who pushed and shoved him, it was the goaltender, who hit him on his back or legs with their stick. Homer refused to give in. He took a severe beating night after night. He was black and blue but did not back down. All his teammates loved him for doing that and creating opportunities for our team when it came to rebounds and blocking the view for the opposite goaltender."

Holmstrom had found a specialty that would later make him famous. It was all a result of hard work and a willingness to do anything for the team. He stayed on the ice after every practice and had teammates shoot pucks, so he could learn how to better direct them into the net. It was a long process, but bit by bit he developed his skills and became the most hated forward among goaltenders. He was in their face every time he was on the ice.

Off the ice he and Lidstrom became close friends, often carpooling to games. Lidstrom's future wife, Annika, and Holmstrom's partner, Annelie, became friends. The couples enjoyed each other's company both during the season and in the summers in Sweden.

"Annelie became my 'sister' during the 16 years Nicklas and Tomas played together," Annika said. "We really became close friends and still are to this day. With two more kids later on in Detroit, I had to learn how to be strong and handle a lot of the day-to-day necessities. I was glad to have family and friends that came to visit us on a regular basis, staying for a week or two. It helped a lot when Nicklas was on a long road trip with the team. I didn't feel so lonely then."

Getting ready for the 1997–98 season was a different challenge for Lidstrom and his Red Wings teammates. Playing hockey into June, celebrating the Stanley Cup, and worrying about their injured teammates made for a short summer and offered little time to regroup. The time for rest was limited before preparation for the next season began at home in Sweden with off-ice training.

"Your body must have a chance to rest before you start building up the muscles again," Lidstrom said. "It is mentally very tough to be focused already when training camp starts in September and be ready to be at your best for the regular season opener in early October after a long playoff the season before."

He and his teammates were aware of the task that was awaiting them when the 1997–98 season started. To capture the Stanley Cup two years in a row is one of the biggest challenges in all of sports.

"After winning the Stanley Cup, all the other teams put an extra effort in beating you," Lidstrom said. "Everybody wants to see how good they are compared to the champs. It's a way to measure the strength of their team, to give them a lift. There's no nights off if you are the reigning champions in the NHL."

There was also another challenge waiting for the Red Wings when they came back to Detroit in the fall of 1997. Their teammate Konstantinov was so badly injured after the June limousine crash that he would be unable to continue his hockey career. But the Wings were determined to ensure that their teammate would not be forgotten.

"I had the place next to him in our dressing room at Joe Louis Arena and we made a decision to let his equipment hang there exactly as he had left it," Lidstrom said. "It stayed that way for the whole next season. Dave Lewis, our assistant coach, had placed a stone there with the inscription BELIEVE. We were reminded daily of what had happened and what Konstantinov went through. In a way, I think it motivated us. We were playing for him, too."

The Red Wings finished third in the NHL standings with 103 points. Lidstrom had 59 points (17 goals and 42 assists) in 80 games to lead all NHL defensemen in scoring, two points ahead of Scott Niedermayer of the New Jersey Devils and Sergei Zubov of the Dallas Stars. Lidstrom's status as an elite player in the NHL was solidifying. It was the first time he was the NHL's top-scoring defenseman.

As was the case in 1997, the Wings started slowly in the play-offs. They actually fell behind 2–1 to the Phoenix Coyotes in the opening round before rallying to win in six games. Six games were also required to eliminate the St. Louis Blues in the second round. The third game in that series developed into a thriller at the Kiel Center in St. Louis. It took until the second overtime period before Shanahan scored the winner after 11:12 of OT, assisted by Larionov and Lidstrom.

As the Wings moved into the Western Conference Final for the fourth successive spring, a new opponent awaited them—the Stars. After splitting the first two games in Dallas, Lidstrom took control of Game 3, with two goals and an assist to lift the Red Wings to a 5–3 win. Lidstrom was named first star of the game. With two more wins in the next three games, Detroit was on to the Stanley Cup Final for the second year in a row.

This time they were up against the Washington Capitals, an experienced team that had beaten the Boston Bruins, Ottawa

Senators, and Buffalo Sabres on its way to the Final. Washington was coached by Ron Wilson and had a forceful captain in Dale Hunter. The Capitals had finished third in the Atlantic Division with 92 points, behind the New Jersey Devils (107) and Philadelphia Flyers (95), but they surprised a lot of people in the postseason.

Washington had a balanced roster with stars like forwards Joe Juneau, Adam Oates, Brian Bellows, and Peter Bondra; defensemen Sergei Gonchar and Calle Johansson; and a solid goalie in Olaf Kolzig. He had been the starting goaltender for the German Olympic team at the 1998 Winter Olympics in Nagano, Japan.

Detroit had made a couple of small changes in the lineup from the previous year but the key players were still there, and they were mostly in their prime. "We had an equally strong team compared to the year before," Lidstrom said. "The nucleus was still there; some role players had changed. It was hard to find a successor for Konstantinov, so it took two players to replace him, the defensive Jamie Macoun and an offensive defender in Dmitri Mironov. Both of them came to us on trading deadline on March 24 that year. Brent Gilchrist was another new member of our 1998 team, a hardworking forward that took on a big role in our penalty killing and was important for our balances."

Another new member of the Detroit defense this season was Lidstrom's fellow Swede, Anders Eriksson. He had spent most of the previous two seasons in the American Hockey League with the Adirondack Red Wings but was ready for a regular spot on the Detroit blueline during the 1997–98 season. He remembered how easy it was to fit into such a cohesive unit.

"We had a well-synchronized team where everybody knew their role and assignments," Eriksson said. "There were no egotistic members on that team who wanted more ice time or had other complaints. Everybody went to work night after night. It was all about teamwork. It was a unique group of guys. We knew that if we did what was expected of us, we would win every game. We had the best coaching staff in the league, led by Scotty Bowman; we had a room full of champions after the win the year before; and the star power was amazing."

The 1998 Final was over in four games, but the Wings had to work for it. They beat Washington 2–1 in the opener at Joe Louis Arena. The second game two days later went into overtime before Draper scored to give Detroit a 5–4 victory and a 2–0 lead in the series.

Game 3 was played at the MCI Center in Washington, D.C., and the Red Wings got the start they wanted with a goal after 35 seconds. That lead held until the third period when the Capitals tied it, but Sergei Fedorov scored the winner later in the period and Detroit was up 3–0 in the series. Detroit finished the sweep with a 4–1 victory in the fourth game and had won its second consecutive Stanley Cup.

"They were so much better than the three teams we had knocked out on our way to the Final," said the Capitals' Johansson. "The Red Wings played on another level. They were so damned good. And a lot had to do with Nicklas Lidstrom. He joined their attack, so when they came with speed through the neutral zone and over the blueline it was hard for us to stop them. They controlled the puck, had an amazing passing game where their forwards received the puck at full speed. I remember thinking, 'How are we going to be able to compete with this team?'

"To be honest, we weren't even close to beating them. They had the puck 75 percent of the time. They had a solid lineup right through, from goaltender, defense, to forwards—with players like Lidstrom, Sergei Fedorov, Steve Yzerman, Vyacheslav Kozlov, and Igor Larionov in their prime. I've never seen anything like it."

Lidstrom felt the experience they'd gained from winning it all the season prior made it almost impossible for the Capitals to dethrone the Wings. "We kept our system from the year before, the famous left-wing lock, as Scotty Bowman liked to call it," Lidstrom said. "In my opinion, it felt like we had the same capacity as the previous year. The only difference now was that we understood what it took to go all the way and become champions."

When NHL commissioner Gary Bettman handed over the trophy to Detroit team captain Yzerman, an emotional celebration started. Konstantinov took the ice in a wheelchair and was handed the Stanley Cup by Yzerman. Konstantinov's teammates then helped him carry the Cup around the ice in a wild celebration in which the Detroit players were both hugging him and each other.

"Of course, we played for Konstantinov," Lidstrom said. "He was in everybody's thoughts that whole year. We really wanted to win it for him."

The Red Wings dedicated the 1997–98 season to Konstantinov and Mnatsakanov and wore patches on their jerseys with the word "Believe" in English and Russian, above the initials VK and SM. The Red Wings arranged it with the league so that Konstantinov's name could be engraved on the Cup even though he hadn't played a game that season.

Another Stanley Cup parade came down Woodward Avenue and ended at Hart Plaza. Police estimated that 1.2 million people came out and jammed the mile-long parade route. Some fans arrived at 6:00 AM, more than four hours before the beginning of the celebration. Michigan governor John Engler and Detroit mayor Dennis Archer were also in the parade. Yzerman was holding the Conn Smythe Trophy he was awarded as the most valuable player in the playoffs. The Stanley Cup was carried by goaltender Chris Osgood in a red Jeep. To the cheers of the fans, he raised it over his head most of the time along the way down to Hart Plaza.

For the players, it was an emotional repeat. So much had happened since the 1997 Cup victory a year earlier. Fedorov sat out the first 59 games of the 1997–98 season in a contract dispute. He then signed an offer sheet with the Carolina Hurricanes worth $38 million that was matched by the Red Wings on February 26, 1998, ending Fedorov's holdout. It ended up being an expensive six-year deal for the Red Wings, but Fedorov came back and delivered. He was Detroit's best goal-scorer during the playoffs with 10 goals, and his 20 points was second only to Yzerman's 24 points.

Eriksson remembers a team party at the home of team owners Mike and Marian Ilitch. "They had a cake made looking like a hockey rink," Eriksson said. "It was just surreal. I just couldn't grasp how big this thing was. It was a celebration that brought the whole city of Detroit on its feet and people talked about us being the first dynasty since the Edmonton Oilers in the '80s."

Lidstrom had a sensational playoffs in 1998 and increased his totals from eight points in 20 games the year before to 19 points (six goals and 13 assists) in 22 games. It was a club playoff record for a defenseman.

"Once again, I was paired with Larry Murphy, and we had developed a really good chemistry after two seasons together on the blueline," Lidstrom said. "We read each other well and had a trust, so we always knew what the other one was doing on the ice."

Lidstrom was the runner-up for the Norris Trophy for the 1997–98 season. It was the first time he was nominated as a finalist and he was now mentioned as one of the top defensemen in the league. The Norris went to Rob Blake, the star blueliner with the Los Angeles Kings. Lidstrom also got recognition when he was selected to the NHL First All-Star Team for the 1997–98 season. It was Lidstrom's first of many appearances on the First All-Star Team; he would be selected the next five years and retired after being selected 10 times. Only Ray Bourque has been selected more often (13). Lidstrom shares second place on that list with Doug Harvey.

With his play and stats from the 1998 playoffs, Lidstrom started to get more attention around the league. "I don't know if Nick stepped up more after we lost Vladimir Konstantinov or if we just simply noticed his excellence more," Shanahan said. "Regardless, the rest of the league seemed to notice at that moment."

Bigger recognition for Detroit's slick Swedish blueliner was just over the horizon.

5
NORRIS NICK

AFTER ANOTHER LONG SEASON AND BACK-TO-BACK CHAMPIONSHIPS, IT was time for Nicklas Lidstrom to go home to Sweden for a short vacation.

The summer of 1998 ended with Nicklas and Annika getting married in Sweden in front of 150 guests at Folkarna kyrka, a historic church in Avesta that first opened its doors in 1853. Among his teammates attending the wedding with their wives were Bob Rouse, Tomas Holmstrom, Tomas Sandstrom, and Anders Eriksson.

"We got married in August and had to leave for Detroit two weeks later, so there was no time for a honeymoon," Lidstrom remembered.

The respect for Detroit's No. 5 was growing year by year in the NHL. A player of Lidstrom's caliber is a scary opponent for any goaltender with his poise, quick thinking, and poker face.

"I felt fear every time Lidstrom had the puck, because he always made the right play," former NHL goalie Kevin Weekes said. "He seldom made the wrong read, which is remarkable with the amount of minutes he played. That's pretty scary. Even when he was in the defensive zone you had to keep an eye on him with his ability to make an outlet pass or flicking out the puck in the air for Henrik Zetterberg or Pavel Datsyuk to pick up.

"I tried to be alert as soon as Lidstrom had the puck. With other defensemen, you kind of jump up and pay attention when they are in the offensive zone, but with Lidstrom it was different. Paul Coffey could fly by everybody, Sergei Zubov could slow it down, Ray Bourque and Brian Leetch were smooth. Lidstrom did everything so easy. He never tipped you off about what he was about to do. He was the ultimate card player in poker. You never knew what card he was about to put on the table."

Weekes was impressed with Lidstrom's ability to utilize his positional excellence to corral opponents. "Nick played the angles in the defensive zone as good as a goalie," Weekes said. "He was always in the right angle. He never chased the game. Never. And that is a big part of the game for a defenseman. I never saw that guy sweat."

With two straight Stanley Cup wins in 1996–97 and 1997–98, the Red Wings had turned into a powerhouse in the National Hockey League. And hockey people were beginning to take notice of Lidstrom's role in that success.

"He had so much patience and such an outstanding level of skill," Winnipeg Jets coach Paul Maurice said of Lidstrom. "And it didn't matter what type of game it was—hard-hitting, high skill, grinding—his game never changed. He had tremendous tempo out there."

The wedding of Lidstrom and Annika wasn't the only coupling the team had in mind when it came to their star blueliner. His teammates felt a marriage of Lidstrom to the Norris Trophy as the NHL's best defenseman was long overdue.

The courtship officially began during that championship season of 1997–98. For the first time in his career, Lidstrom had been nominated as a finalist for the award.

"It had been a long time coming," Detroit winger Darren McCarty said. "He'd always been the most underrated player in the league—our little secret."

The final balloting that year saw the Norris go to Rob Blake of the Los Angeles Kings, who garnered 401 points, including 27 first-place votes. Lidstrom was runner-up with 369 points that included 15 first-place ballots.

His teammates never believed that getting his name inscribed on the Norris was an incentive that lit a fire in Lidstrom, nor did it frustrate him when others were awarded the trophy over him.

"I'm sure he'd be happy to accept the award, but I don't think the drive for him is to win it," longtime defense partner Larry Murphy said. "The drive for him is to just play well."

Still, everybody had a feeling that Lidstrom's time was coming. Blake was one of the players who noticed the Swedish star on the Red Wings' back end.

"I just think it took the league longer to recognize how good he was," Blake said. "I don't think he was much different from the age of 26 to 30, it was just that people weren't sure how good he was. But once you started watching him every game, and how he constantly put up points and constantly won games, you knew this guy is really good."

Blake admitted to being overcome by a sensation that he was only holding on to the Norris until the time came that Lidstrom made it his own personal possession.

"He was so much better," Blake said. "I was lucky that I won my Norris Trophy before he got recognized for being so good. I think it took a while for the league to recognize how good he was, because he was so steady."

In 20 NHL seasons, Lidstrom missed only 44 games. He played every game of the season seven times, including two of his final three NHL campaigns. "He was always playing, he was never injured," Blake said. "If he missed a game, it was at the end of the regular season and he got some rest before the playoffs. To be able to play that much without getting injured was astonishing."

Lidstrom's role as a Norris bridesmaid would continue for two more seasons. He finished the 1998–99 regular season with 57 points (14 goals and 43 assists) in 81 games. He added 11 points on two goals and nine assists in 10 playoff games.

Again, when the Norris finalists were announced, there was Lidstrom's name alongside that of Al MacInnis of the St. Louis Blues and Bourque of the Boston Bruins. And again, when the ballots were tabulated, Lidstrom was a runner-up, finishing a distant second, garnering 234 points to MacInnis' 548. The Blues defenseman received all 54 first-place ballots.

Another strong campaign followed for Lidstrom in 1999–2000. In fact, from a personal standpoint, he enjoyed a record-setting season. For the first time in his NHL career, he reached the 20-goal plateau, adding 53 assists for a career-high 73 points. Lidstrom joined Bill "Flash" Hollett and Reed Larson as the only Detroit defensemen to record a 20-goal season.

Yet, for the third year in a row, Lidstrom was nominated for the Norris Trophy but didn't win the prize. The honor went to St. Louis Blues rearguard Chris Pronger, who would also win the Hart Trophy, the first defenseman to win both awards in the same season since the legendary Bobby Orr in 1971–72. Pronger received 565 points in Norris voting and 53 first-place ballots. Lidstrom picked up five first-place votes and 400 points to finish second in the voting for the third straight season.

Lidstrom's teammates could only scratch their heads in disbelief over the hockey world's apparent inability to recognize his unique brand of excellence.

"We'd look at the Norris voting every year and we'd think, 'Why hasn't he won it?'" Brendan Shanahan recalled. "We didn't know what else they were looking for. The guy did it all—played the power play, killed penalties, was always out against the other team's best players, and he put up numbers."

Coming so close without getting to light the proverbial cigar might leave some players with a significant level of frustration, but Lidstrom simply wasn't that kind of guy. "It was an honor just to be a finalist," Lidstrom said. "The guys who won the Norris all had outstanding seasons and deserved it."

In fact, he offered a suggestion as to why he was continually overlooked. "When you play more physical, [people] notice that a lot more than a guy who plays strong positionally," Lidstrom explained. "Both Pronger and Blake had different styles than I did. They were bigger guys. They used that to their advantage. My game was always good positioning and being in the right spot."

He made a valid point. Lidstrom's quietly effective game seldom drew rave reviews. He didn't lead the rush like Leetch or level players with a devastating hip check like Blake. He merely performed with steadfast efficiency.

While some might question Lidstrom's graciousness toward those who kept beating him for the Norris, like an Oscar loser who says through gritted teeth that it's merely an honor to be nominated, those closest to Lidstrom can attest to the fact that it was no performance. He wasn't putting on a show. Lidstrom was showing the world his true character.

"When you met his parents, Gerd and Jan-Erik, you could understand where his calmness and harmony came from," former teammate Eriksson said. "He reminded me of other Swedish hockey stars, like Borje Salming, Mats Sundin, Peter Forsberg, and Markus Naslund. Nick had an honesty aura around him. Things were good, but he never wanted too much of fame or too little of something. He was his own worst critic and never appeared to be on Cloud Nine. 'You're never stronger than your weakest link' was kind of his way of looking at things."

It was around this time that the genesis of Lidstrom's nickname—the Perfect Human—was beginning to unfold. "It all started with me and a couple of the other guys calling Nick just Swede, which later became elevated to Super Swede," Kris Draper recalled. "There were many great Swedish players in the league at that time with Mats Sundin, Peter Forsberg, Henrik Lundqvist, the Sedin twins [Henrik and Daniel], Daniel Alfredsson, and Erik Karlsson, to name a few, but in our mind Lidstrom was the best of them all. He was *the* Swede.

"Why? Because of the way Nick played the game. His composure, his poise, and the way he dressed. He looked so good in his suits. One day we were just kidding around, and I called him the Perfect Human. The guys laughed, and it stuck in the room."

Draper doesn't remember exactly when he said it for the first time. "It was probably when Nick started winning all those Norris Trophies," Draper said. "He had the nickname for sure when he became the captain in 2006, so it must have been a couple of years earlier. It went from Super Swede to the Perfect Human and that took it to a whole new level."

Off the ice, Lidstrom also seemed incapable of a misstep. Draper and his teammates were always impressed with Lidstrom's test results every training camp. "He came back from his summer vacation in Sweden in great shape and the test results always showed low body fat on Nick," Draper said. "He took a lot of pride in what he did on and off the ice. He was a sharp dresser, wearing high-end fashion that was always pressed well."

Naturally, such a highfalutin handle led to some good-natured ribbing, with Lidstrom always being teased for his apparent infallibility. "We had fun at his expense now and then," Draper admitted. "If we were on the road and went out to dinner with a bunch of guys, we would wait to see what he ordered and then we said, 'Of course, the Perfect Human is gonna order that.' It was funny, because Nick was such a loveable guy. He probably didn't like the nickname, but that's how it was."

"First of all, that nickname doesn't paint a fair picture of me and who I am," Lidstrom said. "I'm not perfect. I wasn't the perfect player on the ice and I'm not the perfect person off the ice. I can see myself being a likable guy, but the rest is just a label that was put upon me."

Shanahan remembered how easy it was to get along with Lidstrom and how quickly they bonded as friends after Shanahan's 1996 trade to Detroit, a closeness that remains to this day. "Nick was quiet, but always came out with the guys for dinner or what-ever activity was going on," Shanahan said. "He liked to be around the guys and we liked to be around him. Nick was a great team-mate and a great family man. His boys were always around the room. It was a very close team. None of us had children when we met and now we all had big families."

Lidstrom had long ago won over the Wings room, and now he was about to win over the entire NHL. In 2000–01, a new millennium was dawning, and a new Norris Trophy winner was about to be crowned. Lidstrom's time would finally arrive.

Lidstrom finished the 2000–01 regular season second in scoring among defensemen with 71 points. Only Brian Leetch of the New York Rangers was ahead of him with 79 points. When the Norris Trophy finalists were announced, Lidstrom was right there again, along with Scott Stevens of the New Jersey Devils and five-time winner Bourque, now a member of the Colorado Avalanche.

"Nick Lidstrom deserves to win this year," proclaimed ABC and ESPN analyst Brian Engblom, a former NHL defenseman, on the eve of the NHL Awards banquet. "It's funny how it works. With a lot of the awards, you have to be around for a couple of years to get acknowledged. Rob Blake went through that."

Engblom evidently wasn't the only one thinking that way. Even those he was up against for the honor were in Lidstrom's corner. "I remember Ray Bourque, who also was nominated, came up to me before the award show in Toronto and said, 'It's a slam dunk for you,'" Lidstrom recalled. "That a player of his caliber, who I had admired for so many years, said that I would easily win, it was a fantastic feeling."

It turned out that it was also an accurate feeling. When the winner was announced, Lidstrom was the guy who heard his name called. After three consecutive years as the runner-up, the Norris was finally his. With his ascension to wear the crown as the NHL's top defenseman, Lidstrom also broke new ground. He was the first

European to win the Norris Trophy. "To be the first European player to win the Norris Trophy was huge," Lidstrom said.

His hockey brethren viewed it as both worthy and long overdue recognition. "It's amazing that he didn't win the Norris Trophy last season," close friend, fellow Swede, and Toronto Maple Leafs captain Sundin said. "Lidstrom was Detroit's dominating player during the two seasons they won the Stanley Cup."

In typical Lidstrom fashion, even at the moment of his biggest individual honor as a player, he wasn't the one everyone was talking about. Actress Tia Carrere, famous for her roles in the Wayne's World films and the television show *Relic Hunter*, was assigned the task of presenting the Norris Trophy to Lidstrom during the awards ceremony at the Toronto Convention Center, and she turned heads and left jaws agape when she appeared wearing a low-cut dress designed to look like a Toronto Maple Leafs jersey.

Even Lidstrom had to admit that she stole the show. "I remember Tia Carrere being the presenter with the Norris the first time I won it," Lidstrom said. "That sticks out. That's one of my favorite memories from the awards shows I attended."

Now that he'd finally gotten his hands on the Norris, Lidstrom wasn't about to let go. He made the trophy his. It was almost as if it became part of his family.

Lidstrom won the Norris in 2001–02 and again in 2002–03, joining Orr, Doug Harvey, and Pierre Pilote as the only defensemen to win the Norris at least three years in a row.

Veteran NHL rearguard Steve Duchesne, who knew Lidstrom only as an opponent through his first eight NHL seasons, marveled at his work after joining the Wings in 1999.

"When you didn't see him that often, you'd wonder, 'Is he really that good?'" Duchesne recalled. "When you played with him, you realized how good he was. He was even better than people said.

"He should have won the Norris every year. He was that good. He was the most talented player I ever played with. Plus, he was such a nice guy, too, and that made him even better. He was not flashy, kept a low profile, and didn't want it to be all about him."

New Jersey's Scott Niedermayer finally broke Lidstrom's hold on the award when he won the Norris in 2003–04 but seemed to realize that he was only borrowing the bauble. "He was recognized a number of times for good reason, because he was a very, very good defenseman, a smart player with great skills, and a good leader," Niedermayer said. "He was everything that you needed to be in his situation. It's tough to say there was anybody better."

Lidstrom got right back to his winning ways in 2005–06, capturing the Norris for the fourth time. He'd win again in 2006–07 and 2007–08, and some in the game felt he was worthy of an even higher honor. "A number of guys put him down not only as best defenseman but also as the NHL's most valuable player," NHL coach Ken Hitchcock said. "That's how highly he was regarded."

Lidstrom was the third Red Wings defender to win the Norris, joining Red Kelly (1953–54) and Coffey (1994–95) but there was another award that Kelly had won and many in hockey felt should have definitely gone to Lidstrom at some point in his career, and that was the Lady Byng Trophy.

To that point in NHL history, just two defensemen had won the Lady Byng, which, according to the NHL, goes to "the player adjudged to have exhibited the best type of sportsmanship and gentlemanly conduct combined with a high standard of playing ability." Both of those defensemen awarded the Lady Byng were Red Wings—Kelly and Bill Quackenbush—and Kelly counted himself a Lidstrom admirer and felt that he most certainly warranted the honor.

"I never thought of the Lady Byng being about penalty minutes," Kelly said. "People look at the penalty minutes aspect, but to me it's an award which goes to a player who displays sportsmanship. Don't tell me about Lidstrom's penalty minutes. Tell me how many goals are scored against the team when he's on the ice. That's what matters. Not that he doesn't get penalties, but that he doesn't get penalties and still gets the job done."

Six times during his NHL career, Lidstrom accumulated fewer than 20 penalty minutes for an entire season. For a defenseman to do that and still be an effective performer, never mind the best in the league as Lidstrom was, is nothing short of astonishing.

"Defensemen use their stick more than most players," explained former Detroit associate coach Dave Lewis, a former NHL defenseman himself. "Usually, when a defenseman gets penalties, it's because of his stick—you cross-check someone at the net, you get beat and give the guy a tug. Since Nick rarely got beat, he didn't have to rely on that. He was such a good positional player that he rarely had to take penalties."

Lidstrom was such a gentleman that even when he was incorrectly accused of an infraction, he accepted his sentence without complaint. In a game against the Vancouver Canucks, Lidstrom was assessed a double-minor for high-sticking by referee Mick McGeough. Those who were at the game, or saw televised highlights, realized that it was the puck, not Lidstrom's stick, which cut the nose of Vancouver forward Alexander Mogilny.

"I didn't know what they were talking about," Lidstrom said of that penalty call. "I wasn't even close enough to touch him, but the linesman said he clearly saw my stick hit Mogilny in the face."

Nevertheless, Lidstrom headed to the penalty box to serve his undeserved penalty without complaint. "What are you going to do?" he said at the time.

A half dozen times, Lidstrom was among the finalists announced for the Lady Byng, and on five occasions, he finished as the runner-up in the voting. The winners in the years Lidstrom was the second-place finisher were Wayne Gretzky (1998–99), Pavol Demitra (1999–2000), Joe Sakic (2000–01), Mogilny (2002–03), and Martin St. Louis (2010–11).

"What really disappointed me is that Lidstrom wasn't the annual winner of the Lady Byng," said *Sports Illustrated*'s Michael Farber. "He almost always had my vote. Given his ice time, the matchups against the best forwards in the league, and his low penalty totals, he was an obvious choice practically every year."

"It would have been a huge honor to win the Lady Byng," Lidstrom said. "I must say that I am a little surprised that I didn't win it after being nominated six times. I thought that I would get it one of those years. The reason could be that very few defensemen have won it throughout the years." In 2011–12, Brian Campbell of the Florida Panthers ended a 57-year drought, becoming the first defenseman to win the Lady Byng since Kelly in 1953–54.

Lidstrom had clearly developed into the best defenseman in the league. The only surprise about his place at the top of the heap was that it came so late in his career. Lidstrom didn't win his first Norris Trophy until 2001, when he was 31 years old. His seventh Norris at the age of 41 in 2011 made him the oldest winner of the trophy.

"I thought the last Norris in 2011 was a career achievement award," Farber said. "Yes, Lidstrom led NHL defensemen in scoring in 2010–11, but he was a minus player that season. I thought [Boston's] Zdeno Chara had a better year."

When it comes to the Norris Trophy, only Orr, an eight-time recipient, won it more times than Lidstrom. "I don't compare myself to Bobby Orr," Lidstrom said. "He is untouchable and someone I still look up to. He's someone I'd like to take a picture with."

Harvey is tied with Lidstrom as a seven-time winner. "To have been nominated so many times and able to win seven Norris Trophies is something I'm very proud of," Lidstrom said. "Just to win it once would have been a thrill for me."

Those closest to Lidstrom aren't surprised by his unassuming modesty in the face of such a great achievement. "He never concerned himself with individual awards and this made him such a great teammate," former Detroit coach Scotty Bowman said.

Those closest to Lidstrom are also happy to provide the superlatives that he is too humble a man to offer. "It was an incredible feat to win that many Norris Trophies with 30 teams in the league," Brendan Shanahan said. "I don't think it will happen again."

Chris Chelios was on Detroit's Stanley Cup–winning team in 2002 and was the runner-up to Lidstrom for the Norris Trophy that year. "Our team was loaded with future Hall of Famers, so the expectations were high," Chelios said. "Nick was our leader both off and on the ice. He was terrific in every sense." Lidstrom suggested that they had hoped for a tie in the voting. Both of them were named to the NHL First All-Star Team and Chelios has said publicly that sitting with Nicklas and Annika at the awards banquet in 2002 was a moment that he and his wife will never forget.

Igor Larionov played both with and against Lidstrom and is amazed by his winning seven Norris Trophies, perhaps summing up the accomplishment the best. "If you win seven Norris Trophies, you deserve a spot on the greatest-ever list," Larionov said. "This is the NHL, nothing is for free here. He dominated an era, year in and year out. And got rewarded for it."

Opposing teams always sought to rattle Lidstrom, but it seldom was a strategy that paid dividends. "You always said, 'Dump it in his corner and make him play all game and get all the pucks,' but when you got to the third or fourth game in the series, you said, 'Just dump it in the other corner. He'll get it back anyway,'" Blake remembered. "There was always a game plan to make him play too much, to be hard on him, to put it in his corner, to do this or that, but none of it worked. He was too good. He was better than anybody else. He was smarter. He never exerted himself too much. He stayed very calm. He played well defensively, he knocked pucks out of the air, he was physical, fast. Whatever style you wanted to play against him, he could counter."

Instead, most nights it was Lidstrom who would put the other teams back on their heels. "To me, he was the hardest defenseman to play against in the league," longtime Colorado captain Joe Sakic said. "He was the best in the game. It was just his hockey sense—his smarts. He was always in the right spot. It was almost like he knew what you were going to do before you did.

"He wasn't flashy on the ice, but he'd play 30, 35 minutes a game and do everything well. You'd see Lidstrom on the ice and you knew you were going to have a tough night."

There was one area of the game where Lidstrom's brilliance truly shone: the power play. In man-advantage situations, Lidstrom's subtle genius was apparent.

A big part of the Wings' sustained success was Lidstrom's anchoring of their power play. He had grown into the role as the quarterback during the man advantage—a calm, effective puck-mover with a sense of where the openings would come and where to pass the puck. Also equipped with a hard and precise shot, Lidstrom always had a string of options when he made his plays from the blueline.

The Red Wings power play was dreaded around the league from the mid-1990s until Lidstrom left the NHL after the 2011–12 season. Henrik Lundqvist, the New York Rangers' Vezina Trophy–winning goaltender, sat through many pregame talks when Lidstrom's name was the focus of the coaches. "There was always talk about him and his ability to move the puck just inside the blueline on the power play," Lundqvist recalled. "He patrolled that area with such authority. He was so calm when he controlled the puck and had a knack for getting his shots through.

"A lot of defensemen can shoot the puck hard, but Lidstrom was so tough to stop with his ability to find openings for the puck. He seemed to find the net most of the time or set up teammates like Henrik Zetterberg or Pavel Datsyuk. Nicklas gave Detroit's power play another dimension."

Lidstrom marvels as he recounts all of the future Hall of Fame options he had at his disposal over the years while running the Detroit power play. "We had so many fantastic power play units during my time in Detroit, so it is really hard to name the best one," Lidstrom said. "I mean, how do you choose between Brendan

Shanahan and Brett Hull when it comes to having the best one-timer? But if I have to pick my favorite setup, I will go with this one—Brendan Shanahan, Steve Yzerman, Sergei Fedorov, Tomas Holmstrom, and myself as the quarterback on the blueline. I have Shanny on my left side and Fedorov to my right, Stevie plays down low on either side, and Homer is positioned in front of the net. The strength with this formation was that both Shanny and Sergei had good one-timers and Stevie was a good weapon with his ability to play the puck from the corners or down low.

"Homer did a fantastic job blocking the view of the goaltender, but he could also move if Stevie or Sergei delivered a quick pass. What made us so dangerous was that we could shoot the puck really well, but also that we were able to move the puck fast if the opponents were good at blocking shots. In that case, we just increased our passing speed and finished off the attack from down low."

Holmstrom's development into a menacing presence in front of the net helped Lidstrom lift the Detroit power play to a new level. The two of them would stay on the ice after practice and fine-tune their shot-deflection goal strategy. It made Holmstrom black and blue, but they found a weapon that opponents had a hard time defending against. The two Swedes delivered a one-two-punch that was effective, including a ploy where Lidstrom sometimes used the backboards at Joe Louis Arena to get the puck to Holmstrom, much to the surprise of the opposing defenders and goaltenders.

"Homer and I worked almost daily on our concept," Lidstrom said. "I would stand at the blueline shooting pucks after practice and he stood in front of the net and tried to tip them in. I aimed the shots at his forehand, backhand, and then high or low. He had unbelievable hand-eye coordination and hit more or less seven out of every 10 shots. After a while, it became a routine that all of our defensemen lined up at the blueline and bombarded Homer with pucks to try to tip in. More and more of our forwards took after him and wanted to learn how to be better at deflecting pucks. Homer paved the way. It was fun to see."

Weekes still shudders at the notion of facing Detroit's dynamic Swedish duo when the Wings enjoyed the man advantage. "The way he could find Holmstrom for a tip-in on the power play was scary," Weekes said. "It was like Holmstrom was a hitter in baseball. He had unbelievable hands. I played with Dino Ciccarelli and Dave Andreychuk and they both had great hands in front of the net, but Holmstrom had unbelievable hands. And Lidstrom could beat you clean with his wrister without having a rocket shot. Or put it on the end boards at the old Joe Louis Arena for Holmstrom to pick it up in front of the net. They were so in sync with each other on the power play. Lidstrom had so many options, and as a goalie you try to anticipate what he was going to do. But he had one, two, three ways to beat you. It was scary. He was so decisively great."

Based in Michigan, *USA Today* hockey writer Kevin Allen followed Lidstrom's entire NHL career, attending many Red Wings home games. He compares Lidstrom's cognitive ability on the ice to that of the great chess masters like Bobby Fischer and Garry Kasparov.

"We say that really good chess players think three moves ahead and Nick Lidstrom thinks 10 moves ahead," Allen said. "To me, it always seemed others were playing checkers and he was playing chess. It is a very thoughtful game and his version of that is he was the first defenseman I saw who started banking shots off the back boards like he was shooting pool. I don't know if Nick knows geometry, but he bounced it off the boards and the puck would come out right in front of the net. He figured that out. I joked with him that if he ever needed a million and a half dollars, he should send a memo out to all teams and say that for $50,000 he would come in and teach all of the defensemen how to get the puck to the net, because nobody could get the puck to the net, and Nick always got the puck to the net.

"When he left, everybody talked about how much he meant to the Red Wings and how terrible it was. I noticed it immediately; the Red Wings never got the puck to the net, because they always counted on Nick to do that. That to me indicated how he just really played the game far differently than anyone else."

NBC analyst Keith Jones, an opponent of Lidstrom as a player, looks at Lidstrom's combination of genius, continued success, unparalleled excellence, and longevity and compares the stellar Swede to a similar mastermind in a different sport, New England Patriots quarterback Tom Brady.

"I just think that Nicklas Lidstrom was smarter than everybody else," Jones said. "It was the one thing that he had the skill set that he had, but his level of intelligence was beyond belief to me. It was Tom Brady-like, just like how Brady sees the game playing football. Nick saw the game and played the game in a similar way. And they had almost similar careers when you look at it. Quarterback on the power play and the guy that everything ran through on the back end. He had a very good supporting cast, but he made everybody else better."

One of Lidstrom's contemporaries and a fellow Norris Trophy winner, Los Angeles Kings defenseman Drew Doughty, a two-time Stanley Cup winner, agrees with Jones on the Brady parallels.

"That makes sense," Doughty said. "Obviously, he had some other great players around him, too, that made that power play successful. His head was up, he walked that blueline, he didn't stickhandle, he just had the puck gliding with him. I don't know how he did it.

"Not only was he the quarterback on their power play, he was the quarterback on that team. He made that whole engine run. He helped make that team become what they were, so I can't say enough good things about him, really. He is an idol of mine, a legend. One of the best ever."

Even as he neared the end of his great career, Lidstrom was still making history. In 2010–11, as he won his seventh and final Norris Trophy, Lidstrom became the first 40-year-old defenseman to score more than 60 points in an NHL season when he finished the year with 62 points (16 goals and 46 assists).

The thought that he ended up a seven-time Norris Trophy winner brings a smile to Lidstrom's face today, but if anyone had suggested to him when he arrived in Detroit in 1991 that this was the fate the hockey gods had in store for him, it would have sounded ridiculous.

"I probably would have laughed right in their face," Lidstrom said. "I would have been honored just to get one. This is really something I'm proud of—to have been able to be nominated for so many years and able to win the Norris seven times. It's been a great honor for me."

6

A GENERATIONAL TALENT

HOW GOOD WAS NICKLAS LIDSTROM? WHAT IS HIS LEGACY IN THE annals of the NHL? It's not a subject he likes to dwell on.

"It's very hard for me to talk about myself and kind of rate my performance over the span of my career in the NHL," Lidstrom said. "What I can say is that I'm proud to have played for the same organization during my whole time in the league and that I stayed so healthy. I was a reliable player. The coaches could trust me."

For all his accomplishments, Lidstrom remains a humble man. Self-promotion is not in his nature. Luckily, many others in the game are happy to do the boasting for him.

There's a constituency that will forever suggest that Steve Yzerman was the greatest player to wear the Red Wings sweater in this era, but Stevie Y is not one of them.

"Nicklas Lidstrom is the greatest player I ever played with," Yzerman said. "He was just consistently the workhorse of our hockey team, kind of the backbone of the whole team.

"There was a fantastic group of defensemen who I got to play with and against throughout my career. From my early days, Larry Robinson, Denis Potvin, and Borje Salming. In my age group, Scott Stevens, Paul Coffey, Ray Bourque, Chris Chelios, and

Brian Leetch, and to younger guys like Nick and Chris Pronger. They were all tremendous players, who were major contributors to Stanley Cup–winning teams and elite players throughout their career. All were slightly different in their own style of play.

"Based on the consistent and long-term level of excellence Nick played at, I would consider Nick at the top of the list of Hall of Fame players. He was excellent in all aspects of the game and position."

The commonly held perception of Lidstrom is that he was the best defenseman to ever play the game—aside from Bobby Orr. Orr was in another era, but he changed the game forever. He added offense from the back end like nobody had before.

It's been often said of Wayne Gretzky that what made him the Great One, the most creative offensive player the game has known, was an uncanny sixth sense for recognizing where the puck was going next before it got there.

Lidstrom brought that same level of hockey ESP to the defensive side of the puck. "He was smart," Gretzky said. "He might have been the smartest defenseman in the game. He didn't ever have to overcompensate. He was always in the right position.

"When you played against Nicklas Lidstrom you soon became aware of the fact that nobody on the ice worked harder than him. But if you sat in the stands or watched the game on TV, it appeared that it looked effortless for him. That is a fantastic skill to have, and it always fascinated me when I played against him. He really was a special player, extremely skilled in everything he did on the ice.

"What Nicklas did during his career speaks for itself. It's not often that we see a player of his caliber. He was truly special. He was the first player Detroit sent out on the ice to kill a penalty and he was the first guy out there on the power play. That is very rare, but it says it all about Lidstrom's qualities."

Robinson, a two-time Norris Trophy winner and among the greatest defensemen of his era, put Lidstrom right there alongside the legends of the game.

"He doesn't take a back seat to a lot of great players that ever played in the league," Robinson said. "I mean, his longevity and his accomplishments winning Stanley Cups, I think when you talk about all of that, for me he is the epitome of an all-around defenseman. He didn't only play great offensively, he was terrific defensively as well.

"Remember that he played at a time when it was a lot tougher, with more fighting and everything else, and there was the so-called knock on Swedish defensemen who came over for being too soft. Well, he certainly wasn't soft. He could play in a tough game, he could play in a wide-open game. And he played a lot of minutes. He was durable and over the course of his career he didn't have many injuries and probably, in my mind, had one of the better shots on the power play. The way he quarterbacked their power play was terrific.

"He was the key player during the championship run in Detroit. And not just because of the things that he did, but because of the position he played. The only other position where there is more pressure on you is the goaltender, and as they say, you are only as good as the people in front of you. Not only did he block a lot of shots, but he defended a lot of two-on-ones and three-on-twos and allowed the goaltender to be able to make the stops. Again, I think you talk about one of the greats of all time."

Few players in NHL history offered the unique combination of high performance and low maintenance that Lidstrom brought to the rink on a daily basis. "Anyone connected with our team always said about Nick, 'There is no maintenance needed in coaching Nick,' and it is still amazing to me how he stayed so healthy in such a long and distinguished career," former Wings coach Scotty Bowman said. "Players like Nick do not come our way very often."

Psychological warfare was ineffective against Lidstrom. "He was a frustrating guy to coach against, because you could never get to Nicklas Lidstrom," former NHL coach Darryl Sutter said.

Physical warfare was also a waste of energy. "You wanted to put this guy through the boards every time he touched the puck, but he'd find a way to slither around you," former NHL forward Jeff O'Neill said. "You'd never see him get crushed, because he was so smart positionally. It's not like he bailed out or anything. He always maneuvered himself in the right way."

With or without the puck, Lidstrom set an incredibly high standard with every passing game. Others could only step back and admire his combination of offensive skill, defensive acumen, positional soundness, calm exterior, and steadfast character. "He was by far the best all-around player in the league for 15 years," longtime teammate Igor Larionov said. "It you look at the defensemen of that era, Nick was in every aspect the best."

"Nick has paved the way for all defensemen," added Brendan Shanahan, another longtime teammate. "He was excellent always. He was durable. He was a winner. You could count on him. He was incredibly humble. Nick is hard to describe, because he made outstanding plays look simple. Nick did all this yet made it all look easy."

Having an ice cream as a four-year-old back home in Hogbo.

I was a happy kid. This portait is from our time in Hogbo. I'm about six years old.

In middle school back home in Sweden.

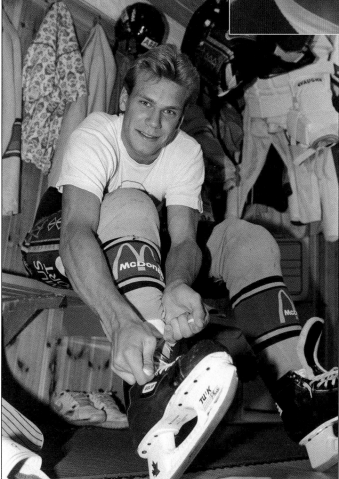

Lacing up my skates for Vasteras in 1990.
(Bildbyran/ZUMA Press/Newscom)

Walking the streets of Finland in 1991.
(Bildbyran/ZUMA Press/Newscom)

Celebrating our victory in the 1991 World Championships with my teammates. From left: Fredrik Stillman, Bengt Gustafsson, Kenneth Kennholt, me, and Jonas Bergqvist.
(Bildbyran/ZUMA Press/Newscom)

My rookie season in Detroit. (Getty Images)

Congratulating Brendan Shanahan, along with Martin Lapointe, after scoring a goal against Philadelphia in Game 2 of the Stanley Cup Final in 1997. We swept the Flyers in four games. (AP Images)

Vladimir Konstantinov skating with the Cup. Six days later, Vladimir, Viacheslav Fetisov, and Sergei Mnatsakanov were involved in a car accident that ended Vladimir's career. It was devastating. (Getty Images)

Me, Tomas Holmstrom, and Anders Eriksson holding the Cup after beating the Washington Capitals in 1998. (Bildbyran/ZUMA Press/Newscom)

Show me the Cup!
(Getty Images)

Celebrating another Stanley Cup with Annika and our sons Kevin and Adam in the Red Wings locker room in 2002. (Getty Images)

Riding the parade route down Woodward Avenue in Detroit with the Conn Smythe Trophy. An estimated 1 million people attended the celebration. (Getty Images)

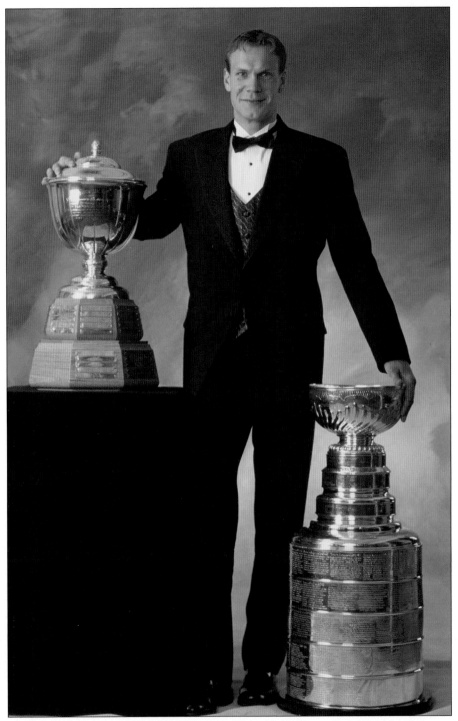

Posing with my second Norris Trophy and Lord Stanley's Cup at the NHL Awards in 2002. (Getty Images)

"The mark Nick left on the NHL and the hockey world is that he was a picture of perfection," said former NHL coach and current NBC commentator Pierre McGuire. "His offensive, defensive, and puck-moving efficiency may never be matched. I'm not sure if he ever really had a bad game. Not only was Nick one of the best players to ever play his position, but he is also one of the greatest gentlemen to ever play in the NHL."

That sentiment is echoed all the way to the top, to the man who runs the NHL. "Nicklas showed tremendous respect for the game and how it should be played," NHL commissioner Gary Bettman said. "Coaches today talk constantly about playing, 'the right way.' Nicklas did that every shift of his career. While he clearly aspired to the highest standards of excellence and lived up to those standards on the ice and off the ice, Nicklas did it in a way that was very understated.

"He didn't go for the big hit or flashy play, but he was so effective and committed to the team concept that he was universally admired by teammates and opponents. He was a fantastic competitor and champion."

Lidstrom is the first to quickly deflect any attempts to compare or parallel his career to Orr, the man he considers to be the best defenseman the NHL has ever seen. Other hockey people are in lockstep on this topic, but they will go this far—no, Lidstrom isn't Orr—but he's the next closest thing. "If it was not for Bobby Orr, who do you get to that level?" asked former Wings defenseman Chelios. "I can't see anybody else than Nick. His consistency was off the charts."

Chelios isn't the only one willing to draw that conclusion. "I grew up a Bobby Orr fan and I always thought Bobby Orr was the best player that ever played the game," said Jim Fox, on-air TV analyst for FOX Sports West and a former NHL player. "I still believe that. But I believe Nick Lidstrom's name is in that same category.

"The control and poise that he brought to a game is unparalleled. I've heard from many coaches who told me when they wanted to teach a young defenseman how to play, what they do is that they pull clips of Nick Lidstrom and then say, 'Watch this. Watch the economical movement, understanding the tempo and flow of the game, how to exert yourself on to that game.' And no one did that better than Nick Lidstrom."

Lidstrom can continue to insist that he's not comparable to Orr, but like Orr, he inspired a generation of NHL defensemen who followed in his footsteps, including fellow Norris Trophy winners.

"For sure Lidstrom was an inspiration for me," Los Angeles Kings defenseman and Norris Trophy winner Drew Doughty said. "Nick Lidstrom was obviously a legend in this league and in the hockey world. He was somebody I looked up to as a young player. I really wanted to be him. I'm not close to being there, but I'm working hard at it.

"He is definitely an idol of mine. He is one of the best defensemen of all time, and you know, I would love to sit down with him one day, and just hang out with him and pick his brain a little bit."

"I think he is probably one of the best ever as far as defensemen go," said Pittsburgh Penguins star Sidney Crosby. "Just in general, the way he played all the way until he finished. He was brilliant. He was so smart and knew when to step up and make plays, score big goals. He was just kind of the ultimate leader. Playing against him as a young guy, you learned a lot."

Crosby's teammate and fellow superstar Evgeni Malkin agreed.

"He is the best I ever played against," Malkin said. "He is the No. 1. If you go back 100 years and start counting Bobby Orr and others, Lidstrom is top five, for sure. But during my career, and if you include Shea Weber, Zdeno Chara, and Drew Doughty, my No. 1 is Nicklas Lidstrom."

Asked Al MacInnis, another Norris Trophy winner, "Has there been a smarter player, ever, than Nick Lidstrom?"

Former NHL defenseman Sergei Gonchar, who competed against Lidstrom in three Stanley Cup Finals, doesn't think so. "What can you say about a guy who is probably one of the best defensemen to ever play hockey?" Gonchar asked, before proceeding to answer his own question. "He controlled the puck on the power play. He was great defensively. He was always pretty much in a perfect position. He played a lot of minutes. He did everything."

Others in hockey looked at Lidstrom's comportment, class, and the manner in which he put the team and the game above himself and drew a parallel with another legendary NHLer.

"I think Nicklas Lidstrom is one of the greatest defensemen to have ever played in the game," said Brian Hayward, on-air analyst for Prime Ticket and a former NHL goalie. "It goes beyond that, too. He did it in a way…I guess the word is 'elegant.' That is the way I would describe the way he played. It always struck me, and I don't know the man at all, but it always struck me that he was such a gentleman. The way he conducted himself on the ice, just his manner, I was so impressed with. I think his legacy is that. He is one of the greatest players to ever play the position of defense in the NHL, and he always conducted himself with tremendous class.

"I played in Montreal for a while and the team there was surrounded by a lot of ex-Canadiens. Jean Beliveau reminded me of a guy like Nick Lidstrom and the way he carried himself, and that's a very high compliment."

Beliveau was a Hall of Famer, an NHL MVP, and Montreal's captain for five Stanley Cup wins; he won 10 Cups in all. In all areas of his life, he set the bar in terms of class and dignity.

TSN's Ray Ferraro, another former NHL player turned TV analyst, also recognizes those Beliveau-like character traits in Lidstrom. "When I think of Nick and playing against him for so long, there was such an elegance that he played with," Ferraro said. "But I don't know if people understand how hard he competed, because he made it look so easy or so smooth.

"I don't really recall many players in the 18 years that I played in the league that would have been as respected as Nick. Nobody took a cheap shot at him, nobody took an extra run, and it wasn't that they would let him off the hook. That wasn't it. It was just that he played the game with class. From my childhood, the guy I always knew who was like that was Jean Beliveau."

Bowman also saw traits of legendary Canadiens in Lidstrom's game, but being a coach, he instinctively compares him to a pair of Hall of Fame Habs rearguards. When Bowman looked at Lidstrom, he saw Serge Savard.

"He didn't get the attention of the other guys in Montreal, but I saw him play almost a perfect game," Bowman said of Savard, like Lidstrom a Conn Smythe Trophy winner. "Guys like Serge and Lidstrom didn't make mistakes. They played at their own pace."

Of course, the other all-time great from Montreal's defense was Doug Harvey, like Lidstrom a seven-time Norris Trophy winner.

"They both had the same concept," Bowman said. "The resulting play they made was not to give the puck away. They made plays. They had the ability to control the game, mainly because of their ability to pass the puck at the right time and play the point."

Bowman can only smile as he recalls his years coaching Lidstrom. "He made my life pretty easy, I'll tell you that," Bowman said. "He was just a wonderful player. One of a kind. As to who's the best ever, it's tough to rate this guy here and that guy there. I will say I don't rate anyone ahead of Lidstrom, though."

New York Islanders GM Lou Lamoriello has watched his fair share of quality defensemen over the years in a career in NHL management that extends back into the 1980s, but he's never seen anyone comparable to Lidstrom before or since.

"When you look at the career Nick had, it's something extremely special," Lamoriello said. "No one will duplicate it, you know. There will always be somebody who comes out and has a style of his own, but he had everything. Not only on the ice, but off the ice, the way he carried himself. He was an elite player, an elite individual, but more important—he finished. He won. A lot of players have great careers, but he won on every level he was at. And he was instrumental as not only a piece of that; he was the driving force.

"It was just pleasant watching him, but not so much playing against him because he was so good at what he did. And he made it look effortless. That was one of the traits that was special about him. It just looked like it was so natural, but so efficient."

Even at times when consternation would have been entirely understandable—during contract negotiations, for example—Lidstrom's mood never soured. He never made demands to be paid a monstrous amount, even though his ability and presence could have rightfully demanded a king's ransom. Lidstrom never held the team hostage in pursuit of a record-breaking deal. Bargaining was done behind closed doors and not through the media. And not once did he take advantage of unrestricted free agency to see what his services could bring on the open market.

"I really enjoyed my professional relationship with Nick," said Don Meehan, Lidstrom's agent. "We had a series of contract negotiations over 20 years and we never argued. We always agreed on the options we should pursue and what offers we could expect. He asked a lot of questions and wanted the necessary research to be done, but he was a true gentleman. We certainly had some challenges; some negotiations were lengthy with a lot of back and forth between us and the Red Wings. I presented the offers from the club, Nick referred them to Annika and came back to me after they had talked, and we got the deal finished.

"The leverage we always had was how important Nick was to the franchise. He was so recognized by the industry and [Red Wings GM] Ken Holland always understood how good Nick was. After every deal, he said, 'I can now sleep better at night.'"

Detroit's general manager from 1998 to 2019, Holland often joked that the day Lidstrom retired would also be the day he called it quits. He understood that Lidstrom was the key cog that made the Red Wings engine purr. He was the straw that stirred Detroit's drink.

"If you want the short answer, I can sum it up in these words: Superstar. Franchise player. Low maintenance. Humble. Respectable. Made a difficult game look easy," Holland said. "Nick was the best player in a very difficult position on both sides of the puck. If you were up or down by a goal at the end of a game, Nick played.

"The thing with Nick was that he could do it night after night; remember that he had a tough matchup every night. He always played against the other team's best player his whole career. He was a great offensive defenseman and an even better defensive defenseman, who never got beat. And he could always pass the puck tape-to-tape.

"He is a generational player, one of the greatest ever. That kind of star that comes along every 10 to 30 years. When he retired it was a massive hole to fill. It might take us 20 years to find another player of that stature."

Lidstrom was the complete package. There wasn't one defining quality in his game that stood out above all others, but he also had no glaring weaknesses. Each and every element of his game was situated somewhere between the solid and the spectacular, and most of them trended toward spectacular.

"He is the second-greatest defenseman in NHL history—none will ever surpass Bobby Orr, just because of the era he played in and how he changed the game—but Nick Lidstrom in my mind was probably the prototype of the perfect defenseman," *USA Today* hockey writer Kevin Allen said. "By that I mean he didn't crush people like Shea Weber, he couldn't skate like Paul Coffey, he didn't have the amazing shot like Al MacInnis or something like that, but he did all these things well above average.

"Sometimes in America, we use the word 'incomparable' and we use it a lot because we don't understand what it means. We just say that a person is as good as incomparable, but Nicklas Lidstrom really is incomparable. There's really been nobody that does all the things that he could do.

"I remember Steve Tambellini, when he was the general manager of the Vancouver Canucks, had this description of the way Lidstrom played. He said it was like if you play racquetball, there's always a cagey veteran there who can play forever, but he stands in the middle of the court and waits for the ball to come to him and lets all the younger players chase the ball around. And that's how Nick played defense. He had such a high degree of understanding of what was about to occur that he didn't have to chase things. He waited for it to come to him. He sorted it all out in his head."

For all his achievements and accolades, perhaps what's most impressive about Lidstrom is that as he went to the head of the class among NHL defensemen, it never went to his head. He changed the game. The game didn't change him.

Anders Eriksson recalls a moment during the time he and Lidstrom were teammates in Detroit that said it all. "Nick had signed a new contract worth millions of dollars and told me he was thinking about buying a new car, a [Volkswagen] Cabriolet," Eriksson said. "I thought it was a great idea and well deserved, but then he told me that he was looking at a Mazda Miata."

A Japanese car in the Motor City, home of the Big Three, would not have been a good look, and it didn't take Lidstrom long to recognize that.

"I couldn't believe it, and said, 'If you do that, I will never speak to you again. Are you kidding me? You can't do that in Detroit.

That is out of the question,'" Eriksson recalled. "He changed his mind and got another car instead. Thank god."

Even the financial windfall from a career as an NHL star couldn't make a dent in Lidstrom's stellar character. "Money is nothing we think about, but it has its advantages and has given us financial security," Annika Lidstrom said.

As Lidstrom's stature in hockey grew, especially after he began taking over the Norris Trophy as if it were a personal possession, the media spotlight began to find him with increasing regularity. Lidstrom was no quote machine. Nothing of a controversial nature was ever going to pass through his lips, but he was always polite and accommodating and did his best to be up front and truthful in his dealings with reporters.

"I wasn't somebody who craved the spotlight, but I didn't have any problems dealing with the media," Lidstrom said. "Sometimes it was hard when the journalists were let into the dressing room right after a big or embarrassing loss and you were frustrated. At the same time, I like that availability and openness. As everybody knows, it gets more intense during the playoffs and the amount of media increases.

"As a leading player on the team or captain, they swarm around you and you have to answer the same question over and over again. That was definitely more straining. I knew it was part of the job as a player in the league. The more years you played, the more experienced you got with handling the media and how to answer all the questions. I always tried to be as honest as I could. If it was about injuries you couldn't say as much, but otherwise I tried to give straight and honest answers about the games."

Allen grew to respect how Lidstrom handled the daily demands on his time, as well as how he carried himself, and also how he treated his inquisitors with equal respect. "As a journalist, he was so cooperative," Allen said. "He was sort of the Lou Gehrig of hockey. Lou Gehrig of the New York Yankees was sort of the quiet man, a dominant performer who carried himself with dignity, and that's how Nick was all the time. Nick was very, very quiet. He didn't like the spotlight, but he wasn't afraid of it. If I asked him to do a story, he was always cooperative.

"Nobody ever had a conflict with Nick. I remember Niklas Kronwall telling me one time that he had never met anyone that had anything bad to say about Nicklas Lidstrom. Everybody just loved him."

To the hockey media that saw him on a regular basis, Lidstrom's unflappable nature on and off the ice was beyond comprehension. "Just words are not enough to describe Nicklas Lidstrom's greatness, but let me try," TSN's Bob McKenzie said. "He personified elegance and class. He made everything look so easy, even as he performed at the absolute highest level."

Chris Johnston, a senior writer for Sportsnet Canada and a regular on *Hockey Night in Canada*, always appreciated Lidstrom's approach. "He was certainly not the most colorful quote or someone that made headlines, but what stands out was him being a gentleman and always there and available to talk after the games and never really making you feel like he didn't want to do it. I'm sure there were days when he didn't, but I think he understood the responsibility of being a star player and a captain, and eventually in his career that was part of his job. I thought he was very good at it.

"Not that he wasn't big in Detroit, but had he been in Toronto… well, that would have had a whole other level to it."

People lined up to shake Lidstrom's hand, take a picture with him, and have him sign photos and jerseys. Was he ever starstruck himself?

"I met Michael Jordan a number of times," Lidstrom said. "Chris Chelios, my teammate, was a close friend of Jordan's, so we did hang out a couple of times and had a beer together with Michael. That was special and something I will always remember. When Jordan left Chicago for the Washington Wizards and came to Detroit to play the Pistons, Chelios and I had a chance to sit courtside on behalf of Michael. That was very exciting. You could hear how the players talked on the court and get a different feeling for the pace of the game."

Lidstrom is a music lover and has met some of rock's biggest bands, as well.

"One of my best memories was when I met the Red Hot Chili Peppers in Detroit," he said. "It happened a couple of days after I had announced that I was retiring from hockey and they were performing at Joe Louis Arena. Together with Annika and Chelios and his wife, we had made plans to see the concert, but before heading over to the Joe we were at a basketball game with the Pistons. During that game the Red Wings PR director, John Hahn, called and said that Chad Smith, the drummer of the Red Hot Chili Peppers, had heard that we were coming and wanted to meet me before the show. So we left the Pistons game before it was over and rushed over to see Chad before they were going on stage.

"When we were done with our meet-and-greet, Chad took me to the side and asked if it was okay if he brought me up on stage after the show. I told him I was fine with that. I was thinking he would bring me up for a couple of seconds and stand there with the band and wave to the fans. But that was not Chad's plan.

"The security guy took me to the side when the band came off the stage and after they all had given me a high-five, Chad brought me up and introduced me to the fans. Then he pointed to the microphone in the middle and wanted me to say something. As you can understand, it made me nervous to stand alone on the stage in front of a sold-out Joe Louis Arena. But it was a cool experience to feel like a rock star for a minute. I know the clip is on YouTube."

Lidstrom also had a chance to meet some of Hollywood's biggest stars during his years in the NHL.

"One time Chris Chelios took me and a number of my teammates to dinner in Malibu when we were in Los Angeles," he said. "Chelios had also invited his friend Cuba Gooding Jr. to the restaurant, whom I had met before a couple of times. He is a true hockey fan and attended some of the All-Star Games that I participated in.

"This place in Malibu was a smaller restaurant with a karaoke machine and after we had finished our dinner, Cuba went up and sang some James Brown tunes. He is such a great entertainer and it was just so fun to see him put on a show for us. We also had Cindy Crawford come by our table that evening to say hi, another friend of Chelios'. Yes, I was heavily starstruck that night."

The lack of controversy around Lidstrom may have frustrated some writers who didn't understand him. Michael Farber of *Sports Illustrated* knew Lidstrom was not the one to go to if one were looking for a headline. "Lidstrom was always humble," Farber said. "He was also careful, anodyne in his public speech. He didn't make noise when he pickpocketed an opposing forward and didn't have much memorable to say in front of a notepad."

Lidstrom was the same person whether he was in the Red Wings dressing room or mingling amidst the other parents at one of his son's youth hockey games.

"It was a pleasure dealing with Nicklas Lidstrom all those years," said Red Wings equipment manager Paul Boyer. "As everybody says, he is a gentleman. Not vocal or loud at all. Even out in a social setting, like a team dinner or something like that, it was always good to sit beside him. He was always good and enjoyable all the time.

"He was never hard on the training staff—not on me, anyway, as an equipment manager. He never had any issues with skates, never had issues with sticks. He was very consistent, he rarely changed patterns. He switched brands only once. The most he asked for was having his stick pre-cut, so he didn't have to cut them. That was the hardest thing he asked for. He never changed the hollow on his skates, he was always $\frac{9}{16}$.

"He was so well respected. He was a good leader, too. A very quiet leader, but he was respected, and he was successful. I think the Perfect Human was a fitting nickname for Nick. If you wanted someone for your kids to grow up and learn how to be a good human being from, it would be him. I know his father is very proud of him. Nick is what guys in the league should be. They could learn a lot from him."

Lidstrom often sought Boyer's sage advice, especially after he became captain of the Wings in 2006. He knew that every player spent time each day inside Boyer's workshop. Lidstrom recognized that Boyer was someone who had his finger on the pulse of the team and he could be vital in ensuring any problems could be nipped in the bud before they had time to fester into something of a serious nature.

"Paul became a trusted friend when it came to feeling the mood of our team," Lidstrom said. "You could walk into his office and talk to him, knowing he always gave honest answers when it came to things of concern around our team."

Analytics have developed to a place where they are playing an ever-increasing role in how teams assess players, but long before Corsi came into the hockey vernacular, a couple of Swedish researchers and hockey fans, feeling Lidstrom's perennial excellence was underappreciated, sought to create a methodology to explain the impact Lidstrom had on the game.

Carl Lindberg and Jan Lennartsson are two Swedish scientists who started studying Lidstrom's movements with the Red Wings. After going through 40 hours of video from his games with Detroit, they contacted him and asked for a meeting. When presented with their theory, Lidstrom gave his approval to the researchers' conclusions and became a co-writer on their thesis, "Game Intelligence in Team Sports," which was published by Chalmers University of Technology and the University of Gothenburg.

"It all started with me signing up for a team in an adult recreation league in Sweden," Lindberg explained. "I wasn't very good but wanted to become a better defenseman, so I thought that it would be a good idea to study the best player in the world in that position to see if I could learn anything.

"That led me to look at all angles of Lidstrom's game and I soon was fascinated by how smart he acted in different situations on the ice. He seemed to always play simpler than everybody else, as if he chose between fewer alternatives than other players would have in the same situation."

Lindberg sat down and analyzed a number of situations that occur in a hockey game and how Lidstrom acted when he had to face them. When somebody seemingly always does the right thing, there has to be a pattern. That was Lindberg's thought process as a scientist.

Lindberg, a former adjunct professor at Chalmers, and Lennartsson studied Lidstrom's way of playing a large number of situations, including his method of playing the puck out of his defensive zone, the so-called breakout pass. They also studied how he dealt with one-on-one situations, one-on-twos, two-on-ones, and how he handled being under pressure with the puck along the boards or behind his own net.

"There was a clear pattern to how he solved every situation and he did it differently than others," Lindberg said. "He always wanted to play so that, in each situation, he had the best odds to not be scored on. Often, this meant that he made his opponents' best choices as limited as possible by holding back instead of charging. Nicklas was thinking like a statistician. In deciding how to play in each situation, decisions that evolved and were fine-tuned over the years, he always chose the low-risk alternative and was therefore so hard to beat."

While other defensemen took chances and fiddled with the puck behind their own net, trying to find open space to make a pass up the ice, Lidstrom just shot it along the boards around the corners when he was under pressure. A teammate would then pick up the pass at the blueline or in the neutral zone. When Lidstrom was alone trying to defend against two opponents coming over the blueline at full speed, he always made sure that the pass did not go through. This was because he felt that it was better for the goalie to defend a shot one-on-one rather than having to move across the crease to defend a potential one-timer or tip-in.

"Nicklas' explanation was very simple," Lindberg said. "He had decided on how to play each situation beforehand and had, based on his analysis, limited his number of alternatives to choose from. This allowed him to make faster and better decisions in game situations. He therefore limited the risk of making bad plays, and as a consequence seldom gave up the puck. He never wanted to end up in a situation where he was cornered by the opposite team and had to make a blind pass or lose the puck.

"This was a way of playing that he developed, and we can't figure out why the league hasn't interviewed him about it or analyzed it properly. It's like saying that Einstein is a nice guy, but whatever you do, don't ask him anything about physics."

When the two researchers presented their findings and theory to Lidstrom, he admitted that they had found the key that unlocked his thinking on the ice. "He said nobody had ever asked him before about his thinking and strategy on the ice," Lindberg said. "We were the first ones. It was mind-boggling, for many reasons. Why hadn't other defensemen picked up on his secrets, and why hadn't the National Hockey League found a way to use Lidstrom's smartness? His greatness is really easy to spot if you just know how to gather the right data and how to analyze it. Why hadn't anyone done it before us?

"He should have got more credit for this. They talk about Corsi and all the other hockey analytics programs they use, but Lidstrom's analysis of his game was so far ahead of them. In my mind, Florence Nightingale did more advanced things than you would find in a Corsi report. Hockey is so underdeveloped. Nicklas Lidstrom was a pioneer like Dick Fosbury was in the high jump or Jan Boklov when it comes to the ski jump, two athletes that really changed their sports."

It was Fosbury, the 1968 Olympic gold-medal winner, who was the first to go over the high jump bar backward, the so-called Fosbury Flop. Boklov, the 1988–89 World Cup champion, popularized the V-style of ski jumping in the late 1980s.

Lindberg actually put his findings into practice, implementing Lidstrom's tactics into his own rec hockey games, with astonishing results. "I became a much better player on my team," Lindberg said. "It was amazing how you could copy Lidstrom's concept and lift your own game. I don't understand why nobody had picked up on this after Nicklas played for 20 years in the NHL and was regarded as the best defenseman for so many years."

The report Lindberg and Lennartsson filed was the most downloaded article on the Chalmers website for two years and was also published in *PlosONE*—a peer-reviewed open-access scientific journal published by the Public Library of Science since 2006. What happened next was…nothing, which still bothers Lindberg. He is convinced that this mathematical theory on game intelligence in team sports could be a game-changer for many players and teams. In short, the paper gives a method for how you can measure your own performance, and more importantly, how you can change your game to become a better player.

Lidstrom was impressed with the results Lindberg and Lennartsson presented him with when they met. "It sounded very interesting and I was curious to know how they could apply a mathematical formula to their study of my movements on the ice," Lidstrom said. "I have to say that they got everything right when it comes to my thought process and approach to every situation."

That would be an apt description of how Lidstrom played the game. He did everything right. Better than most every player who's ever played the game.

"Everyone's going to know who he was long after he's done playing," Babcock said. "He's one of the easiest players I've coached, for sure. You just put him on the ice and got out of the way."

Perhaps former NHL defenseman and fellow Swede Douglas Murray summed up Lidstrom the best. "He was about as perfect of a hockey player as anyone could be," Murray said.

7

THE GREATEST
TEAM

FOLLOWING BACK-TO-BACK STANLEY CUP WINS IN 1996–97 AND
1997–98, Lidstrom and the Wings set out in pursuit of a bit of history as the 1998–99 NHL campaign got underway. Not since the 1979–80 to 1982–83 New York Islanders had a team won more than two successive Stanley Cups, and it had happened just five times in the existence of the NHL.

Detroit looked primed for another Cup run when the 1998–99 season began. The key members of the team were still there—Nicklas Lidstrom, Steve Yzerman, Brendan Shanahan, Sergei Fedorov, Igor Larionov, Chris Osgood, Larry Murphy, Tomas Holmstrom, Vyacheslav Kozlov, Darren McCarty, Martin Lapointe, Kris Draper, Kirk Maltby, and Doug Brown.

The coaching staff was also intact, with Scotty Bowman's strong leadership backed up by assistant coaches Barry Smith and Dave Lewis. It certainly looked like a dynasty had been born at Joe Louis Arena. Detroit's roster seemed to have everything in place to win more championships, but just to be sure, Red Wings general manager Ken Holland engineered a series of blockbuster moves at the NHL trade deadline, getting Wendel Clark, Bill Ranford, Ulf Samuelsson, and Chris Chelios.

Clark was a five-time 30-goal scorer and the longtime captain of the Toronto Maple Leafs. Samuelsson was considered among the NHL's nastiest defenders. Ranford won the Conn Smythe Trophy as playoff MVP in 1989–90 as he backstopped the Edmonton Oilers to the Stanley Cup, and was the only goalie in hockey history to win the Stanley Cup, Canada Cup, and World Championships.

But Chelios, a three-time Norris Trophy winner, was the biggest name and came to Detroit after a long and successful career in the league with the Montreal Canadiens and the Chicago Blackhawks, winning a Stanley Cup with the Habs in 1985–86.

"Chelios meant a lot for us when he came to Detroit," Lidstrom said. "He was the kind of player we had been missing since Vladimir Konstantinov's injury, a tough defenseman who you didn't like to play against but was worth gold to have as a teammate. I think he also wanted revenge after the Blackhawks had traded him."

As great as Lidstrom was, he always sought ways to improve, and in Chelios he found a sterling example of someone taking the right approach to the game in order to succeed both as a teammate and an individual.

"Chelios was an unbelievable team player who always focused on the group and pointed out the importance of sticking together on and off the ice," Lidstrom said. "We only played together on the penalty kill and at the end of games where we had to protect a lead. Otherwise we had different defense partners.

"What I learned mostly from him was his preparation before the games and his excellent work ethic in the gym and on the stationary bike. He was always in great shape and was very proud of it."

Detroit finished the season third overall in the Western Conference behind the Dallas Stars and Colorado Avalanche, but after Detroit's trade blitz, the Wings closed out the regular season on a 9–2–1 roll, sweeping aside the Mighty Ducks in the opening round of the playoffs. Next up was a familiar foe; Detroit would face the Avs in the postseason for the third time in four springs.

The conference semifinal against Colorado was another renewal of the long war between the two teams that now had a not-so-loving history. The Avalanche had home-ice advantage after finishing ahead of the Red Wings in the Western Conference, so the first two games were scheduled to be played at Denver's McNichols Sports Arena.

Detroit won Game 1 on an overtime goal from Maltby. The opening game had some hard hits. McCarty crushed Claude Lemieux from behind into the glass in the third period and Colorado's Peter Forsberg was kicked out of the game with a misconduct penalty after hitting Shanahan into the boards. Shanahan got a cut over his right eye. McCarty got a five-minute major for the Lemieux hit but didn't get kicked out of the game.

Game 2 also went to Detroit, this time a 4–0 shutout behind Bill Ranford, playing in place of the injured Osgood, and Colorado looked like a beaten team. The home fans in Denver booed them off the ice after their coach, Bob Hartley, sent out tough guys Dale Hunter and Jeff Odgers during the final minutes of the game to try to intimidate the Red Wings.

The Wings were 15–2–1 since acquiring Chelios, Ranford, Clark, and Samuelsson at the trading deadline. They'd won 11 straight playoff games, including the last five games of the Stanley

Cup playoffs the year before. It seemed like the Red Wings would make it to the next round without much extra effort.

But Colorado got winger Valeri Kamensky back from injury before Game 3, while the Wings lost Larionov to injury, and that had an impact on the outcome of the series. Hartley made some line changes, and with Patrick Roy playing better in goal, the visitors took advantage of a rare Lidstrom double-minor high-sticking penalty on Theoren Fleury. Lemieux tied it up at 1–1, and Colorado went on to dominate the game en route to a 5–3 win.

Ranford was injured in Game 4, giving way to third-string goalie Norm Maracle in Colorado's 6–2 win. Suddenly, the series was tied 2–2 and things were unraveling for Detroit. Back home in Denver, with the ailing Osgood suiting up and bravely trying to stem the changing tide, the Avalanche won their third straight game, this time with a 3–0 victory, and now Detroit was up against the wall.

Forsberg had been moved to the left wing of Joe Sakic's line and suddenly the Avalanche could not be stopped. Colorado knocked out Detroit with a 5–2 win. The series was over. The Wings were done. There would not be a third straight Cup for Lidstrom and company.

The disappointment in Detroit was huge. Everybody had prepared for a third straight title, but the team ran out of gas. "I don't know if it had something to do with the amount of energy it takes. I just think the energy level to win another Stanley Cup wasn't there," Lewis said.

"The funny thing is, the team in '99 might have been our best team," Shanahan said. "We were real strong. I disagree we ran out of gas. We didn't run out of gas. Our No. 1 goalie was hurt, and our

No. 2 goalie got hurt. It might have looked like we ran out of gas, but when you know your top two goalies are hurt, and the other team is scoring two or three soft goals early, it takes the wind out of your sails."

During the summer, Lidstrom signed a new three-year contract with the Wings, after some thought that he and Annika might return to Sweden to raise their children in their homeland. "We were glad we made the decision we did," Lidstrom said. "It was the right decision to make."

Lidstrom had endured persistent media speculation, both in North America and Sweden, about whether he would leave the NHL. "It was incredible," Lidstrom recalled of the daily questions. "Now, there was one less thing to think about. One big thing. It was a big relief."

The Lidstroms bought their first house in the Detroit suburbs of Novi in 1996. They stayed there for nine years before moving to a bigger house they built from scratch in 2005 in a gated Northville community. "Living in a neighborhood with many young families made it easier for both our kids and Nicklas and I to make new friends outside of hockey," Annika said.

Annika gave birth to four sons during their years in Detroit. "Kevin and Adam were both born in the spring, in the middle of the hockey season, so we had to do some planning there with the delivery dates so Nicklas would be able to be there at the hospital with me," Annika recalled. "Samuel was born in May of 2000 and that was the tricky one, with Nicklas being in Denver where the Red Wings were in the middle of a playoff series against Colorado.

"I remember him calling home, saying he might not make it back for my delivery. They were down 3–1 in games in the series and he felt he couldn't ask management for permission to leave the team and travel home, even if they would have given their approval. Luckily for me, I didn't have to make it to the hospital that night and he came home the next day in time for me to give birth to Samuel a couple of days later. Our fourth son, Lucas, was born in September, so that time we didn't need any planning, as the regular season hadn't started."

The support from the other wives meant a lot to Annika during her 20 years in Detroit. "The hard part was saying good-bye when somebody suddenly had to move after their husbands had been traded, and that happened a lot in Detroit," Annika said. "You build a relationship and learn how to be there for each other. Then they're gone. It can be heartbreaking, but I stay in touch with many of them today even as we are spread out all over the world. Without cell phones during our early years in Detroit, it was a little more complicated to keep up with everybody after they left, but I have reconnected with many of them since."

Annika Lidstrom has been there for each moment of her husband's journey from a talented rookie to becoming a superstar in the league. "It's been fantastic to have been there every step of the way with Nicklas," Annika said. "I knew he was very talented, and with his calmness and the focus he always has, I wasn't surprised that he reached so many milestones in his career, but I have to say that it was a joyful experience to do it together with him. Who would have thought all this success was coming when we moved to Detroit in 1991?"

Players are known for being moody and Annika admits that there were days when her husband wasn't happy with his or the team's performance. As Nicklas has pointed out, she more than anyone else could dispute the notion of her husband as the Perfect Human. But even in the bad times, Lidstrom would internalize his frustration and disappointment, rather than burden his family with it.

"Nicklas could be down on himself when the Red Wings weren't winning, but he learned how to leave those emotions at the rink," Annika said. "Of course, he was happy when they were winning, but the next day he was focused on the upcoming game. That's just how he handled it."

Lidstrom had also learned how to develop other passions outside of hockey. Growing up on an NHL team makes young boys become men in a hurry. Larionov remembers how he taught Lidstrom and some of his other teammates to be lovers of the vine.

"The Swedes and the Russians on our team often went out to dinner together when we were on the road," Larionov said. "They were all first-class guys and we always had interesting conversations. Maybe not so much about current affairs, but we definitely talked about other things than hockey off and on.

"Once when we were in Vancouver, Brendan Shanahan had signed a new contract and took everybody out to dinner. We were ordering appetizers at a really nice restaurant, and I couldn't hold myself when I heard the guys ordering beers. I said, 'Hold on, what are you doing? You need a good glass of wine for this meal.' All of a sudden, everybody looked up and I convinced them that we had to order a bottle of wine or two.

"I think I got Nick interested in wine then, and I remember later on during our time together on the Red Wings, I took him to a wine tasting. That really got him interested."

Lidstrom confirms that Larionov was the one who helped him develop his passion for wine. "Yeah, I remember that team dinner in Vancouver and the wine tasting he later took me to during our time together in Detroit," Lidstrom said. "It made me a wine collector. I installed a wine cellar in our house in Northville. When we moved back to Sweden in 2012, I shipped 350 bottles of wine to our new home in Vasteras, where we have a built-in wine cellar.

"Living in the U.S. made me like wine from Napa Valley. My favorite is Silver Oak, but I also have a couple of Larionov's brand. I like them, too. My wine collection grew at the end of our stay in Detroit when a teammate of mine, Brian Rafalski, and I had a chance to buy bottles from a restaurant nearby that went from a five-star to a four-star and wanted to get rid of some of their more expensive wines. We got a good deal."

Lidstrom felt that the early playoff exit in 1999 might benefit the Wings in the long run by helping to reenergize the team. "I thought the extra month off really helped, mentally and physically," Lidstrom said. "It gave us a chance to get in shape, too, to get ready for training camp. Everyone came into camp ready and rested."

They may have come in ready for the 1999–2000 season, but the final result remained the same. Things started in the playoffs just like they had the previous spring, with Detroit sweeping aside a team from California, this time the Los Angeles Kings. And just like the year before, Colorado awaited the Wings as a second-round opponent. It wasn't even close. The Avs dumped the Wings in five games.

Detroit won the Central Division in 2000–01 with 111 points and finished second in the Western Conference behind the

Avalanche, who took home the Northwest Division after collecting 118 points. There would be no rematch between the heated rivals.

The Red Wings entered the postseason with high hopes but collapsed in the first round against the Kings after winning the first two games at home by the scores of 5–3 and 4–0. Lidstrom had two assists in each of the two games, but both Shanahan and Yzerman were injured.

Lidstrom scored Detroit's only goal in a 2–1 loss when the series moved to Los Angeles. Game 4 saw the Kings rally from a 3–0 third-period deficit, winning in overtime 4–3. Lidstrom registered his sixth point in the first four games, but it was evident that just like in the spring of '99 against Colorado, the wheels were coming off Detroit's train.

Detroit had a chance to take back control of the series at Joe Louis Arena in Game 5 but lost 3–2. The Kings closed out the conference quarterfinals after a 3–2 OT win at home in Game 6. Detroit had lost four straight games after taking a 2–0 lead in the series. Lidstrom had at least one point in every game and a total of eight points (one goal and seven assists).

As difficult as that loss was to stomach, it's another episode from the 2000–01 campaign that haunts Lidstrom to this day. The most frightening moment for Lidstrom during all the years of traveling around North America with the Red Wings happened on January 15, 2001.

The Red Wings had taken off from San Jose after a game against the Sharks and were on their way to Vancouver when one of the engines of the team charter plane died. "I've never been so scared during all my time while flying on the team charter," Lidstrom said.

He was listening to music on his headphones with teammate Holmstrom seated next to him, playing a video game on his computer. "Everything had been normal so far," Lidstrom said. "We got to the airport in San Jose after the game, the team bus took us out all the way on to the tarmac. Our plane was ready for takeoff and we departed San Jose without any problems.

"I think we had reached 35,000 feet when we suddenly heard a bang and the engine on one side went out. The pilot made a dive with the plane down to 8,000 feet to try to restart the engine. The maneuver succeeded, but then the other engine died. Homer and I got really nervous. We immediately understood that this was more than regular turbulence. The airplane was shaking and tilted. We got permission for an emergency landing in Sacramento and that's where we spent the night. We were picked up with a new airplane the next day and taken to Vancouver for a game that same night."

There was another incident on the team charter that Lidstrom will never forget. "We were flying into Buffalo from Chicago or St. Louis one winter night in the late '90s or early 2000s and ended up in a vicious snowstorm," Lidstrom said. "We were landing in the middle of the storm, and the heavy winds made our plane shake and vibrate on the way down. It became so bad that the pilot had to abort the landing and we were redirected to Cleveland, which was the closest airport open with decent weather at that time.

"I remember hearing afterward that the Sabres trainers were at the airport in Buffalo, waiting to pick up our equipment, and saying to each other that they didn't think we were going to make it. That's how high the winds were at the airport in Buffalo. We couldn't make a safe landing there."

Holland had been appointed Red Wings general manager before the 1997–98 season, after being the assistant general manager for three years. He got a great start as the hockey boss when Detroit won the Stanley Cup in 1998 and continued what his predecessor Jimmy Devellano had started—building a dynasty in Detroit.

But Holland was not happy with the results in the playoffs for three straight seasons. He had made changes, but even with the addition of a number of quality players, his team had not returned to the Stanley Cup Final. The biggest disappointment was the loss to the Kings in the first round of the 2001 playoffs. Holland knew he had to make more changes. He was an aggressive and innovative manager, and unafraid of looking for untraditional solutions.

"Kenny made some unbelievable signings before the 2001–02 season when he got us Dominik Hasek, Brett Hull, Luc Robitaille, and Fredrik Olausson," Lidstrom said. "We already had a good team, but it boosted our lineup in a big way. We went from being a star-filled team to becoming a super team. And don't forget that we also had Pavel Datsyuk, who was a rookie that year but played like a veteran. We went on to win both the Presidents' Trophy, as the team with most points during the regular season, and the Stanley Cup."

The Red Wings won 51 of 82 regular season games and ended up with 116 points. They were a powerhouse now and had four 30-goal scorers in Shanahan (37), Fedorov (31), Hull (30), and Robitaille (30). Five of their players reached 50 points, with Shanahan on top at 75 points. Lidstrom had 59 points (nine goals and 50 assists) in 78 games and was a rock on the blueline.

Lidstrom had a lot of respect for the goaltenders in the league. Some of them he found more difficult to solve than others. "I thought

Martin Brodeur was really good. The same with Roberto Luongo, especially when he was in Vancouver," Lidstrom said. "Dominik Hasek was exceptional when he played for Buffalo and made a huge impression on me even if we didn't face them that often, as we were in the Western Conference at that time. Colorado's Patrick Roy was somebody we battled with and he was another goalie that was hard to beat, but you could get in under his skin.

"We had guys like Kris Draper and Darren McCarty who were good at doing that. It was possible to throw him off his game. He had a temper and sometimes he just lost it. I remember a playoff game, I think it was in 2002, when he thought he had made a save and raised his catching glove in the air, only to see the puck fall down behind him and into the goal."

Lidstrom played in front of a number of quality goaltenders during his 20 seasons in Detroit, starting with Tim Cheveldae when he arrived in the fall of 1991 and ending with Jimmy Howard when he left after the 2011–12 season. In between were names like Osgood, Mike Vernon, Ken Wregget, Manny Legace, Hasek, Curtis Joseph, Ty Conklin, and Joey MacDonald.

"I adjusted my play in front of our goaltenders depending on who was in the net," Lidstrom said. "If it was somebody like Chris Osgood, who was good playing the puck, I acted differently than if Hasek was in there. Ozzy was like a third defenseman and could make good passes with his stick. Hasek did not play that way. But he had quick reflexes and was very aggressive in the crease."

Looking back at the goalies he played with, Lidstrom ranks Hasek as the best. When Hasek came to the Red Wings before the 2001–02 season from Buffalo, he was at the top of his game. He had won the Vezina Trophy six times in Buffalo (1994, 1995, 1997,

1998, 1999, and 2001). Hasek had also won the Hart Memorial Trophy as the league's MVP in 1997 and 1998, the first time a goaltender had won the award since Montreal's Jacques Plante in 1962.

"He had a different style, but he was an exceptional competitor," Lidstrom said. "He just hated to let goals in. It didn't matter if it was at practice or in a game. It upset him if he couldn't make the save."

Bowman coached the Red Wings to three Stanley Cups in six years, including the 2001–02 triumph. It's an amazing achievement, but Lidstrom believes credit should also go to assistant coaches Lewis and Smith. "Scotty was of the old school and delegated a lot of work to his assistant coaches when it came to our special teams and how they should be set up," Lidstrom said. "He let Dave Lewis and Barry Smith run the penalty kill and the power play. Scotty gave them a lot of responsibilities, even if it was his thoughts and strategy that set the tone.

"Scotty was a great game coach. He was quick to respond to different situations on the ice and knew right away who he should match against the opponent's key players. His hockey IQ was off the charts."

Lidstrom was known as someone who never complained about anything, and most certainly not the play of a teammate. But on those rare occasions when Lidstrom raised a point of concern, the coaching staff listened. "I was called into Bowman's office once after I had asked Dave Lewis, who was responsible for our defensemen, if they had any thoughts about making some changes," Lidstrom recalled. "We were playing a fast team and one of our defensemen couldn't keep up. I made my point to Dave Lewis before a very important game and he told Scotty what I had said.

"When he called me into his office and when he asked what my thoughts were, I repeated what I thought. Scotty told me that he trusted older and experienced players and promised to think about it. I didn't hear more about it, but when the next game came, he had made the adjustment I had suggested, and we won the game. That was the only time during his years in Detroit that he talked to me about a specific player on our team."

For Lidstrom, having a coach like Bowman was a privilege. "Scotty has meant so much for me, and he wasn't just one of the many coaches I had during my career," Lidstrom explained. "Look at his merits and Stanley Cup wins over the years, and the respect he had in the league.

"I felt that Scotty had enormous confidence in me. He showed it by giving me all that ice time and he never talked to me that much about the way I played. He showed his trust in me by putting me out on the ice more and more. Specifically, after Vladimir Konstantinov was injured, my role on the team increased.

"He was a special coach and I'm happy that I had a chance to play for him during my time in Detroit. I couldn't have asked for more from Scotty."

Smith could see how Bowman's trust in Lidstrom grew from year to year. "Scotty loved him and was never in his face," Smith said. "He didn't need to be. The guys who cheated their game were the ones who had trouble with Scotty. Nick was never one of them and Scotty never wanted him to change his game.

"Nick was always the go-to-guy, because he was so responsible and never lost his temper, even if he was upset. His emotional level was so consistent. After Konstantinov got injured, Nick had to take on a larger role on our defense and he made that adjustment so easily."

The Red Wings were stacked with stars and Bowman made them winners. Robitaille was one of the additions to the 2001–02 team. At the age of 35, Robitaille left the Kings when he saw a chance to finally get his name on the Stanley Cup, signing a two-year contract with Detroit.

Robitaille was a highly regarded goal-scorer in the league, and still had that knack for finding the net. He played 81 regular season games with Detroit in the 2001–02 season and finished with 50 points (30 goals and 20 assists), the 12th time Robitaille had reached 30 goals in an NHL campaign. Only Shanahan and Fedorov scored more goals on the Red Wings that season. Robitaille added four goals and five assists in 23 playoff games.

Hockey experts have often called the trio of Robitaille, Larionov, and Holmstrom the best fourth line in NHL history. "We called it a fourth line, but look at the names on that line," Lidstrom said, pointing out that Robitaille and Larionov are in the Hockey Hall of Fame and Holmstrom was a great goal-scorer for many years in the league. "That is a top trio on almost any team."

Holmstrom is still in awe over that 2002 lineup. "It was a team packed with All-Star players," Holmstrom said. "It was unbelievable, and the great thing was that nobody showed any ego. We all played for the team."

Nine players from the 2002 team have made it into the Hockey Hall of Fame—Hasek, Lidstrom, Chelios, Yzerman, Larionov, Fedorov, Shanahan, Hull, and Robitaille. Pavel Datsyuk will be the next member from that team to be inducted.

"The reason I went to Detroit was to win a Cup," Robitaille said. "We had an All-Star team, so it was a dream to be part of that '01–02 season group. I played with Igor and Homer and we just did feed off each other so well."

Playing alongside Lidstrom was another attraction. Robitaille had played against Lidstrom for years in the league and knew how good the Swede was. But it took some time for Robitaille to see how great the star defenseman really was.

"I remember asking Stevie Y when I got to Detroit who he thought was the best player he had ever been on a team with," Robitaille said. "I knew he had played with [Wayne] Gretzky and [Mark] Messier and all those stars in the Canada Cup and so on. Stevie's answer was Nick Lidstrom. When I asked him why, Stevie said, 'I have never seen Nicklas Lidstrom have a bad game.' After six months of playing with Nick, I realized what Stevie had said was true."

Heavy favorites to win the Stanley Cup, the playoffs started off with disappointment and consternation for the Red Wings. They lost Game 1 of their opening-round series to the Vancouver Canucks 4–3 after leading 3–2 with less than 10 minutes left in the third period. Henrik Sedin scored the winner 13:59 into overtime. Two nights later, Detroit lost a second straight game at Joe Louis Arena to the Canucks, this time by a lopsided 5–2 count.

Lidstrom vividly recalls the heartbreaking Game 2 loss. "I remember one of our fans threw a game jersey on the ice as the buzzer sounded," Lidstrom said. "That really stung. It was tough to fly to Vancouver being down 0–2 in games. They had a really good team with Markus Naslund as their superstar.

"Before the first game in Vancouver, our captain Steve Yzerman asked for everybody's attention in the dressing room. He didn't speak to the team much, but when he did it, everybody listened. Stevie made it clear that we were a very good team and that we needed to go out on the ice with confidence and show that. If we did that, we would turn the series around and win it, he said."

The long shot Canucks looked to have turned the series in their favor, but it would be a long shot that would swing things in Detroit's favor. Lidstrom played a big part in turning the series around with his game-winning goal in Game 3, a shot from just across center that shockingly eluded the grasp of Canucks goalie Dan Cloutier.

"We were tied 1–1 nearing the end of the second period when I rushed the puck up the ice and was thinking about letting off a low shot at their goalie Dan Cloutier's catching side to get a rebound," Lidstrom recalled. "I could see Brett Hull coming in from the right side, so I thought he would be in the perfect position to pick up the rebound. To my surprise, the puck sneaked in behind Cloutier and we were suddenly leading 2–1."

Detroit won the game 3–1 after an early third-period goal from Shanahan. The Red Wings went on to win three more games and took the series 4–2. "I'm the first one to admit that we were in deep trouble against Vancouver that year," Lidstrom said.

Detroit had a smoother ride through the conference semifinals against the St. Louis Blues after opening the series with two victories at Joe Louis Arena, 2–0 and 3–2. The Red Wings lost the third game at the Savvis Center 6–1, but left St. Louis with a 4–3 win in Game 4. Detroit finished off the Blues with a 4–0 victory back home and were back in the Western Conference Final. To nobody's surprise, their opponent would be an old foe, the defending Stanley Cup champion Avalanche.

"Another hockey war awaited us," Lidstrom said. "Colorado was at least as good as we were, that we knew."

The Avs had added Rob Blake, their own Norris Trophy–winning defenseman, in the hopes of countering Lidstrom. When Blake came to Colorado in February of 2001, the rivalry with Detroit had been going on for years.

"It was pretty intense," Blake said. "I had been watching it for all those years [playing in] Los Angeles and seeing it firsthand now, you could see how much they really disliked each other. It wasn't just TV stuff. It was real when you became part of it.

"The year we won the Cup in 2001, we didn't have to go through Detroit, but I remember the next year they also had added Luc Robitaille, Brett Hull, and Dominik Hasek, while we had played two seven-game series against the L.A. Kings and San Jose and were pretty beaten up."

The teams split the first two games in Detroit and were tied 2–2 after the next two in Denver. Peter Forsberg then scored an overtime winner to give Colorado a 2–1 win at Joe Louis Arena in Game 5. Colorado was going home looking to close out the series in Game 6.

"We knew we were in trouble when we left for Game 6 in Denver and that we could not afford any mistakes," Lidstrom said. "But then we got a little lucky. During a penalty for us in the second period, their coach Bob Hartley asked for a measurement on Dominik Hasek's stick. Hartley thought it had an illegal curve and was trying to get a five-on-three power play. But Hasek had checked his stick before the game and knew that it was legal, so Colorado got the penalty and we ended up four-on-four instead."

The Red Wings won the game 2–0 after goals from Shanahan and McCarty and the series went back to Detroit for a seventh and deciding game. Everybody expected a tight and hard-fought game; it turned out to be the opposite. Holmstrom gave the home team a lead just 1:57 into the game and before the first period was over, Detroit had gained a 4–0 edge. Colorado had run out of steam and the Red Wings won 7–0. Hasek had another shutout, only having to save 19 shots. Roy, on the other hand, was replaced in the second period by David Aebischer.

Despite the lopsided Game 7, the series was a close one. "They beat us pretty bad in Game 7," Blake said. "Three of the seven games went to overtime, though. It was always a big rivalry. The team that won the series between us had a pretty good chance to win the Cup."

This time, that team was the Red Wings, who were back in the Stanley Cup Final for the first time since 1998.

A new acquaintance awaited Detroit: the Carolina Hurricanes, a team that had put together a strong regular season, winning the Southeast Division. The Canes then dispatched the New Jersey Devils (4–2), Montreal Canadiens (4–2), and Toronto Maple Leafs (4–2) on their way to the Final.

Led by coach Paul Maurice, Carolina had a roster filled with established players such as Ron Francis, Rod Brind'Amour, Sami Kapanen, Sandis Ozolinsh, Glen Wesley, former Wing Aaron Ward, Bret Hedican, and goaltender Arturs Irbe. The Hurricanes showed they were for real in the opening game at Joe Louis Arena, winning 3–2 in overtime. Detroit came back two nights later and tied the series with a 3–1 win. Lidstrom played an astonishing 34:38 in Game 2, beating Irbe for a power play goal. "He's awesome every game," teammate Boyd Devereaux said at the time. "He's just unflappable. He's so poised and so collected. I've never seen the guy make a poor pass, hardly ever. He's been that way through the whole playoffs."

The first game in Raleigh, North Carolina, was a thriller. Long into the night, Larionov scored the winning goal in the third extra period for a 3–2 win. Lidstrom played 52 minutes in the game. "With the dramatic win in Raleigh in Game 3, we felt that we had turned the series around and that we would bring home the Cup," Lidstrom said.

Detroit won the fourth game by the score of 3–0 and flew home to Michigan with a 3–1 lead. "When we landed in Detroit after the fourth game, Steve Yzerman gathered us right after we got off the plane and said, 'Everybody is going to say that we now will win this easily, but we haven't won anything yet. Remember that,'" Lidstrom recalled. "His message was that there was a lot of work left to do and I thought that helped us. Everybody understood that we had one more game to win before we could start to celebrate.

"In that way, Yzerman was a great leader. He said the right things at the right time. Nobody was allowed to get ahead of themselves. We all got the point."

The Red Wings won Game 5 at home 3–1 to clinch another Stanley Cup. Before NHL commissioner Gary Bettman handed the Cup to Yzerman, the winner of the prestigious Conn Smythe Trophy was announced. The trophy is awarded each spring to the player judged most valuable to his team during the National Hockey League's Stanley Cup playoffs.

In front of his hometown fans, Lidstrom heard his name announced and skated up to the trophy table to receive it from Bettman. For the first time in league history, the Conn Smythe Trophy went to a European player.

"It was a huge accomplishment for me," Lidstrom said. "Not only being the first European player to be awarded it, but also the competition from players on our team. Brett Hull was the best goal-scorer in the playoffs and Dominik Hasek was unbelievable in goal. Both of them could have won it. To be the Conn Smythe winner, you have to be at the top of your game when it counts the most. It's a significant honor."

Lidstrom was the fifth defenseman to win the playoff MVP in the past 25 years, joining New Jersey's Scott Stevens (2000), the New York Rangers' Brian Leetch (1994), Calgary's Al MacInnis (1989), and Larry Robinson of the Habs (1978).

"Nick turned it all around for us in Game 3 with that 2–1 goal against Vancouver," Robitaille said. "We were a team of All-Stars, but he was the one that lifted us. And he kept on playing unreal hockey throughout the playoffs. St. Louis tried to go after him and put Keith Tkachuk on Nick, but that didn't work, either.

"He dominated every game and was clearly the MVP, not only of our team but the whole 2002 Stanley Cup. No question about it."

"Some guys in this league have a presence," was how Wings equipment manager Paul Boyer explained it. "Steve Yzerman had a presence. Wayne Gretzky had presence. Mario Lemieux had presence. You know when Mark Messier is in a room, he has that presence.

"Nick had a presence. I guess it is felt maybe more in Sweden, but when Nicklas Lidstrom is in a room, the presence is there. It's just who he is."

Lidstrom moved into fourth place on Detroit's all-time playoff scoring list with 107 points, three ahead of longtime captain Alex Delvecchio. "All the minutes he plays, he's just the perfect player," Bowman said. "He scored big goals for us, he was out there against all the other team's best lines."

As the celebration engulfed the ice at Joe Louis Arena, there was something else getting everybody's attention beyond the presence of the Stanley Cup. As soon as the game ended, Bowman disappeared into the dressing room. A couple of minutes later he came out again and took to the ice. To everybody's surprise, he was wearing his skates.

A smiling Bowman, the legendary NHL coach who seldom showed any extra emotion behind the bench, looked like he was having the time of his life. Sure, the victory over Carolina gave him a record nine Stanley Cups. But there was something else going on, something not many knew about at that moment. Bowman had coached his last game. The Master was done.

"He told me on the ice during the celebration," Lidstrom said. "It came as a big surprise to me, even if there had been rumors among us players that he might retire after the season."

A couple of weeks later, at the NHL Awards in Toronto, Lidstrom won his second Norris Trophy and joined Bobby Orr as the second defenseman in league history to bring home the triple—the Stanley Cup, the Conn Smythe Trophy, and the Norris Trophy.

"It was a dream come true," Lidstrom said. "Something I could never have expected."

8

THE GOLDEN
GOAL

ON THE WORLD HOCKEY STAGE, NICKLAS LIDSTROM MIGHT BEST BE described as an international man of history. He was the first European player to win the Norris Trophy and Conn Smythe Trophy and would eventually become the first European captain of a Stanley Cup championship team.

But none of it would have happened if not for the groundwork laid down back home in his native Sweden. Lidstrom is the first to say he owes much of what he's achieved in the game to his homeland and the hockey infrastructure of the Swedish system. And his countrymen will be the first to tell you that Lidstrom has paid them back handsomely, and then some.

As a youngster, the Stanley Cup wasn't the object he dreamed of one day holding. His hockey dreams centered around donning the Tre Kronor jersey, as the Swedish uniform is known due to the three crowns that adorn its front.

"I grew up watching all of the different World Championships and the Olympics, because every kid in Sweden dreams of playing for the national team one day," Lidstrom said. "I was one of those kids.

"I wanted to play for Team Sweden and I finally had a chance to do that when I put on that national team jersey. It's a special feeling. You feel very proud, especially when you're representing your country. To be able to do that was a big thrill for me."

Lidstrom's first taste of international competition came at the 1987–88 European under-18 championship. He would also play for Sweden at the 1989–90 World Junior tournament, but much bigger stages soon awaited him.

In the spring of 1991, the Red Wings were weighing whether to give Lidstrom another year of seasoning in Sweden, or if he was ready for North American hockey. The Detroit brass ventured across the Atlantic Ocean to Finland to watch Lidstrom play for Sweden in his first World Championships.

When the tournament was over, the Swedes wore gold around their necks for just the second time since 1962, and Lidstrom's stellar work along the blueline was a big reason why.

Sweden and the Soviet Union met in the final game of the tournament, which was conducted under a round-robin format in those days. A tie would give Canada the gold medal, and the game was deadlocked 1–1 in the third period when Mats Sundin, who would finish as the tournament's leading scorer with 12 points (seven goals and five assists), tallied the deciding goal in Sweden's 2–1 victory.

Lidstrom finished with six points (three goals and three assists) in 10 games, but two defensemen who would later be his teammates got attention along the blueline ahead of him. Jamie Macoun of Canada was named the tournament's top defenseman, and Slava Fetisov of the Soviet Union was named to the All-Star team. All three would win the Stanley Cup together with the 1997–98 Red Wings.

"Of course, winning the gold medal in my first big tournament was huge for me at that point in my career," Lidstrom said. "I just got an offer from the Wings to come over and play for Detroit and that was a fairly big tournament for me to kind of showcase myself. Then on top of that, winning the gold medal was huge and a big stepping stone for me in my career."

There would be one more international stop for Lidstrom before settling in Detroit. He suited up for Sweden in the 1991 Canada Cup, pairing on the defense alongside childhood hero Borje Salming and wearing No. 4, because on the Swedish national team at that time, No. 5 belonged to Salming.

Lidstrom's next sampling of international hockey wouldn't arrive until the spring of 1994, when he played for Sweden at the World Championships after the Wings were knocked out of the playoffs by the San Jose Sharks. He got to Italy in time to play four games. Sweden beat the host Italians in the quarterfinals but were whitewashed 6–0 by Canada in the semifinals. The Swedes rebounded to dump the United States 7–2 in the third-place game and Lidstrom and Sweden went home with the bronze medal.

Lidstrom would heed his country's call once again to play in one more World Championships tournament in 2004 in Prague. Lidstrom came over to the Czech Republic toward the end of the tournament after Detroit had lost 4–2 in the Western Conference semifinals to the Calgary Flames. The last two games of the series ended with 1–0 wins for Calgary, and the second one went to overtime before Martin Gelinas beat Curtis Joseph with only 47 seconds left in the first extra period.

"After we lost, I got on a plane and rushed over to Prague to be able to join the national team on the last weekend of the tournament," Lidstrom said. "I was there only three days. The semifinal and final were played back to back at that time. It was exhausting."

Lidstrom assisted on Dick Axelsson's game-winning power play goal as Sweden edged the U.S. 3–2 in the semifinals. But Canada proved too much for the Swedes to handle in the gold-medal game, taking a 5–3 decision. Lidstrom flew back to Detroit with a silver medal as a reward for the weekend trip, and now he had a matched set to go with the gold medal he won in 1991 and the bronze medal from 1994.

New York Rangers goalie Henrik Lundqvist first got to know Lidstrom during this event. Lundqvist was the starting goaltender on the Swedish team and was selected to the tournament All-Star team.

"He played at an extremely high level," Lundqvist said of Lidstrom. "Outside the rink he was a very sympathetic person who was easy to get along with. We lost the finals against Canada, but it was a great experience for me. We had a good team with additions arriving late from the NHL, like Lidstrom, Peter Forsberg, Daniel Alfredsson, Michael Nylander, and Samuel Pahlsson."

Lundqvist quickly came to appreciate the many benefits of having Lidstrom playing in front of him. "Nicklas was such a smart player," Lundqvist said. "I was always fascinated by his position play. He was so intelligent and could read the play at any time and at any place on the ice. He knew on what side of the opponent player he should be and with his long stick he was so effective in getting the puck out of the way. Not many defensemen had his skills."

Ottawa Senators forward Alfredsson had previously teamed alongside Lidstrom on the Swedish team at the 1996 World Cup of Hockey, and also grew to appreciate the subtleties of Lidstrom's understated game. "I didn't know much about him, to be honest," Alfredsson admitted. "I had one season in the NHL and had played twice against him. I guessed he was a pretty good player but didn't know too much about him."

Alfredsson soon recognized that studying Lidstrom was a good way to get ahead of the game. "Early in your career you watch and pick up stuff all of the time," Alfredsson said. "Obviously, with Nick—having been so successful in the NHL as well, winning four Cups and being around as long as he had been and around so many great players—there's lots to learn.

"But the biggest thing I found was how he was able to push himself as much as he did, day in and day out, to be better all the time, even though he had been so good. That's a talent in itself and something I admired."

The landscape of the hockey world changed in the winter of 1998. The NHL took a break in its schedule to allow its players to participate in the Winter Olympic Games in Nagano, Japan. For the first time in hockey history, the best players in the world would play on the biggest stage in sports, and Lidstrom would be a part of the festivities.

Lidstrom felt that sending NHL players to the Winter Olympics was a concept that was both brilliant and long overdue. "I think it's real important to players from all ends of the world," Lidstrom said. "Having a chance to showcase the best players in the world in such a big event, I'm all for having a chance to play in the Olympics for NHL players."

Although he'd eventually get the chance to skate in four Olympic Games, Lidstrom viewed the opportunity as a once-in-a-lifetime experience. Part of that was due to the unique accommodations.

"I liked the Olympic Village with all the other athletes," Lidstrom said. "I liked the atmosphere in the Olympic Village and the chance you had to mingle with athletes from other sports and countries. It was a much bigger stage, with all kinds of other things going on. It was a new and different experience, compared to the international hockey tournaments I had taken part in earlier, like the World Championships, Canada Cup, and the World Cup. It wasn't just hockey. I really enjoyed playing in the Olympics."

The Swedes found themselves in the toughest pool of the tournament, alongside the favorites from Canada and the United States, who'd won the 1996 World Cup of Hockey, as well as minnow Belarus.

Sweden opened with a solid 4–2 decision over the U.S. Lidstrom collected a goal and an assist in the next game, a 3–2 loss to the Canadians. Sweden completed pool play by outclassing Belarus 5–2. The Swedes drew their archrivals from Finland in the quarterfinals, and two goals from Teemu Selanne sent Lidstrom and his teammates packing after a 2–1 defeat.

"My first Olympic experience in Nagano, Japan, had been pleasant," Lidstrom recalled, "except for the loss to Finland."

By the time he came back for his second attempt at an Olympic medal, four years later at the 2002 Salt Lake City Winter Games, much had changed in Lidstrom's life, and in the perception of Lidstrom within and outside of hockey circles. He'd won a pair of Stanley Cups and the first of his seven Norris Trophies. He wasn't just one of the players who would help carry the Swedish team;

Lidstrom was a key element of the team's core, a national icon in his homeland.

The Swedish Olympic Team boasted a strong roster, missing only Forsberg, who had taken the season off to heal an injured foot. But the rest of the Swedish stars in the NHL were there, including Markus Naslund and Mattias Ohlund from the Vancouver Canucks, Alfredsson of the Senators, and Sundin of the Toronto Maple Leafs. Lidstrom was joined on the Swedish roster by two of his Red Wings teammates—best friend Tomas Holmstrom and Fredrik Olausson, Lidstrom's defense partner in Detroit that season—as well as a future Wing, 21-year-old forward Henrik Zetterberg from Timra IK, one of only two players on the team who played in the Swedish Elitserien.

Zetterberg was a star back home in Sweden and had won the 2002 Golden Puck as the best Swedish player in the country's top league. The prize is given out every year by national newspaper *Expressen* with a jury consisting of hockey writers and members of the Swedish Hockey Association, including the coach for the national team. Selected by Detroit in the seventh round as the 210th overall pick in the 1999 NHL entry draft, Zetterberg had been voted rookie of the year in Sweden in 2001 and would meet Lidstrom for the first time as a member of the national team for that 2002 Olympiad.

Lidstrom noticed early on what a great talent they had in Zetterberg, who would join the Wings in time for the 2002–03 NHL season. In Sweden, Zetterberg is referred to by the letter Z (pronounced "zaeta"), but he soon became known as Hank among his teammates in Detroit.

"I was impressed with Hank's work ethic," Lidstrom said. "He wasn't the biggest body on the ice, but he never backed away from heavy traffic or the boards. He played a smart game. Nobody could intimidate him. He just kept coming and showed us all that he was a team guy. That gave him respect in the dressing room and on the bench. He had come to stay and be a big part of our team for years to come. We all knew that."

The chance to play in Salt Lake City not only enabled Zetterberg to perform alongside his Swedish hockey heroes, it presented him the opportunity to measure his game against the top players on the planet.

"It helped me tremendously that I had been on the Olympic team with Nick and Homer in February that year," Zetterberg said. "When I arrived at training camp in Detroit in September for the 2002–03 season, at least I was familiar with two of the guys on the team."

He learned a lot from Lidstrom during his rookie year. "Nick was my roommate on the road," Zetterberg said. "I was very shy in his presence and he isn't a big talker either, so not much was said when we were in our hotel room. It was pretty quiet, from what I remember. But Nick and Homer made sure that I got adjusted to the team and life in the NHL. They took me out to dinners on the road and it was good to have two countrymen on the ice during practices in the beginning, so they could explain what the coach wanted us to do before the next drill. I am forever thankful to them for what they did for me."

Zetterberg enjoyed an impressive first season in Detroit with 44 points (22 goals and 22 assists) in 79 games, best among all rookies in the league. He was runner-up for the Calder Trophy, losing the vote to St. Louis Blues defenseman Barret Jackman.

The bond he developed with Lidstrom continued to play a large role in Zetterberg's career and life in the U.S. "These are things you start to think about when you get older," Zetterberg said. "Today I'm aware of what a big part Nick played in my career, both on and off the ice. It's hard to find a better defenseman in this league. For sure, I have not played with anyone better. Just look at what he has accomplished. It's mind-boggling.

"Four Stanley Cups, seven Norris Trophies, a Conn Smythe Trophy, and all the nominations to All-Star Teams and All-Star Games. Add to that his Olympic gold medal and also a gold from the World Championships. You can go on and on."

In February of 2002, all that Lidstrom and Zetterberg were thinking about was winning an Olympic gold medal. Sweden started the 2002 tournament in Salt Lake City with an impressive 5–2 victory over Canada. Sundin was the captain and leader, and he played a fabulous game, leading a line with Alfredsson and Per-Johan Axelsson. "We played real well in the opening game against a strong Canadian team with players like Martin Brodeur, Scott Niedermayer, Paul Kariya, Jarome Iginla, Brendan Shanahan, Steve Yzerman, Mario Lemieux, Eric Lindros, and Joe Sakic," Lidstrom said. Both Lidstrom and Zetterberg collected assists in the win over the Canadians.

Sweden continued the round-robin play with a 2–1 win over the Czech Republic. Lidstrom drew another assist in this game. A 7–1 rout of Germany followed, as Sweden clinched the top spot in Group C with a 3–0 record. Lidstrom set up two goals in this game, including a tally by Holmstrom.

"We started the tournament so well," Lidstrom said. "We beat Canada in the first game 5–2, and we played real well. We played real well in the following games, too, right up to the quarterfinals when we were a huge favorite against Belarus and then we didn't play up to par. I thought we were close to doing something great and we collapsed in the quarterfinals."

Nobody thought Belarus would give the Swedes any problem in the quarterfinals, but what happened put a black eye on Swedish hockey for years to come. The Swedes lost 4–3 after a late goal from unknown Belarus forward Vladimir Kopat, who launched a high, looping shot from the neutral zone that oddly bounced off the head of Swedish goaltender Tommy Salo and into the net. The 7,240 fans in the E Center in Salt Lake City were stunned. The goal came with 3:24 left in regulation time; Lidstrom, Sundin, and the rest of Team Sweden tried desperately to even the score and take the game to overtime but fell short.

"We didn't play as well as we knew we could," said Lidstrom, who had a goal and an assist in the loss. "Losing in the quarterfinals was tough. It was tough for everyone on the team. Still to this day, you remember the loss. It was a tough loss because a lot of people in Sweden are passionate about the national team and there was a lot of disappointment from the people in Sweden."

The loss to Belarus caused an uproar among the hockey fans and media back in Sweden. A headline in one of the biggest newspapers read THEY LET THEIR COUNTRY DOWN, with pictures of all the players. Lidstrom was one of the players who made himself available for the media after that game. He stood there with his friend Salo and tried to explain what had just happened. It was late at night back in Sweden and people were furious.

One reporter asked, "Would the players tell the hockey fans back home that they were sorry and ask for forgiveness?"

Lidstrom recalled pausing to take a couple of seconds to think about his answer before responding. "No, I don't think we should ask for forgiveness," Lidstrom said. "We did our best, as we always try to do, but it wasn't enough today, unfortunately."

He felt badly for Salo, who everybody knew was going to be the scapegoat. Nine times out of 10 he would have saved that game-winning shot. This time he misread it badly and the puck flew over his catching glove, hit his mask, and landed in the net. Salo was vilified back in Sweden and stopped talking to the national media for months.

Lidstrom was appalled by the way Salo was treated by the press and by the Swedish people. "Salo took a lot of heat from letting in that goal," Lidstrom said. "I felt bad for Tommy. People didn't say a whole lot. It was more from reading the newspapers and learning of their disappointment that way. I actually stopped reading the papers after that. I saw one headline and I knew there was going to be a lot of disappointment, so I stopped reading the stories about that tournament."

Lidstrom and Salo had just become partners in a restaurant in their hometown of Vasteras, a sports bar where the game had been broadcast that night. The timing could not have been worse. "I thought we were on our way to a great tournament," Lidstrom said. "We had a really good team. The first three games had been evidence of how well we could play. Then we collapsed against Belarus. I still think about that game off and on."

The truth was that Salo wasn't the only player who had a bad game that day in Salt Lake City. Belarus had taken 2–1 and 3–2 leads in the game before Sundin tied it at 7:54 of the third period. Losing to Belarus, after outshooting them 47–19, was an upset it took years for Swedish hockey to regroup from. It was worse than the disappointing finish in Nagano in 1998. Bringing in the NHL players to the Olympics had not paid dividends for Team Sweden. They didn't even have a medal to show for it after two appearances at the Olympics with their Dream Team. The three crowns on the chest of Sweden's jersey were seriously devalued.

Four years later, there would be redemption for a devastated hockey nation, and Lidstrom would lead the healing process in heroic fashion.

Sweden sent a powerhouse team to the 2006 Olympic Games. This time, the Olympiad was held in Torino, Italy, and the national team included the names of Lidstrom, Sundin, Forsberg, Lundqvist, Alfredsson, Holmstrom, Zetterberg, Fredrik Modin, and the Sedin twins, Daniel and Henrik. It was a star-filled lineup and the mission was clear—revenge for the fiasco in Salt Lake City and the heartbreaking loss to Finland in the quarterfinals of the 1998 Nagano Olympics. The window for what media in Sweden called the Golden Generation was closing. The country's three major NHL stars were getting older—Lidstrom and Sundin were 35, and Forsberg was 32—and fans were wondering, could they deliver the gold medal this time?

Lidstrom, who'd endured years of heartbreak with the Red Wings before finally getting to drink from the Stanley Cup, understood better than most that talent alone wouldn't get the job done for the Swedes.

"We knew we had a great team, but we also had great teams in Nagano and Salt Lake City and that wasn't enough to reach the medal rounds," Lidstrom said. "It was something that was in the back of our minds, for sure. We definitely had something to prove. In Torino, suddenly everything came together for us as a group. We clicked and got better and better from game to game."

Sweden was situated in Group B together with Slovakia, Russia, the U.S., Kazakhstan, and Latvia. They beat Kazakhstan in the opening game 7–2 but lost against Russia 5–0 in the next game. Sweden came back with a 6–1 win over Latvia and secured a playoff spot after beating the U.S. 2–1.

The last game for the Swedes in group play was against Slovakia. A win would set up a matchup with Canada in the quarterfinals; a loss would give them Switzerland. The speculation began: would Sweden tank its game against Slovakia to avoid the Canadians?

In the end, Slovakia shutout Sweden 3–0. The result started a flood of rumors and to this day, many hockey writers and experts are convinced that Sweden did not give its all. More fuel was added to the fire when Forsberg, in an interview with the filmmakers behind the Swedish documentary *#21 Peter Forsberg* in December of 2011, more or less confessed that they hadn't done their best against Slovakia.

Michael Farber, who was the main hockey writer at *Sports Illustrated* at that time and was covering the tournament, has his own explanation of how Sweden got away with it. "I've always teased Lidstrom and some of the other Swedes about the two-minute five-on-three that Sweden had against Slovakia in the last round-robin match in Torino 2006, a game the Tre Kronor were obviously not interested in winning," Farber said. "Better matchup in the knockout, Switzerland or Canada?

"The power play of Lidstrom, Forsberg, Sundin, Modin, and Alfredsson didn't register a single shot in those minutes. Lidstrom did, however, hit the post. I swear he was so good that he hit the post on purpose, so it would sort of look like Sweden was trying, which it wasn't."

Lidstrom dismisses Farber's claim. "I know that Michael thinks that, he told me his theory some years later," Lidstrom said. "My answer is that I'm not that good. I can't do that. I did not purposely hit the post on that power play. What I can say is that it wasn't a game of life or death for us. A loss wouldn't kick us out of the tournament. I think it was Ken Holland who compared it to a semifinal in the 100 meters in track and field and you finish second. That is totally fine, because you make it to the finals anyway.

"It was a similar situation for us in the game against Slovakia in Torino. We weren't going to throw ourselves on the ice to block a shot with our face. We knew we had already made it to the final rounds. Under those circumstances, you don't want to get injured, but of course you want to win every game."

In the quarterfinals, Lidstrom and his teammates rolled over Switzerland in a 6–2 win, Lidstrom collecting two assists, and then defeated the Czech Republic 7–3 in the semifinals, with Lidstrom dishing out another helper. The Swedes had made it to the finals and, much to their surprise, they would not be up against Canada. The Canadians lost 2–0 to Russia in the quarterfinals and then Finland knocked out Russia 4–0 and came storming into the gold-medal game.

"That we were up against Finland felt really good for a number of reasons," Lidstrom said. "First of all, the hockey rivalry between our countries is intense. Sweden and Finland, that's huge. It's one of the greatest rivalries in all of sports. It goes way back. And we also had a score to settle after the loss in Nagano."

Kimmo Timonen gave Finland the lead 14:45 into the opening period, but Sweden came back with two power play goals in the second by Zetterberg and fellow Red Wing Niklas Kronwall. Ville Peltonen tied the game with five minutes left in the second period.

The third period started with a four-on-four and that's when the Golden Generation stepped up. Saku Koivu broke his stick during a faceoff against Sundin, and suddenly the Finns were one man short. The deciding moment had arrived. Sundin passed the puck to Forsberg, who dropped it back to the Swedish team captain.

"I immediately noticed that Koivu had gone to the bench to get a new stick and that it would create space for me inside the blueline for a shot," Lidstrom recalled. "I just waited for Mats to get me the puck. When the pass came, I was so ready. Peter had told us at the pregame meeting that we should aim high on their goaltender, Antero Niittymaki, his teammate on the Philadelphia Flyers. Forsberg knew everything about Niittymaki's weaknesses and told us that he was extremely hard to score on low, that he covered most of the ice there. So, the best chance to get shots past him was to shoot high. That was on my mind when Sundin's pass landed on my stick."

Lidstrom could see the puck leave his stick and go straight to the far high corner. "It almost felt like watching the whole sequence in slow motion," Lidstrom said. "After playing so many years as I had, you have memories from situations like this where the puck often hits a stick or an opponent in front of the goal and suddenly moves in another direction and misses the net. This time, I could see how the puck went in under the crossbar on Niittymaki's stick side. It was magic."

Holmstrom saw the goal from the penalty box. "From the angle where I was sitting, I could see how Nick put all the power on this slap shot and I knew before it reached the net that it was a goal," Holmstrom said. "It was the perfect shot."

Lidstrom's goal after 10 seconds of the final frame turned out to be the winning goal in a 3–2 victory. It was fitting that the assists on the goal came from Sundin and Forsberg.

"Yeah, of course it was special having Peter and Mats assisting me on that winning goal," Lidstrom said. "We had been through so much together and to have a chance to end our time together on the national team with an Olympic gold medal was so special. A fairy tale ending."

As soon as the final buzzer sounded in the Torino Palasport Olimpico Stadium, Lidstrom and his teammates went crazy. Helmets, gloves, and sticks were thrown in the air. They were hugging each other and celebrating with the huge number of Swedish fans in the stands as they all released years of pent-up feelings. Annika and their two oldest sons, Kevin and Adam, were there to share in Lidstrom's relief and happiness.

In the past many observers had wondered how Lidstrom could be so good in the NHL, yet unable to lead Sweden to gold at the Olympics. Farber admitted that this was a notion that crossed his mind. "Curiously to me, Lidstrom was never the bell cow in international play, at least not when I saw the Swedes," Farber said. "I don't know if that was because of personality or style of play. Sundin was that main guy because he could always find another gear, which made him perhaps their best international player for nearly a 15-year period. Lidstrom didn't seem to have that extra gear. He was always so good, so proficient, and so calm, that every night seemed like a Friday in Detroit against the Sabres. Maybe he didn't have, or need, that extra gear because he always was at his best, although often in those Olympic tournaments you just wanted a little more. Maybe scoring that goal to start the third period against Finland in 2006 is all anyone could ever expect."

After the medal ceremony, national anthem, and team picture on the ice, it was time for the champions to celebrate behind closed doors in the dressing room. "I will never forget the emotions inside the dressing room when fans and media couldn't see us," Lidstrom said. "Everybody walked around with their gold medals around their neck. It was just awesome. We were such a tight group. I think all of us felt what a very special moment that was. It is hard to describe."

In the middle of the celebration, Lidstrom snuck out into the arena to make a phone call to his parents back home in Sweden. "I was standing alone on the ice, where I had scored the winning goal a little earlier, talking to my mom and dad," Lidstrom remembered. "It was very emotional. My mom answered the phone and I just wanted to tell them where I was standing at that moment, alone on the ice in the arena. It was hard to hold back the tears.

"I'd rank it right up there with winning the Stanley Cup. The Stanley Cup is played every year. The Olympics are played every fourth year. That's what makes it so tough to win. I'm just glad we finally did it. Finally being able to wear the gold medal was just an unbelievable feeling."

The Olympic gold at the time made Lidstrom and Fredrik Modin the 17th and 18th members of the prestigious Triple Gold

Club; members are winners of a Stanley Cup, an Olympic gold medal, and a World Championships. "That's very special, too," Lidstrom said. "Not a whole lot of players have been able to do that, win two different tournaments with the national team, then winning the Stanley Cup as well. It's a special feeling and something that I'm very proud of, to be a part of that Triple Gold Club."

Forsberg had also won gold at the 1994 Olympics in Lillehammer, Norway, but at a time when NHL players weren't participating.

"To be able to win the Olympics with the old guys in Torino was unbelievable fun," Forsberg said. "Just unreal. I call us the Old Boys Club because we were all in our 30s. For myself, I had gone through a number of problems with my feet in the years before Torino, but all the surgeries felt worth it after we won. Having Nicklas scoring the winner was the perfect ending."

Sharing such a moment with his longtime international teammates was as vital to Lidstrom as was the winning goal. "That tournament was special for all of us, because we didn't know if we would play in that big of a tournament together again," Lidstrom said. "It turned out that we didn't play together again, because Mats didn't play in Vancouver [at the 2010 Olympics].

"To have those two assist on the goal that I scored to be the deciding goal was the best. I thought it was a perfect ending that they assisted on my goal."

When it was all said and done, Swedish national team coach Bengt Gustafsson summed it up with his comment in Torino. "It was our turn," was all Gustafsson said.

There was another hero on the winning team who was almost forgotten: goaltender Henrik Lundqvist. With 25 seconds to go in the game, Lundqvist made a spectacular save, flying through the crease with his stick raised to stop a shot from Finland's Olli Jokinen. "That's the gold, right there," said Swedish forward Modin afterward.

Coach Gustafsson recalls another key moment at the ending of the game. "Henrik Zetterberg went down and blocked a slap shot from Teemu Selanne with just seven seconds left in the game," Gustafsson said. "It was really the last thing that happened. When people ask me today about Lidstrom's winning goal in Torino, I always come to think of Lundqvist's remarkable save and Zetterberg's unselfish shot-blocking. Everybody was a hero that Sunday in Italy."

Coaching Sweden's Dream Team at the 2006 Olympics was a once-in-a-lifetime experience for Gustafsson. "It was a wonderful group to coach," Gustafsson said. "They all had such a respect for each other and they all accepted their roles on the team. As a coach, I wanted to take advantage of their experience. We had a lineup full of leaders with Sundin, Lidstrom, Alfredsson, Forsberg, to name a few. They all had tons of experience from years in the NHL and were used to performing under pressure against the best players in the world.

"At the same time, they created a fun atmosphere in the dressing room and off the ice. They knew how to have fun. Nobody was above the team. I was aware of the fact that I really couldn't teach a guy like Lidstrom much. He had already won three Norris Trophies or something like that and was a multiple Stanley Cup champion. For me, it was more about creating a game plan and an environment where he could thrive. And he sure did."

Lidstrom was the top-scoring defenseman with six points (two goals and four assists) and was voted to the Olympic All-Star Team in Torino.

To Swedes, the Lidstrom goal holds the same grip on the nation, the same fond memories, as Paul Henderson's goal in the 1972 Summit Series brings to Canadians and as Mike Eruzione's goal against the Soviets at the 1980 Lake Placid Winter Olympics creates for Americans.

Lidstrom won't put up any argument, recognizing that the goal meant as much to his homeland as it did to him. "Yeah, people still talk about it," Lidstrom said. "When I'm out and about in Sweden, a lot of people want to talk about that goal. They remember where they were when they watched the game and when I scored the goal. It's a great feeling to hear those people talk about the goal and remembering what they were doing that afternoon."

In 2010, Lidstrom would captain the Swedish team to a quarterfinal appearance in his fourth and final Olympics. "The things he has accomplished are remarkable," former NHL defenseman and fellow Swede Henrik Tallinder said. "In my eyes, he's the best Swedish player we've had over here."

Though he no longer wears the three crowns, Lidstrom still answers his country's call. When Swedish national team coach Rikard Gronborg started preparations for the 2016 World Cup tournament in Toronto, he wanted to form an advisory board of former players. Gronborg asked Lidstrom, Sundin, and Alfredsson— all three former team captains in the NHL and members of the Olympic gold-medal-winning team in 2006—and was happy to get them all on board.

The 2016 World Cup team featured a group of defensemen who had grown up idolizing Lidstrom and his style of play, something that Gronborg was very aware of. "Before picking the team, I had Nicklas traveling with me to a number of NHL games, scouting players," Gronborg said. "I wanted to get to know him and as the hockey nerd I am, I wanted to pick his brain. I mean, he is maybe the best defenseman we've seen in the modern era.

"It was amazing to hear his knowledge of the game. He could dissect every play down to the smallest detail. It confirmed to me that he is from another planet when it comes to studying and analyzing the game of hockey. You can compare him to a top-notch architect or engineer, who is drawing and building a house where every space, angle, and security aspect is figured out as far as the last detail.

"We had conversations where he explained how a player should angle his skates to the ice to be able to get maximum efficiency in the defensive zone. He could tell me how you shoot the puck in different situations depending on the possibility of it going straight in or hitting a stick or a leg in front of the net, or giving a teammate a chance for a tip-in."

During a stop in Tampa Bay for a Lightning game, Lidstrom asked Gronborg if he wanted to meet the team's general manager, Steve Yzerman, Lidstrom's former teammate in Detroit. "We were met by Yzerman in the lobby of the arena and he took us to his office," Gronborg remembered. "I thought I would get a chance to hear how the Lightning were using Swedish defense duo Victor Hedman and Anton Stralman and it would be a 10-to-15-minute meeting, but we ended up talking for almost an hour before we had to rush out to the arena to catch the start of the game.

"I could see the respect Yzerman had for Nicklas. The same scenario played out in other NHL arenas we visited during our trip, and I'm talking about people I would call the absolute cream of the crop in the league. Every one of them made themselves available when Lidstrom came to their building for a game."

Gronborg wanted Alfredsson, Lidstrom, and Sundin to attend every team meeting before and during the World Cup. He placed Lidstrom with Peter Popovic, a former NHL defenseman and now Swedish assistant coach, who was responsible for the defensemen on the team and the penalty kill. Gronborg assigned Alfredsson to work with his other assistant coach, Johan Garpenlov, to oversee the forwards and power play. Sundin was a sounding board for Gronborg on the overall strategy, as well as a source of leadership experience.

"I made it clear that it was us coaches who would direct the players, but that I wanted my three advisers to attend all meetings and practices," Gronborg said. "I wanted their contributions across every aspect of our game and was really thankful for the time and work they put in. All three of them would make great coaches if they wanted to, not only for their hockey knowledge but also for their social skills. They are very good people and leaders. First class."

Gronborg paid particular attention to Lidstrom's style of making his way into the group. "He never used the respect everybody had for him to maneuver his way into the heart of the team," Gronborg said. "He didn't have to. Nicklas is a natural when it comes to getting to know people and gain their trust. He was always available and eager to do the job we asked him to do, which was to share his know-how. I did discuss every change I wanted to make with him first, because then I knew it was a slam dunk that the team would buy in on it."

The group of defensemen on the Swedish World Cup team were Mattias Ekholm, Oliver Ekman-Larsson, Victor Hedman, Niklas Hjalmarsson, Erik Karlsson, Hampus Lindholm, and Anton Stralman. For them, it was a privilege to have Nicklas Lidstrom around for a couple of weeks in the late summer of 2016.

"The World Cup was the first time when I really had a chance to be around Nicklas," Karlsson said. "Before that, I didn't know him on a personal level. It was gratifying to spend time with him and see what a funny and well-organized human being he is. That he was smart, I knew since before. We played a couple of rounds of golf and had a lot of fun. I won't say that we talk every week, but when I see him it feels like I know him so much better now. I am very thankful that I had the chance to meet him, and not only hear from other players what a great guy he is."

Lidstrom is proud to be somebody the new generation looks up to. "Erik Karlsson is a different kind of player than I was," Lidstrom said. "He is a better skater and can beat anybody with his speed. That makes him an offensive threat on another level than me. Victor Hedman is more physical with his size, so I don't see that many similarities in his game because of that.

"I would say that Oliver Ekman-Larsson is playing more of my style. He plays in all situations, is good at both ends of the ice, but doesn't step up on the ice to deliver the big hits. Oliver is a good skater and a mobile player, who positions himself well, like I feel I did. So, I see a lot of similarities in his game."

Ekman-Larsson, the Arizona Coyotes' outstanding defenseman, agrees that he has tried to model his game after the way

Lidstrom played. "He was my idol growing up and the reason I became a defenseman," Ekman-Larsson said. "I've been studying how he played, but it is tough to copy him. His success is the main reason that we have so many leading Swedish defensemen on teams around the league right now. The thing with Nicklas was that he made everything look so easy on the ice. One of his strengths was his ability to make that first pass up the ice and always find a team-mate on the blueline.

"It seemed that he made the right choice every time on where to deliver his pass, if it was in the middle of the ice or along the boards. That gift made Lidstrom one of the best in the league ever. What I'm trying to do is have an active stick, like he had, and to position myself well. I had the honor to play against him a couple of times in the NHL and that's when you really saw how good he was and how he made everything look so easy."

Hedman remembers that visit Lidstrom and Gronborg made to Tampa Bay in the spring of 2016. "Stralman and I had the chance to have lunch with them and I think I was sitting through the whole meal with a smile on my face," Hedman said. "I was just trying to take in everything he said. He is so smart and knowledge-able. Even if our playing style is different, I hoped to pick up some details to implement into my own game."

John Klingberg, from the Dallas Stars, is another of Lidstrom's disciples. "What impressed me so much was his complete skill set both offensively and defensively," Klingberg said. "He was never hit, and his defense partner didn't get hit either, because Nicklas was so smart and created time for everybody in all situations, with or without the puck."

A legend and a hero to one generation of Swedish hockey, Nicklas has received many accolades in his home country for his long and successful career.

"I was awarded a medal from the King of Sweden and was part of a ceremony at the Royal Castle in Stockholm," Lidstrom recalls. "That is something I will never forget. I have met King Carl Gustaf in Detroit before, when he was there test-driving cars at General Motors."

Lidstrom had the honor of being invited to the Royal Castle in Stockholm on June 10, 2010, to receive the H.M. The King's Medal from the king himself, King Carl XVI Gustaf and Queen Silvia.

Today, Lidstrom continues to serve as a mentor to the next generation of Swedish stars.

"He has been a great role model for every Swede growing up, myself included," former NHL goalie and Swedish Olympian Johan Hedberg said. "He's a great person and very, very professional. I think he's someone who probably doesn't get the respect he deserves in Sweden. He's a very low-key guy who gets overshadowed by some more marquee personalities.

"If there's anyone who people should want to model themselves after, it would be him."

9
A HISTORIC CAPTAINCY

FOLLOWING SCOTTY BOWMAN'S RETIREMENT, LONGTIME DETROIT associate coach Dave Lewis was promoted to head coach of the Red Wings before the 2002–03 season. The defending Stanley Cup champions had another strong regular season and again won the Central Division, earning 110 points. The Wings were one point behind the Dallas Stars for the Western Conference's No. 1 seed. Nicklas Lidstrom kept dominating the back end and collected 62 points (18 goals and 44 assists) in 82 games and was an impressive plus-40.

Detroit look poised for another deep playoff run, but everything took a dramatic turn for the worse in the first round of the playoffs when the Red Wings were swept by the Mighty Ducks of Anaheim. All four games were one-goal losses. Anaheim won in Detroit 2–1 and 3–2 before returning home to Southern California and finishing off the champions with two more victories, also by 2–1 and 3–2 counts. It was the first time since 1951–52—when the Wings beat the Toronto Maple Leafs—that a reigning Cup champion had been swept in the first round of the playoffs.

"The loss against Anaheim really hurt because we were defending champions that year," Lidstrom said. "I thought [Anaheim coach] Mike Babcock's team did a great job holding us on the outside in all four games and they had a great goalie in Jean-Sebastien Giguere. He was fantastic and won the Conn Smythe Trophy that year as the most valuable player in the playoffs. We had a really hard time scoring against him. For me personally, it was a huge letdown to be knocked out of the playoffs so early after winning the year before."

Though fingers were immediately pointed at Lewis, Lidstrom said, "I don't think we can blame Dave Lewis. He wasn't the reason we lost that series."

Individually, Lidstrom enjoyed another strong campaign. He played in his seventh NHL All-Star Game and won his third straight Norris Trophy that season.

The next season, 2003–04, was almost a carbon copy of the previous one. Detroit won the Central Division and was the first seed in the Western Conference but stumbled again in the playoffs. After a six-game series win over the Nashville Predators in the first round, the Wings lost against the Calgary Flames in the conference semifinals in six games.

The 2004–05 season was wiped out after the owners locked out the players when the two sides couldn't negotiate a new collective bargaining agreement, and when play resumed in 2005–06, the Wings had a new coach. Babcock, the man who beat them in the 2003 playoffs, replaced Lewis behind the bench. Things looked promising under the new leadership, but once again, playoff failure awaited Detroit. The Red Wings lost against No. 8 seed Edmonton in the first round. The Red Wings had now won only one playoff series since their Stanley Cup victory in 2002.

Lidstrom was the top-scoring NHL defenseman in 2005–06 with 16 goals and 64 assists, averaging a point per game for 80 games, and he was plus-21. A fourth Norris Trophy gave Lidstrom proof that he was still a top defender in the NHL, if not the best, but he took no solace from individual success. "In both 2004 against Calgary and 2006 against Edmonton, we were up against teams that made it all the way to the Final," Lidstrom said. "We were not able to reach the level of play you have to be at to be successful in the playoffs."

Things were about to change dramatically in Hockeytown, and it would impact Lidstrom directly. Steve Yzerman, a Red Wings player since 1983 and captain of the team since 1986, announced his retirement. Yzerman was the only captain Lidstrom had ever known during his NHL career.

"Steve had been there all my career and he did a great job," Lidstrom said. "It's not just the fans, but we as players were spoiled having him as captain."

On October 5, 2006, Lidstrom was named the new captain of the Red Wings, joining an illustrious group that includes Sid Abel, Ted Lindsay, Red Kelly, Gordie Howe, Alex Delvecchio, Reed Larson, and, of course, Yzerman. "It was a big honor for me, knowing how many legendary players had been captain for the Red Wings before me," Lidstrom said.

Detroit's captains are a varied lot. Yzerman was known for his steely-eyed determination. Long before him, Lindsay was as fiery as they came. Abel, the consummate professional, was perhaps the closest to Lidstrom in personality. All shared a common bond: each led their team by example.

For Yzerman, it seemed natural that Lidstrom was asked to wear the C when he retired. "I do believe Nick and I had the same values both on and off the ice," Yzerman said. "As captains, there were definitely some similarities. Neither of us were very vocal on or off the ice. Nick was more reserved than I was; he was better at controlling his emotions, good or bad, which enabled him to be extremely consistent game in and game out, year after year. Nick's calming presence was reassuring to us all in the most stressful situations we were faced with. Everyone knew that in the biggest games, Nick would be there, playing his best hockey."

The torch was officially passed at center ice at Joe Louis Arena on opening night of the 2006–07 season. Yzerman was part of the opening faceoff as the ceremonial puck-dropper. The worst-kept secret in Hockeytown was revealed when Lidstrom skated out wearing the C for Detroit to take the faceoff against Vancouver Canucks captain and fellow Swede Markus Naslund.

"I knew my role would change a bit, as I'd have more communication with the coaching staff. I'd be more of a link between the players and the coaches," Lidstrom said of taking on the captaincy. "There would be more responsibility being a captain. You had to be more responsible for the team and have a lot more discussions with the coaching staff."

Everybody who had been part of the inner circle of the team in the years before Yzerman's retirement knew that the choice of new captain was a no-brainer. It had to be Lidstrom. "Stevie was a tough act to follow," Brendan Shanahan said. "I don't think anyone else could have done it."

Lidstrom had been a quiet student of Yzerman's way of doing things for years and the manner in which the man known in Detroit as The Captain handled himself on and off the ice.

"I remember that our general manager, Ken Holland, during the season-ending meetings in the spring of 2006 mentioned that

Stevie might be retiring," Lidstrom said. "The meeting took place in Holland's office at Joe Louis Arena and Ken asked me if I was interested in taking on the captaincy if that happened.

"I told him that it would be an honor to be the captain for the Red Wings. We left it at that. Ken said that we would continue the discussion when we were back after the summer break. Then we met again during the training camp and it was decided that I would be the new captain, but the club chose to not make it official until the opening game of the regular season."

Lidstrom sought out Yzerman's advice before taking on the assignment. "I had a one-on-one-meeting with Stevie in his office at the arena where I asked a ton of questions about the captaincy," Lidstrom said. "What I remember most is he kept saying that I should just be myself, that it all came down to that."

After being a dominating defenseman for years, when the 2006–07 season started Lidstrom was also now the ultimate leader of the Red Wings. He was the one dealing with the media and serving as the connection between the players and the coaching staff. He was the one making sure that everybody in the dressing room felt appreciated and was ready to go when the puck was dropped.

"I held a number of players-only meetings when we were struggling or lost games we should have won," Lidstrom said. "Sometimes I started talking and then Henrik Zetterberg, Niklas Kronwall, or Kris Draper filled in. I distinctly remember a game where we lost at home against St. Louis, I think it was 10–3, and I was really mad afterward of how we had played in front of our own fans. I felt we had embarrassed ourselves and that I needed to address the situation.

"I think that was the only time that I asked our equipment manager to keep the door closed to the dressing room for a couple of extra minutes before the media was let in. We needed to clear the air. Except on that occasion, I don't think there were really any other incidents or crises on the team that I had to take care of during my time as the captain."

The addition of the captaincy certainly did not affect Lidstrom's performance on the ice. He had 62 points in 80 games, which was third on the team behind only Pavel Datsyuk (87) and Zetterberg (68), and he was the best plus-minus player with a plus-40 rating. Detroit was the top seed in the Western Conference and advanced to the conference final after first beating Calgary and then San Jose, each in six games. Without Yzerman, who had retired after 22 seasons, and Shanahan, who had left for the New York Rangers in the summer, Detroit could not make it past Anaheim, though. After taking a 2–1 lead in the series, the Red Wings lost three straight and were sent home by the Ducks, who would go on to win the Stanley Cup.

Niklas Kronwall, who was one of Lidstrom's defense partners and later also an assistant captain to him on the Red Wings, saw the way the rest of the team looked to Lidstrom to show them the way.

"The reason the transformation of the leadership from Stevie to Nick went so smooth was that Nick was so respected," Kronwall said. "He was without question the best defenseman in the league at that time. He had a very good relationship with our fans and the media. Nick was a down-to-earth guy with a rock-solid status on the team, so the change from Stevie to him was an easy one.

Nothing much changed. Nick spoke when he needed to, and he had good support from Z and Draper.

"I became an assistant captain later on and it was always easy to communicate with Nick. He listened to his teammates and he had a good awareness of what was going on. Nick was a natural leader who showed up for work every day and cared about the club. I don't think the captaincy had any negative effect on his play. It was probably the other way around, if it was even possible for him to play better than he had done in previous years. He had been taking on bigger responsibilities already under Stevie."

It also became Lidstrom's job as the new captain to be the connection between Babcock and his staff and the players. "Babcock had an intensity in all he did as a coach," Lidstrom said. "He was very particular with details in the way he wanted his team to play. There was a script for every situation that could occur on the ice for us players. His teams always come well prepared.

"I have talked to players that had him on other clubs and everybody has had the same experience. You could say that Babcock and his assistant coaches do such a good job preparing the players before games that it is up to the players themselves if the team will win or lose. If you lose, the players haven't paid attention during the pregame meeting or read the memo that's been handed out."

Babcock frequently sought out input from his captain on the mood of the team, and also turned to Lidstrom and his alternate captains to help identify areas in need of shoring up and problems that required addressing.

"There were a lot of meetings where Babcock wanted to know how the mood was among us players in the dressing room and why certain players didn't perform up to expectations," Lidstrom said. "Sometimes my assistant captains were also asked to attend. He also could ask for our input on the traveling schedule or other things that would affect the team's performance. Babcock wanted a lot of feedback before he made his decisions. I felt that I had a good relationship with him as the captain."

Babcock was not afraid of making controversial decisions. One example was when he benched Dominik Hasek during the first round of the 2008 playoffs against Nashville and replaced him with backup goaltender Chris Osgood.

"It was a pretty bold move by Babcock," Lidstrom said. "I mean, he benched Hasek in the middle of the playoffs, but he was willing to take the chance. Osgood played really well and carried us all the way to the Stanley Cup."

The communication between Babcock and Lidstrom was often intense during these years. "Babcock could call me and my two assistant captains into his office and request us to act in a special way in front of the rest of the team to set the tone," Lidstrom said. "It could be about getting specific players to stop cheating during games, like skipping defensive assignments to gain offensive chances.

"Babcock's opinion was that if our best players took these kinds of liberties, everybody would follow. That was unacceptable behavior in Detroit and something I had learned during my years with Stevie as the captain. It was a tradition that was carried on from generation to generation in Red Wings players and one that I hope I was able to carry on, too."

Lidstrom became captain at the age of 36. He doesn't think that the C on his jersey changed him in any way or increased the pressure to produce magic on the ice. "I felt like I could continue to play the way I had done before," Lidstrom said. "In my mind, the captaincy was a challenge, and of course it made me proud to be the leader of one of the Original Six teams in the league. It was a good challenge during the latter part of my career, but I never felt that it took anything away from my game. My role on the team just got a little larger."

Lidstrom's calm exterior, perennially on display for public consumption, was also how he operated behind the scenes—most of the time. Zetterberg insists that he never heard Lidstrom raise his voice or scream in the dressing room. "I can't recall a single time Nick did that," Zetterberg said.

Lidstrom begs to differ. "It didn't happen often, and I don't think that I ever screamed at a teammate, but for sure I raised my voice a couple of times when we stunk," Lidstrom said.

Draper was another teammate who insists he didn't see any changes in Lidstrom's behavior when he was named captain. "Taking on the C after Steve Yzerman could not have been easy," Draper said. "In my mind, Stevie is one of the greatest captains and leaders of all time. To me, Nick was so consistent with his game, so he did not need to change. He was never a rah-rah guy who screamed in the dressing room. We had those guys in myself, Holmstrom, Maltby, and McCarty.

"Nick led by example and did not change a bit when he succeeded Yzerman as our captain. He played 30 to 35 minutes a night, but was back in the gym the next morning, anyway. I remember a triple-overtime game we had against Carolina in the Final in 2002 where Nick played like 50 minutes. The next morning, I saw him at the breakfast buffet like nothing had happened. I had maybe played half the minutes and I could hardly make it down there. These things were the stuff Nick impressed us with."

The man called the Perfect Human by his teammates was the perfect choice to follow Yzerman, someone who had perfected the qualities of leadership—even if Lidstrom would be the first to insist that he's never been perfect.

"Osgood mentioned to a reporter once that he thought that I had played a perfect game," Lidstrom laughed. "A game without one single mistake." His own harshest critic, Lidstrom can't recall playing a perfect game during his career.

"I remember an interview I did with Swedish journalist Mats Olsson after a World Cup game in 1996 where he had tracked all my moves on the ice and told me after the game that I had made 35 of 37 passes tape-to-tape," Lidstrom said. "I immediately knew which two passes I had missed.

"I don't know about perfect games, where I did not make a single mistake. For me, it was more about the feeling of accomplishment after a big win in a championship game. Then it didn't matter if I made a small mistake or two. Sometimes, nobody else would notice what I counted as a miss. It could be that my pass hit the skate of my teammate instead of the blade of his stick. That was my mindset."

Lidstrom admits that there were occasions when he was driving home after a game at Joe Louis Arena thinking that he had played better than ever before. "Yeah, that did happen," he said. "More than once, I would say. Usually after a game against somebody like [Sidney] Crosby or a player of his caliber. If you could stop them from scoring and end up with a plus rating yourself for the night, it always felt good.

"It could also be driving home after playing 30-plus minutes and not feeling tired. When everything, both mentally and physically, felt perfect and you had positioned yourself well on the ice for the whole game. Those nights, when you drove home, you congratulated yourself for a job well done."

As much as he appreciates the praise, Lidstrom wants to kill the myth of him being the perfect human being. "I try to treat people with respect when they come up to me and ask for my autograph or a picture," Lidstrom said. "It doesn't bother me to be recognized. In my world, I'm just a regular guy who had a great job for many years. Nothing more. And yes, I can get angry and raise my voice like everybody else. Just ask my children."

Babcock relayed a tale that suggested that Lidstrom might not be perfect, but also that his teammates recognized how much less than perfect they would be without him in their lineup.

"This is one of my best stories," Babcock said. "Tomas Holmstrom and Lidstrom showed up late for a game. Tommy comes running into my office and says, 'We had a big accident. But don't worry, when I knew we were going to get hit I dove in front of Nick and he didn't get touched.'"

The two close friends and Detroit teammates for 15 years usually carpooled to practices and games. "We often stopped at a Starbucks out where we lived before we were getting on the freeway into the city," Holmstrom said. "One morning after we had gotten our coffee, Nick made a left turn on one of those two-lane streets and we bumped into a car from the opposite direction. A couple of scratches on the car, but nobody was injured.

"I spilled my hot coffee and was not happy, while Nick made it without a drop on him, even though he was driving and was holding his coffee cup. I think it was just his hand-eye coordination that kept him from spilling his cup and he could have been steering the car with his knees at that moment.

"Anyway, he blamed me for the accident for not telling him that there was a car in the turning lane. I was supposed to be the lookout. Not true. I was in the passenger seat and far away from the side where he was turning."

Holmstrom got to see a side of his captain that few people outside of Lidstrom's inner circle of friends were privy to. As with any close friends, both men were also instinctively and playfully able to get each other's goat and knew how to push each other's buttons. Holmstrom and Lidstrom had fun at each other's expense. They knew what ticked the other one off.

"Nick is a perfectionist and always had his equipment so well organized and laid out in his locker in the dressing room," Holmstrom said. "His pads were always laying at the same distance from the wall, his gloves had a special place. I was sitting to the left on the other wall, slightly across from him. Sometimes, I turned his pads upside down or put a glove on the floor when he left the room briefly. He smiled and gave me a stare when he came back but didn't say anything.

"For me it was a way of getting back at him for something that had happened earlier on the ice during practice. It was nearly impossible to beat him on the outside when we were doing drills or scrimmaging. Nick was always so well positioned. You couldn't pass by him with the puck, his reach was extraordinary. He used his long stick to hook me. I was so frustrated once that I told him, 'Hit me then!' That would have been easier to take than not being able to go around him time after time again."

Lidstrom and Holmstrom say they never had any big fights during the years on the Red Wings, just a couple of quarrels. The two lived close to each other in the Detroit suburb of Novi and spent hours in the car together driving back and forth to Joe Louis Arena. "What did we talk about? More or less everything," Holmstrom said. "We both had kids at the same age, so we often talked about them and their activities, their hockey practices or games. We talked about life in general—where to go on vacation, how to spend the next summer back in Sweden. We spent the holidays together in Detroit during the hockey season—Thanksgiving, Christmas, and Easter. My wife, Annelie, and Nick's wife, Annika, became good friends, so our families were close."

On game days, they made a habit of eating a pregame meal at the same restaurant, Andiamo Trattoria in Livonia, on the way home after the morning skate. You could say they were superstitious. "Nick always had the same meal, a spaghetti called Pasta alla Andiamo with chicken breast and two different sauces," Holmstrom said. "He ordered both the Palomino and Bolognese sauce. Half of each. I shifted between two to three different pasta dishes on their menu, depending on what kind of game I had just had. If I hadn't scored the game before, I shifted from one kind of pasta to another. But I always had a penne pasta as my go-to if I wasn't sure what I would order. It had chicken breast with a Bolognese sauce.

"Both Nick and I were superstitious. This went on for four or five years. I told Nick that he couldn't eat the same pasta all the time we went there, but he insisted. The waiters knew what time we were coming in on game days and were ready to seat us and had the lunch ready as soon as we walked in the door. The only time

Nick passed on stopping at Andiamo's was if Annika had made him the same pasta at home and he wanted to go home and eat."

On the ice, Lidstrom and Holmstrom took a bite out of the opposition, operating as a devastating combination on the Detroit power play—Holmstrom absorbing endless punishment at the net, creating screens and avenues for Lidstrom's slap shot from the point. High or low, Holmstrom became a master of scoring tip-in goals.

"Nick was so precise with his shot and hardly missed the net, so I just had to keep my eyes open and get my stick on the puck," Holmstrom said. "If I didn't get out of the way, the puck hit my legs or upper body. I felt the pain and we had our arguments about his shooting precision, but I give him credit for his execution. He had such good hands and seldom missed the open net or my stick if I was able to screen the goalie. It was a dangerous spot to be in, but we had a lot of fun scoring all those goals."

Together they won four Stanley Cups and an Olympic gold medal with Team Sweden. Holmstrom credits ownership, smart management moves, and great coaches for the success in Detroit. "There was a red thread from the owners all the way down to us players and the staff in the dressing room," Holmstrom said. "The club had good scouting, made good trades, and found a way to put the puzzle together with pieces that fit from year to year."

Both Lidstrom and Holmstrom retired after the 2011–12 season. Lidstrom moved back to Sweden with Annika and their four sons a couple of months later, while Tomas and Annelie stayed on in Detroit for another year. "Of course, we missed them," Holmstrom said. "We had kids on the same hockey team and Nick and I played golf, tennis, and worked out at the gym together. Not that I ever beat him in tennis, but it was always fun to play."

The Holmstrom family moved back to Sweden in the summer of 2013. Tomas and Annelie had Lidstrom's oldest son, Kevin, living with them later when he played hockey for the local team in Holmstrom's hometown of Pitea. "Nick and I stay in touch on a regular basis," Holmstrom said. "We call and text each other every week and our families get together once or twice a year. It's a friendship that started in Detroit with the Red Wings when I came over in 1996 and it stays strong. Nick is a great guy and we have fun together. I can't believe we ended up winning four Stanley Cups together. Who would have thought?"

Lidstrom wasn't the first European-born-and-trained captain in NHL history, but he was the first in Red Wings history. At the time, there were still critics who believed European players couldn't cut it as leaders in the North American game. It was an archaic way of thinking and a thought process that the man many hockey people consider to be the most outstanding leader in NHL history finds absurd.

Mark Messier won six Stanley Cups and is the only man to captain two different teams to the Cup—the Edmonton Oilers (1989–90) and the New York Rangers (1993–94). As Canadian as they come, Messier never bought into the antiquated notion that Europeans can't lead.

"He was the prototypical leader by example," Messier said of Lidstrom. "I don't know Nick well enough to know what he did behind the scenes in the dressing room, but if you talk about a consistent leader, he was the same guy game in and game out. He was consistent in his personality so that when the guys looked at him, he was always going to be the same guy. He had some tough shoes to fill with Yzerman leaving there and he stepped in and they didn't miss a beat."

The quietly efficient Lidstrom didn't fit the popular image of the captain. Those fascinated by the role of the on-ice leader think it's all about fire-and-brimstone speeches. Those who've worn the C insist this is a total misconception. "Being captain, it's a recognition of leadership," Lindsay said. "A quality that you have to hold your team together, make them perform as a unit. I think Steve Yzerman would be the best illustration. Steve Yzerman didn't kick any butt.

"He used to show guys how to do it. I think this is where lots of mistakes are made by people who think a guy gets in the dressing room and he makes a big show. That's not true leadership. You do it by leading by example."

You do it the way Yzerman did it. The way Lidstrom did it.

"I've never coached anybody this good, never coached anybody as consistent, as intuitive, who has a great understanding of the game and is tuned in to what's going on," Babcock said of Lidstrom. "He was such a professional, when you talked to him as a coach, it was an unbelievable experience for you. He was comfortable to share his thoughts with you."

Brian Rafalski won three Stanley Cups working in a defense pairing alongside Hall of Fame captains; two with Scott Stevens and the New Jersey Devils, and one with Lidstrom in Detroit. Stevens put fear into opponents with his punishing hits. Lidstrom frustrated opponents with the league's best positioning and most active and accurate stick. Otherwise, Rafalski says the two were mirror images.

"You've got a Hall of Famer back there, that's a good cornerstone to build around," Rafalski said. "Obviously, two different style players, but both very dominating at what they did—Scotty through physical play, Nick by controlling the game. As leaders, they were both pretty similar. Scotty wasn't real vocal in the locker room, either. They both led by example on the ice. They'd go out there and they do what they have to do on the ice."

The rest of the team willingly followed Lidstrom's lead. "You'd see the way Nick played at such a high level," Kris Draper said. "You wanted to be there right with him. It was just great to be playing with such a great leader, such a great captain."

Kronwall felt that the same character traits that made Yzerman such a sensational leader were also part of Lidstrom's DNA. It wasn't so much about who they were as it was about what they did day in and day out. They set the tone. "What makes them leaders is they're the hardest-working guys and they show up every night," Kronwall said.

"Nick spoke when he needed to and led by example," added goalie Jimmy Howard.

Zetterberg was in his third season in Detroit when Lidstrom was named captain and could see Lidstrom growing into a leader in Hockeytown. "When Nick took over the C from Steve Yzerman before the 2006–07 season, it was a natural shift," Zetterberg said. "We had many leaders in the room and Lidstrom was one of them. He had been an assistant captain to Stevie and belonged to that inner circle for years already."

When Lidstrom left the Red Wings in 2012, Zetterberg ascended to the captaincy. For the first time ever, one Swedish captain was succeeded by another.

"Yes, that was a very unique transfer of the C and had never happened before in the league," Zetterberg said. "I had gotten my indications that something was up after a chat I had with Ken Holland at a charity golf event during training camp. When it came true a couple of months later, it was a big moment for me. Was I ready? Well, I had been a student of Lidstrom during my whole time in Detroit. Anytime you wondered about something, you could always ask Nick.

"I wanted to do it the way he did it. I tried to copy his way of leading the team, both on and off the ice. He kept himself in top shape and worked hard during every practice, so that was something that I tried to pass on to the next generation of players here. It is hard to see yourself as the older generation, but that is exactly what it is. I was just trying to hand the traditions and ways of handling things here from the way Yzerman and Lidstrom did it to our younger players, just the way he handled himself on and off the ice, how he prepared for every practice and every game, how he led by example. I think a lot about how Nick handled certain situations that occurred. It made me calm. He did it so well."

10
ONE MORE CUP

JUNE 4, 2008, WAS A HISTORIC DAY FOR NICKLAS LIDSTROM AND THE National Hockey League. For the first time, the Stanley Cup was lifted by a European-born-and-raised captain. Lidstrom had reached another milestone in his career with the Detroit Red Wings.

It was his second season as the team's captain and Lidstrom was truly at the top of the hockey world. He was the first European defenseman to win the Norris Trophy, in 2001. He was the first European player to win the Conn Smythe Trophy, in 2002. And now, he stood on the ice at Mellon Arena in Pittsburgh lifting Lord Stanley's Cup over his head.

"It was so special for me to be there on the ice and to receive the Stanley Cup from NHL commissioner Gary Bettman," Lidstrom said. "We had 11 European players in the lineup in the sixth game, which made it even more emotional for me. Being the captain for that kind of team added a lot of pride to winning it that year.

"We had all heard the whispers for years that European players didn't have the same drive as North Americans and that we were cowards. For that reason, it was huge for me to be the first European captain to lead his team to the championship title."

Bettman fondly recalls handing over the Stanley Cup on the ice in Pittsburgh to Lidstrom. "It was a very special moment," Bettman said. "While I was happy for the Red Wings organization and their fans, I was truly happy for Nicklas and for all the fans in Sweden. Presenting the Stanley Cup to Nicklas reinforced the international nature of our game. It reinforced the remarkable strength of hockey in Sweden and expressed the appreciation of the entire NHL that Sweden let us borrow him for a while."

Heading into that 2007–08 NHL campaign, Lidstrom was of the belief that the Wings had the makings of a special squad. "We had lost to Anaheim in the conference finals the year before," Lidstrom said. "They had a really strong team with Chris Pronger and Scott Niedermayer on defense and a strong trio up front in Teemu Selanne, Ryan Getzlaf, and Corey Perry. We weren't able to compete with them, but a year later we were hungrier and wanted to win so badly, which helped us a lot."

Proving Lidstrom to be a prophet, Detroit reached the Stanley Cup Final after knocking out Nashville (4–2), Colorado (4–0), and Dallas (4–2). "I had a feeling that we had gotten better and better for every round of the playoffs," Lidstrom said. "The Dallas Stars were a strong opponent in the conference finals with a hot goalie in Marty Turco, but we felt we were a better team."

The Red Wings and the Pittsburgh Penguins had never met in the postseason before the 2008 Stanley Cup Final. They hadn't crossed paths at all that season, with Detroit playing in the Western Conference while Pittsburgh belonged to the Eastern Conference, and that particular regular season had not involved any games between the teams.

After suiting up against the Russian Five in the late 1990s, Lidstrom, Tomas Holmstrom, Henrik Zetterberg, Niklas Kronwall, and Mikael Samuelsson formed the Swedish Five when the NHL resumed after the lockout for the 2005–06 season, and all five would play significant roles in Detroit's 2007–08 Stanley Cup win.

Following a scoreless first period in Game 1, where Lidstrom had a goal waved off because of goaltender interference by Holmstrom, Samuelsson came through with two unassisted goals. The rugged Swede gave Detroit the lead with a wraparound in the second period and extended the lead to 2–0 early in the third period. Dan Cleary made it 3–0 with a shorthanded goal and Zetterberg finished it off by scoring on the power play to make it 4–0, assisted by Holmstrom and Lidstrom, with just 13 seconds remaining.

Chris Osgood stopped all 22 shots in Game 2 and recorded his second consecutive shutout, lifting Detroit to a 3–0 victory. The goals were scored by Brad Stuart, Holmstrom, and Valtteri Filppula.

The Red Wings arrived in Pittsburgh on a high note after scoring seven goals and not letting a single goal in during the opening two games at home. Things would soon change, however, and to no one's surprise it was Pittsburgh captain Sidney Crosby who lifted the Penguins at Mellon Arena. Crosby made it 1–0 late in the first period in Game 3 and increased the lead to 2–0 on a power play early in the second period. Johan Franzen put the Red Wings on the board with a power play goal, Lidstrom and Kronwall drawing assists. Adam Hall got Pittsburgh back to a two-goal lead in the third period before Samuelsson scored his third goal in the series. The Penguins won 3–2 and had bounced back after the embarrassing two losses in Detroit.

Game 4 saw Lidstrom take charge. He tied the game in the first period after Marian Hossa had given the Penguins the lead on the power play before the three-minute mark. Jiri Hudler delivered the game-winner in the third period of a 2–1 Detroit victory.

Coming back to Detroit with a 3–1 lead gave the Red Wings a chance to close out the series and lift the Cup in front of their home fans, as they had in the 1997 and 2002 Finals. Crosby and the Penguins had other ideas.

Game 5 would be one to remember for both teams. After the first 20 minutes, Detroit found itself down by two goals. Darren Helm cut the Penguins' lead in half in the second period and Pavel Datsyuk and Brian Rafalski put them up 3–2 in the third. Pittsburgh pulled goalie Marc-Andre Fleury with less than a minute remaining in regulation in a desperate try to tie the game and it worked. Maxime Talbot scored with 35 seconds left and forced overtime.

After two scoreless extra periods, the winning goal finally came in the third overtime session; Pittsburgh's Petr Sykora kept the Penguins alive with a power play goal. The triple-overtime game— 109 minutes and 57 seconds in total—was the fifth-longest contest in Stanley Cup Final history. To be so close to lifting the Cup only to have it snatched away was a devastation the Wings needed to rapidly put in the rearview mirror.

"Losing at home when we were in the lead so late in the fifth game was heartbreaking," Lidstrom said. "We had to quickly regroup with so few days between the games in the playoffs, so there wasn't any time to dwell on the lost opportunity to close out the series. We had to focus on the next game immediately and I think that we had learned how to do that after the conference final against Dallas, where we were in a similar situation. We had a 3–1 lead in games and hoped to finish the Stars off at home at Joe Louis

Arena, but Marty Turco stood on his head and won the game for them.

"We went to Dallas very well prepared and full of confidence. Our game plan worked; we had a 4–0 lead after two periods and could ride out the storm we knew was coming in the last 20 minutes and won 4–1.

"I think we had that game fresh in our memory when we took on Pittsburgh in Game 6. I did not feel the need to call any extra pregame meetings in my role as the captain. All that match preparation was taken care of by Mike Babcock and his coaching staff. We all knew how high the stakes were. It was up to us older players to stay positive and lead the way on the ice. We played with confidence, everybody stayed calm and focused. It paid off."

The Wings knew that they were facing the toughest game of the season, but one that they were determined to win. "Oh, yeah, we were totally committed on winning the Cup in their arena, the Igloo, as everybody called it," Lidstrom said. "The Penguins had two superstars leading their first two lines in Sidney Crosby and Evgeni Malkin. We also had two great center-forwards, Pavel Datsyuk and Henrik Zetterberg, so as expected it became a trial of strength between them."

Zetterberg was on fire during the 2008 playoffs and was tied for the scoring lead with Crosby; both collected 27 points. Zetterberg was the best goal-scorer together with teammate Franzen (13 goals). Zetterberg's last goal in Game 6 sealed the win for Detroit. He squeezed the puck through the legs of Fleury, who fell backward and accidentally knocked the puck across the goal line. The goal gave Detroit a 3–1 lead after 7:36 of the third period. Pittsburgh made it a one-goal game with Hossa's power play goal at 18:33 and pulled Fleury at the end in a final effort to tie the game.

"I remember Malkin came storming toward our net with the puck in the final seconds and made his way around Chris Osgood before he made a backhand shot that went along the goal line as the final buzzer sounded," Lidstrom said.

One of the keys to winning the Final was Zetterberg's matchup against Crosby. The diverse Swede shadowed the Penguins captain throughout the series and was still able to score two goals and add four assists in the six games. Zetterberg was plus-16 in 22 games during the 2008 playoffs and was rewarded with the Conn Smythe Trophy as the MVP of the postseason.

"Hank was spectacular at both ends of the rink," Lidstrom said. "He controlled the game."

The two quiet Swedes, who hardly could get a conversation going between them in their hotel room as roommates on the road six years earlier, were now at the center of the hockey universe. Lidstrom was holding the Stanley Cup. Zetterberg stood beside him with his Conn Smythe Trophy. One the captain, the other an assistant captain for one of the league's most historic and respected franchises.

"It felt unreal to be awarded the Conn Smythe when you think of the team we had," Zetterberg said. "I'm very proud of that achievement."

The shy new guy from the 2002–03 season had developed into a bona fide star. He did it with the help of Lidstrom, Holmstrom, and Datsyuk, who became one of Zetterberg's best friends on the team.

It was always an incredible honor to represent Sweden in international play. Waiting for the start of the game in the World Championships in 2004. (Getty Images)

After a goal against Team USA in the World Championships semifinals. (Andreas Hillergren/ ZUMA Press/Newscom)

I scored our third goal in the gold medal game against Finland at the 2006 Winter Olympics in Turin, Italy.
(AP Images)

An incredible moment: on the ice with our gold medals. (Getty Images)

Another Cup! Hoisting the trophy after we defeated the Pittsburgh Penguins in 2008. (AP Images)

With my friend and fellow defenseman Chris Chelios. (Getty Images)

Annika and I got married at Folkara Kyrka outside Avesta in August of 1998.

This was our Chrstmas card in 2006 when we had moved into our house in Northville. From left: me, Adam, Annika, Lucas, Samuel, and Kevin.

Going to another party to celebrate our 2002 Stanley Cup and my Conn Smythe Trophy in a limousine.

On our way to a team Halloween party in the late 1990s with the Holmstroms, Annelie and Tomas.

Saluting the fans in Detroit after collecting my 1,000th career NHL point in 2009.
(AP Images)

Receiving a medal from the King of Sweden, Carl XVI Gustaf, at the Royal Castle in Stockholm in June of 2010.

It was an incredible honor to have the Red Wings retire my No. 5 jersey and raise it to the rafters at Joe Louis Arena. (Getty Images)

With my childhood idol and onetime teammate, Borje Salming, at an alumni game between the Red Wings and Maple Leafs in 2016. (Getty Images)

Stepping on to the ice at Joe Louis for one last time after the Red Wings' final home game there in 2017. (Getty Images)

Zetterberg had established himself as a leader and top player in the league and was praised by people throughout the hockey community. When he scored his 100th career goal, against the Phoenix Coyotes on February 7, 2007, Wayne Gretzky, who was the Coyotes head coach at that time, named Zetterberg "probably the most underrated player in the league." Zetterberg thanked the Great One 10 days later and showed that he was indeed for real with a hat trick and an assist against—yes, Phoenix.

Lidstrom had been asked for months who he would hand the Cup to first if Detroit was ultimately victorious. NBC Sports analyst Pierre McGuire originally brought the subject up with Lidstrom during the NHL All-Star Game in February.

"My answer then was that I had one guy on my mind, but that I wanted to keep his name to myself," Lidstrom recalled. That name was Dallas Drake. A veteran forward in the league who had never won the Stanley Cup, Drake was 39 years old and was finishing his 15th and last season in the league.

"Sometimes you sit in the dressing room before games and read the lineups just to kill time," Lidstrom said. "His name caught my eye on one of these occasions earlier during the season. I looked at his stats and saw that he had played in the league for 15 seasons but had never been on a Stanley Cup–winning team. That's why it felt right to hand over the trophy to Dallas Drake after I had lifted it."

At the age of 38, Lidstrom was still the most dominant defenseman in the NHL and he had his own secret recipe for his longevity. "My objective every summer was not to try to win the Norris Trophy the next year, but to play as well as I had done the season before," Lidstrom explained. "I worked out hard back home in Sweden and came well-prepared to training camp in Detroit.

Another reason that I could keep up so long was that I didn't go and play somewhere else during the 2004–05 lockout season. Many of my teammates left for Europe and played there, but I stayed in the U.S. and skated three times a week in Detroit. Without playing any games that season, I gave my body a chance to rest and regroup after years of increased ice time."

The Red Wings' championship in 2008 was the team's fourth in 11 years and their 11th in total. With their 115 points, they won the Central Division, the Western Conference, and the Presidents' Trophy.

Back in Detroit, Lidstrom and his teammates were treated with another parade in front of hundreds of thousands of fans. Together with goaltender Osgood, Lidstrom flew out to Los Angeles in June for an appearance on *The Tonight Show with Jay Leno*. The taping took place at NBC Studios in Burbank and was a fun experience for the new champions.

"We were on the show together with Justin Timberlake that night and the studio band was playing [Justin Timberlake's 'SexyBack'] so right before the taping the producers came up with the idea that we should be singing, 'I'm bringing Stanley back,'" Lidstrom laughed. "Which was okay with us. It was fun, and we got a chance to talk hockey and take some pictures with Justin, who was promoting the Mike Myers comedy *The Love Guru*, a film where he was playing a goalie for the Los Angeles Kings."

Before heading back to Detroit that evening, Lidstrom and Annika made a stop with Jenna and Chris Osgood for an appearance on another TV show, *Last Call with Carson Daly*. There they met Verne Troyer, another actor from *The Love Guru*. "It was a busy schedule in California," Lidstrom said. "We were only there for eight hours. Doing those two shows made it worth it."

The Red Wings played in the Western Conference during Lidstrom's time with the club and the long road trips out to California twice a year were popular among the players for a couple of reasons. It gave them a chance to get away from the cold and snow in Michigan in the winter as well as giving them a glimpse of Hollywood.

"One year we were able to be in the audience during the taping of *Friends*," Lidstrom remembered. "I think it was John Hahn, our director of communications, who knew somebody on the production team for the show, somebody who was from Michigan. We also visited the set of *24* and had a chance to meet Kiefer Sutherland during the first or second season of the show. It was really fun and a well-needed break from the daily grind at the hockey rink."

Later that month, Lidstrom made the trip to Las Vegas to pick up his sixth Norris Trophy at the NHL Awards. This time, the runner-up was Calgary's Dion Phaneuf. Four months later, the whole Detroit team visited the White House for a celebration hosted by President George W. Bush. Lidstrom presented the 43rd President of the United States with a Red Wings jersey that had No. 43 on its back. The players also brought a jersey for Bush's father, George H.W. Bush, with the No. 41 on it.

It was Lidstrom's fourth visit to the White House. "I was there twice when Bill Clinton was the president after we won in 1997 and 1998 and two times when we were invited by George W. Bush after the wins in 2002 and 2008," Lidstrom said. "Every time you're invited to the White House is special and a nice little bonus after winning the Stanley Cup."

During the 2008 visit, Lidstrom had a chance to go behind the scenes in the White House. "Together with Chris Chelios and Andreas Lilja, I was asked by some of the Secret Service guys if we wanted to go down to the basement and see the bowling alley President Nixon had installed during his time as president," Lidstrom said. "We got a private tour down there and it was really interesting to see that part of the White House."

The Cup win in 2008 was extra special for a quintet of Detroit players, also referred to as the Golden Five. Lidstrom, Holmstrom, Kris Draper, Kirk Maltby, and Darren McCarty were the only players who were on all four Red Wings championship teams in 1997, 1998, 2002, and 2008.

No team had won Stanley Cups back to back since Detroit's repeat in 1997 and 1998, but after the 2008 win, Lidstrom and his teammates felt they could duplicate that achievement in 2009. They had a strong roster and knew what it took to go all the way in the playoffs, which they proved in 2008. Datsyuk, Zetterberg, and Franzen were now the key offensive stars together with Holmstrom. The addition of free agent Marian Hossa on a one-year, $7.4 million contract was made to bolster the scoring up front.

Lidstrom was leading a backline that included Rafalski, Kronwall, Stuart, Brett Lebda, and Lilja. With Osgood in goal, the Red Wings would enter the 2008–09 season as one of the favorites. Ty Conklin had been brought in from Pittsburgh as a backup goaltender to replace Dominik Hasek, who announced his retirement during the summer of 2008.

Nobody was worried after a solid regular season, during which Detroit won 51 games and finished as the top team in the Central Division with 112 points behind only the San Jose Sharks (117 points). It was the fourth consecutive season of 50 or more victories for Detroit. Datsyuk (97 points), Zetterberg (73 points), and Hossa (40 goals) lived up to all expectations, and even if Lidstrom's numbers had fallen (59 points in 78 games), he was still a force on the blueline with a plus-31 rating. The Wings went into the playoffs believing they could get the 16 wins required in the postseason to win the Stanley Cup.

The Red Wings completed a four-game sweep of the Columbus Blue Jackets in the first round. Next up were the Ducks. Anaheim was a great team that had won the Stanley Cup two years earlier, and even if they struggled during the 2008–09 regular season and snuck into the playoffs after finishing eighth in the Western Conference, the Ducks were still a feared opponent. Their lineup included names like Getzlaf, Perry, Selanne, Bobby Ryan, Chris Kunitz, and one of the best fighters in the league in George Parros. The Ducks defensive corps was led by team captain Niedermayer and had another star in Pronger. Goaltender Jean-Sebastien Giguere, who was the key to the 2007 Stanley Cup win over the Ottawa Senators, had lost the starting job to Jonas Hiller by the time the 2009 playoffs were underway.

The Western Conference semifinals featured the last two winners of the Stanley Cup. They had faced each other four times in the playoffs since 1997, with Detroit winning in 1997 and 1999, and the Ducks winning in 2003 and 2007. Now, in the spring of 2009, the Red Wings were eager to reach the Final again and become a dynasty once more. Only the Ducks stood in their way.

Lidstrom scored two goals in the opening game at home, including the game-winner with just 50 seconds left. The next game went to triple overtime before Todd Marchant scored to give Anaheim a 4–3 victory. The series then moved to the Honda Center in Anaheim, where Ducks goalie Hiller stopped 45 shots in a spectacular Game 3. Hossa thought he had tied the game at the end, but referee Brad Watson blew the whistle when he no longer could see the puck and the home team came away with a 2–1 victory.

Detroit regrouped after the controversial call and tied the series with a 6–3 win on the road in California after Hossa and Franzen scored two goals apiece. Back in Detroit, the Red Wings won Game 5 by a 4–1 score. But Hiller was not to be denied in Game 6, making 38 saves at home that carried the Ducks to a 2–1 win. A seventh and deciding game awaited both teams at Joe Louis Arena on May 14.

In another close and dramatic game, the home fans had to wait almost the entire third period before Dan Cleary scored the winner when Hiller couldn't control the puck and inadvertently pushed it over the goal line. Detroit had made it to the Western Conference Final, where the Chicago Blackhawks would be the opponent. The Blackhawks had advanced by beating Calgary (4–2) and Vancouver (4–2) in the first two rounds.

Detroit beat Chicago in five games, but the series was closer than that would indicate, with three of the games decided in overtime. For Lidstrom, the series took a dramatic and painful turn in Game 3. A stick from a Chicago player hit him in the genitals and damaged a testicle.

"It happened on a Friday night and we were playing in Chicago again that Sunday," Lidstrom explained. "I woke up Sunday morning with a fever and I was in extreme pain in my abdomen. Our team doctor gave me a couple of painkillers that I took with a glass of water, but I threw up right away. I knew something was seriously wrong."

He was immediately transported to a local hospital and underwent emergency surgery. "I had to spend the night at the hospital and afterward was ordered to rest for a few days before I was allowed to sit on the exercise bike for the first time after the surgery," Lidstrom said.

His injury was kept secret; the Red Wings told the media that their star defenseman was getting treatment for "a lower body injury." He missed Games 4 and 5 against Chicago on May 24 and 27, ending his streak of 228 straight playoff games played over 17 seasons. On the plus side, his teammates beat the Blackhawks without him and secured their ticket to the Stanley Cup Final.

Lidstrom was back in the lineup a couple of days later for the opening game against Pittsburgh. "I only had a very short time to recover before the Final and played on painkillers during the first four games," Lidstrom said.

There was another concern as he returned to action; Lidstrom had lost a lot of weight the week after his surgery. "I couldn't eat very well for a couple of days and had a hard time playing the games," Lidstrom said. "I was weak and not playing up to par. It took me a number of games before my strength came back, so I was just trying to hang in there. The doctors told me that I was lucky, though. It could have been much worse. I was swollen all the way up to my stomach."

For the second year in a row, Detroit was up against Crosby and his Penguins. The Penguins marched to the Final by beating Philadelphia (4–2), Washington (4–3), and Carolina (4–0). They were really only tested against the Capitals in the second round;

Pittsburgh fought back from an 0–2 deficit to win a series that featured three overtime games.

The home team won the first six games of the series. Detroit took a 2–0 series lead after winning 3–1 twice at Joe Louis Arena two nights in a row on May 30 and May 31. Pittsburgh answered back with consecutive 4–2 verdicts home at Mellon Arena on June 2 and June 4 before the series was back in Detroit, where the Red Wings rolled over the Penguins in a 5–0 rout.

The question before Game 6 was, could the Wings win the Cup in Pittsburgh for a second straight season? The answer was no. The Penguins tied the series with a 2–1 win and the drama continued. There would be a seventh and deciding game at Joe Louis Arena on June 12.

Pittsburgh had never played a seventh game in the Stanley Cup Final before. Detroit had a 3–3 record from its six earlier appearances, but the last time was in 1964 against the Toronto Maple Leafs. Detroit lost that game in Maple Leaf Gardens by the score of 4–0.

None of the Red Wings' championship wins since 1997 had required a seventh game in the Final, and the 2008 series against the Penguins was the only one to extend beyond five games. The Red Wings had beaten Philadelphia 4–0 in 1997, Washington 4–0 in 1998, Carolina 4–1 in 2002, and Pittsburgh 4–2 in 2008. This time, everything was on the line in a winner-take-all showdown. And what a thriller it turned out to be.

After a scoreless first period, Talbot scored on a turnover to give Pittsburgh the lead early in the second. Malkin made a smart move with his skates, blocking a pass from Stuart and the puck found its way to Talbot, who beat Osgood. Detroit had chances to tie the game in the period—the best opportunity belonged to Darren Helm after a quick pass from Rafalski out to the left circle—but Fleury stopped the shot. Later in the period, Detroit's Franzen crushed Crosby along the boards. The Penguins captain only played one more shift in the game after sustaining a knee injury.

Pittsburgh was a team with extensive firepower up front, but to everybody's surprise it was Talbot who struck again in the middle of the third period. The goal came after a two-on-one with Tyler Kennedy that gave Talbot a chance to lift the puck over Osgood.

It took until the 13:53 mark before the Red Wings got on the board. A slap shot from Jonathan Ericsson just inside the blueline finally beat Fleury. Lidstrom assisted on the goal. Four minutes later, Kronwall sent a wrist shot from the right circle toward the Pittsburgh net that ricocheted off Jordan Staal and then hit the crossbar. No Detroit player was there to get the rebound.

Pittsburgh was up 2–1 with only seconds left when Lidstrom got the puck in the left faceoff circle on a rebound from a Zetterberg shot. Fleury was out of position and the net looked open when Lidstrom aimed and let his shot go. The crowd thought that the game was heading to overtime, but the excitement and cheers soon turned into a loud sigh. "Fleury threw himself in my direction and somehow the puck hit him on the chest and bounced down to the corner," Lidstrom said. "The game was over."

It was a devastating loss for the Red Wings and their fans. Nobody could explain what had really happened. How could Lidstrom miss? How could Fleury make that diving save?

Lidstrom didn't let the emotions destroy him. An hour after the game, when he was leaving the arena together with Annika, he stopped by the temporary press room in the corridor behind the

Zamboni entrance on the way to his car and talked to a number of journalists. He already knew that the missed opportunity to score and take the game into overtime would be talked about for years.

"I try not to think about what happened, but when people start talking about that situation I get reminded," Lidstrom said later. "At the same time, with perspective on my career, I had the fortune to play in six Stanley Cup Finals and won four of them. That's a pretty good number."

Malkin was the best player in the 2009 playoffs with 36 points (14 goals and 22 assists) in 24 games. He became the first Russian player to win the Conn Smythe Trophy. Lidstrom was third on the Red Wings in scoring behind Zetterberg (24 points) and Franzen (23 points) with 16 points after playing only 21 games because of the injury against Chicago. As always, he took care of his own end with a plus-11 to show for it.

To this day, Lidstrom thinks about how close he was to a fifth Stanley Cup triumph. Forever a competitor, the memory comes back to him frequently, in much the same manner that his missed assignment on Nikolai Borschevsky's overtime goal from Game 7 of the 1993 playoffs against Toronto still bothers him.

"The situation was a little different in 2009," Lidstrom said. "We were the defending champions then and had a really strong team. It should have been a repeat and a fifth Stanley Cup for us. That one hurts a little more also because it wasn't that long ago, either."

11
SOARING TO THE FINISH

THE RED WINGS MADE THE PLAYOFFS FOR THE 19TH CONSECUTIVE SEASON
in the spring of 2010 after finishing second in the Central Division
and fifth in the Western Conference. Nicklas Lidstrom notched his
1,000th career NHL point on October 15 against Los Angeles. He
was the eighth NHL defenseman to achieve that milestone and the
seventh player to do so while wearing a Detroit sweater, but just the
fourth to collect all 1,000 points while a member of the Red Wings,
joining Gordie Howe, Alex Delvecchio, and Steve Yzerman.

Lidstrom collected 49 points (nine goals and 40 assists) in 82
regular season games. Forwards Pavel Datsyuk and Henrik Zetterberg
were his only teammates with more points, both with 70. The Red
Wings had lost Marian Hossa, Tomas Kopecky, Ty Conklin, and
Mikael Samuelsson to free agency before the season, but had picked
up Todd Bertuzzi as a much-needed power forward.

Detroit knocked out the Phoenix Coyotes in the first round of
the playoffs in a series that went to a seventh and deciding game.
In the next round, the Wings were sent packing by the San Jose
Sharks after five games.

Datsyuk won the Selke Trophy, but Lidstrom was left empty-
handed at the NHL Awards that year. The Norris Trophy went

to Chicago's Duncan Keith, with Mike Green of Washington finishing as the runner-up. Lidstrom was selected to the Second All-Star Team.

The next season, 2010–11, not only saw Lidstrom return to the First All-Star Team but gave him the chance to select his own team of stars for the NHL All-Star Game in Raleigh, North Carolina. Under a new format, it was Team Lidstrom against Team Staal, with Lidstrom and Carolina's Eric Staal as captains for each team.

"This was during a period when the league was experimenting a little with the format for the All-Star Game," Lidstrom said. "I had been part of games with East versus West and the World versus North America. This time, Staal and I could draft our own teams from a group of players that was selected by the fans and the league."

Lidstrom had Chicago's Patrick Kane and Martin St. Louis from Tampa Bay as his assistant captains. Together, they would pick their teams during a live TV broadcast the night before the game.

"This was the first time the league gave us players a chance to form the teams and I thought it was a new and fun way to do it," Lidstrom said. "It added another dimension to the process of picking the teams and me and my assistant captains could see that the other players were a little nervous.

"Nobody wanted to be picked last. Everybody there was a star in the league and I remember Kane telling me not to take his buddy Jonathan Toews from Chicago when we started drafting members of our team. 'Let him sweat a little,' said Kane. And it really looked like Toews did."

Team Staal won the coin toss and started off by picking goaltender Cam Ward from the home team, the Carolina Hurricanes. When it was Team Lidstrom's turn, he let Martin St. Louis make the selection and agreed on taking his friend Steven Stamkos from the Tampa Bay Lightning. With their next pick, Lidstrom took Keith.

"I had played against him for a number of years but had never had a chance to get to know him, so I thought this would be a good opportunity," Lidstrom said. "And Kane really wanted his Chicago buddy on our team." They were able to pick Toews, too, after letting him sit until the eighth round of the draft.

Toronto's Phil Kessel was the last player selected, but there was a consolation prize for him in the form of a new car and $20,000 being given to a charity of his choice. He ended up on Team Lidstrom.

The coaches for the two teams were decided by a coin toss and Team Lidstrom was awarded Alain Vigneault of the Vancouver Canucks and Peter Laviolette of the Philadelphia Flyers.

As is usual when it comes to the no-hitting All-Star Games in the NHL, the 18,680 fans at the RBC Center got to see a high-scoring game. When the final buzzer sounded, Team Lidstrom skated off with an 11–10 victory.

"It was a great night for everybody," Lidstrom said. "The score wasn't that important. We all had a good time and the fans in Raleigh, who had waited so many years for the All-Star Game to come there, seemed pleased after seeing all those goals."

Lidstrom had one assist in the game but was still one of the stars with an amazing plus-seven rating. "It's a matter of being on the ice at the right moments, I guess," Lidstrom said. "They won the skills [competition], so I think we kind of came out even."

Team Staal had a four-goal lead in the first period but could not hold it despite the support from the hometown crowd. Staal, who scored two goals, gave kudos to the winning captain on the other team. "Pretty good night for Nicklas Lidstrom," Staal said. "It's fun to get to know him a little bit more, just doing this whole experience for the first time with him."

For the Sedin twins, this was the first and only time they played against each other in competition. They were both picked in the third round, Daniel by Team Staal and Henrik by Team Lidstrom.

"It was an honor to play for Nick's team," Henrik Sedin said. "Every time you are around him, you notice the respect he gets from everybody. I don't think I have ever met any player that demands less attention from teammates, coaches, equipment managers, trainers, and the media. That's what makes him such a great guy to have on your team."

The 2011 appearance was Lidstrom's last in an All-Star Game. His first time participating in an All-Star Game was in 1996 at the Fleet Center in Boston. After missing the 1997 star-filled showcase, Lidstrom played seven straight All-Star Games between 1998 and 2004. The 2005 contest was canceled because of the lockout, and the next year the Olympic Games in Italy made the league skip the All-Star Game.

Lidstrom made appearances in the 2007 and 2008 All-Star Games but turned down the invitation for the 2009 edition for health reasons. The league suspended him for one game when the regular season continued after the break, a decision that was criticized by Detroit general manager Ken Holland, who in a statement said that Lidstrom had been dealing with tendinitis for a long time and wanted to use the All-Star break to recover. "Nick Lidstrom has been an incredible ambassador for our team and for our game. I respect his decision," Holland said at the time.

Lidstrom was represented by super-agent Don Meehan throughout his professional hockey career. It was a successful partnership and along with Lidstrom's increasing status in the league, it made him the highest-paid defenseman in the world for the 2002–03 and 2003–04 seasons with a salary of $10.5 million.

"I was fortunate to play in the NHL in an era when the salaries skyrocketed and there was no salary cap for many years," Lidstrom said. "I played for a wealthy club that wanted to have a competitive team on the ice. As a player, I also felt the support from the National Hockey League Players Association that had a strong presence and helped us players compare salaries between us.

"I'm not comfortable talking about my salaries, but after they became official, anybody can find out how much they were year by year. I like to keep my private finances to myself and only say that it has been a privilege to have hockey as your full-time job for so many years."

At the end of his stay in Detroit, Lidstrom decided to be his own agent and negotiated his contracts directly with Holland. "I told Meehan that it was something I wanted to do during my last years in the league," Lidstrom said. "I had experienced everything else from a player's point of view, but not this part. It was a way of educating myself, too. I knew my playing days were coming to an end and I thought that having that experience would benefit me when I went on to do something else, maybe in the business world. Meehan had no objections. He was still doing my commercial deals and PR contracts."

Meehan wasn't surprised or disappointed when Lidstrom informed him that he wanted to do the negotiating of his contract himself. "No, we were at a stage when Nick was winding down his career," Meehan said. "These were shorter-term deals and the compensation was acceptable. We still maintained a relationship where Nick consulted with me. We collaborated until we were both satisfied."

The first time Lidstrom sat down with Holland to talk about an extension was in the summer of 2010. "Ken always said that we should meet for what he called a 'fireside chat,'" Lidstrom said. "A friendly sit-down to agree on a new deal, and of course he and the owners were hoping for a hometown discount, which meant that I would not press for the maximum amount to try to get the last penny out of them. He hoped I would sign a two-year deal, but I told him that I wanted to take it a year at a time. He understood."

Behind closed doors at Joe Louis Arena, Lidstrom and Holland met, just the two of them. "Ken told me how he and the owners saw my market value at that time and how much they thought they could pay me for the season," Lidstrom said. "I then presented my offer, based on my role on the team and how I thought I was ranked among defensemen in the league. We met again a couple of days later and made an agreement and signed the papers. It wasn't more dramatic than that."

No other Swedish player had ever negotiated his own contract with an NHL team, so Lidstrom was once again a pioneer. How well did he do? The Red Wings paid him $6.2 million for a one-year deal. "I have to say that I learned a lot from that first negotiation,"

Lidstrom said. "Just to be in the room and take part in the process gave me a new insight into the business of an NHL team."

Holland had gotten to know Lidstrom over the years and felt he was someone he could trust. "Nick wanted to be paid fairly as a player, but also wanted to be fair to the club," Holland said. "He wanted to be on a good team that could spend to the cap."

Holland recalled a point in time prior to the salary cap era when Lidstrom and some of Detroit's other core players opted to make a financial sacrifice in order to benefit the greater good, the pursuit of another Stanley Cup.

"When we made a push for the Cup before the 2001–02 season, there was no cap in the league, but after signing both Dominik Hasek and Luc Robitaille we didn't think we could afford to add Brett Hull, too," Holland said. "So, I called in Nick, Steve Yzerman, Brendan Shanahan, and Chris Chelios to my office and asked them if they could defer a part of their salary until the year after. We were talking about $500,000 each, so it was a significant amount, but they all said yes, and I could go out and sign Brett Hull. Nick worked with me and the club, but he also understood his responsibilities to the NHLPA."

The players' gamble paid off; Detroit won the Stanley Cup in 2002 and newcomers Hasek, Robitaille, and Hull played a big part in making them champions.

Holland had given Lidstrom an increase from $2.1 million in 1998–99 to $6 million the next season. Then, Lidstrom's salary jumped to $10.5 million in 2002–03. "Nick was probably underpaid for two to three years, but he honored every deal," Holland said. "He could have ripped it up, but he went out and played. You gave him the schedule and he always showed up. There were no issues. He was the best player at his position in the league. If Nick had an off night, you were surprised."

Holland was not surprised when his team captain told him in the summer of 2010 that he wanted to negotiate his next contract on his own. "He walked in and told me at the end of his career that he wanted to negotiate himself," Holland said. "I would sit down with Nick and walk him through the dynamics of the salary cap after the lockout in 2004–05, so he was pretty well-informed of the business changes that had taken place. He just wanted to be paid according to his status."

For Meehan, representing Lidstrom over the years had been a smooth ride. It demanded a lot of preparation work, however. "Nick asked a lot of questions and wanted the necessary research to be done before every negotiation of a contract extension with Detroit," Meehan explained. "We always agreed on the options to pursue and the offers we should look at. The leverage we had was how important Nick was to the Detroit franchise and how recognized he was by the industry.

"We certainly had some challenges along the way, and some negotiations were lengthy, with a lot of back-and-forth talks. Ken Holland always understood how good Nick was and after every deal was signed he said, 'Now I can sleep better at night.'"

The Wings were back on top of the Central Division in 2010–11, finishing as the third seed in the Western Conference with 104 points, and Lidstrom was also back on top of his game. He became the first defenseman to record 60 points at the age of 40 in the history of the NHL.

"He played one of the best seasons I've ever seen a defenseman play," frequent blueline partner Brad Stuart said. "It's a pleasure to be able to see him every day. For anybody to have a season like that is pretty incredible, and then factor in he's been playing for 20 years, and it's even that much more amazing."

The voters for the Norris Trophy agreed. After leaving Lidstrom out of the final trio in 2009–10, he was back among the finalists in 2010–11. Lidstrom got word of his nomination just three days prior to his 41st birthday and pushed former teammate Chris Chelios out as the oldest nominee ever. Chelios was 40 years, three months when he got his last nomination in 2002. Lidstrom had been nominated for the award 11 times in 13 years.

While admittedly biased, Lidstrom's teammates left no doubt as to who they felt deserved the Norris. "You know who the three finalists should be?" defenseman Ruslan Salei asked. "Nick Lidstrom, Nick Lidstrom, and Nick Lidstrom."

Defenseman Niklas Kronwall added, "There are a lot of good defensemen, but they're in a different league than he is."

Also a finalist for the Lady Byng Trophy, being up for two awards past his 40th birthday offered a strong indication that Lidstrom's game hadn't slipped.

Detroit coach Mike Babcock remembered being certain that it was Lidstrom's Norris to win. "You mean the 62 points he got playing on our team at age 40 when half the team was minus and we were like we were?" Babcock asked. "To do at 40 years of age what he did was absolutely phenomenal and incredible."

When the final balloting was made public at the NHL Awards, to no one's surprise the silky-smooth Swede walked away with his seventh Norris, besting himself as the oldest winner of the trophy. He was 38 years, two months for his 2008 Norris Trophy win. Montreal great Doug Harvey, who is tied with Lidstrom for second all-time with seven Norris Trophy wins, is the third-oldest winner at 37 years, five months.

"I never set out the goal of being nominated or trying to win the Norris," Lidstrom said. "I always looked at it as being a bonus."

Lidstrom didn't argue about being left out of the finalists for the Norris in 2009–10. "The season before, I could've contributed more offensively," he said. In fact, the only thing that disappointed Lidstrom was finishing as a minus player (minus-two) in 2010–11 for the first time in his career. "It's something I wasn't very happy about," Lidstrom said.

Still, he took great pride in his latest Norris triumph. "They're all special," Lidstrom said. "The first one was very special, being the first European to win it."

As he picked up his Norris Trophy, Lidstrom also delivered a sigh of relief to everyone in the Red Wings organization, confirming that he intended to play the 2011–12 season.

Zetterberg felt it was the right decision for his friend and teammate. "He was the best player for us every night," Zetterberg said. "He had a lot of hockey in him still."

For Lidstrom, his strong 2010–11 campaign convinced him that he had more hockey left in him. "Coming off [the previous] season, I thought I could've played better," Lidstrom recalled of his personally disappointing 2009–10 season. "I wanted to prove I could still play at a high level and be an impact player. It was important. If I'd taken another step back that season, it would've been a difficult decision for me."

It wasn't the actual games that Lidstrom found to be the most taxing on his body in his later years as an NHL player. Rather, it was the amount of prep work necessary in the summer months to hone himself for the long grind ahead that was most demanding.

"Preparing for a long year, you had to start in June," Lidstrom said. "As I got older, it got even harder. I learned you couldn't cut corners. You had to be ready to play in October and you had to be ready to keep doing it in April and May.

"I appreciated it even more as I got older, knowing how hard it was in the off-season."

Lidstrom's return was even more critical to the Red Wings because Brian Rafalski had opted to retire from the Detroit defense. "If we'd have lost both, it would have probably been devastating," Holland admitted. "You're talking about two elite, puck-moving defensemen."

The 2011–12 season did not turn out to be the success the Red Wings had hoped for. They finished third in the Central Division with a 48–28–6 record and fifth in the Western Conference. It was the first time since the 1990–91 season, the year before Lidstrom joined the club, that Detroit did not finish first or second in its division.

There was plenty of change to the team, and some familiar faces who'd been there almost from the beginning of Lidstrom's time in Detroit were stepping aside to make room for younger players. Chris Osgood had announced his retirement in the summer of 2011 after 17 seasons in the league; Jimmy Howard took over the job as the team's No. 1 goaltender. Detroit lost two additional core players via retirement that summer when Rafalski and Kris Draper also decided to hang up their skates.

Draper was an assistant captain for many years and a signif-icant voice in the dressing room. He had been part of all four

Stanley Cup–winning teams during Lidstrom's time in Detroit and played a key role on the checking line, as a penalty killer, and on faceoffs. Osgood had won three Cups during his time on the team and Rafalski played a big part on defense on the 2008 championship squad with his 14 points in 22 games, one point better than Lidstrom and second among the Red Wings defenders behind Kronwall's 15 points. They all had played a big part in making the Red Wings an NHL dynasty. Now they were gone and left big holes to fill.

"Losing three experienced players like them at the same time obviously hurt us, not only on the ice, but also the leadership they provided in the dressing room," Lidstrom said. "It's hard to replace veterans with newcomers that need some time to adjust to the new environment and their new teammates. You have to give them time to find their way."

Holland signed defenseman Mike Commodore from the Columbus Blue Jackets and Ian White from the San Jose Sharks to beef up the back end. Commodore was injured during the preseason and never found his rhythm; he only played 17 games before he was traded to the Tampa Bay Lightning. White got a chance to play with Lidstrom on a regular basis and enjoyed his most productive season in the NHL with 32 points and a plus-23 rating in 77 games.

The hopes of a long playoff run in the spring of 2012 were bolstered in the middle of the regular season when Detroit went on an unbeaten streak of 23 straight home games. It started with a win against the Anaheim Ducks on November 5, 2011, and ended with a 4–3 shootout loss to the Vancouver Canucks on February 23, 2012. The Philadelphia Flyers held the NHL mark of 20 consecutive home wins before Detroit broke the record after beating the Dallas Stars on February 14. The Red Wings extended the streak to 23 games after wins over Nashville (2–1) on February 17 and San Jose (3–2) two days later.

The regular season ended with two home losses against New Jersey and Chicago, leaving Detroit stumbling into the playoffs. Lidstrom's 34 points (11 goals and 23 assists) was his lowest point total in his 20 seasons in the NHL, and he missed 12 games due to injury. His plus-minus rating was still impressive at plus-21. He played his 1,500th career NHL game on October 22, 2011. On February 12, Lidstrom participated in his 1,550th career NHL game, surpassing former Red Wings captain Alex Delvecchio's mark for the most NHL games played by a player who spent his entire career with one team.

On March 26, Lidstrom beat Steve Mason in the second period of a 7–2 rout of the Columbus Blue Jackets. No one knew at the time, but they'd just witnessed the 264th and final goal of Lidstrom's NHL career. He scored 11 goals in 2011–12, the same number that he had tallied 20 years earlier in 1991–92 as a Red Wings rookie, yet another example of his remarkable consistency. Two nights later, again against the Blue Jackets, Lidstrom figured in a Kronwall goal for what would turn out to be his farewell NHL point.

"The Central Division was really strong that year, with four teams collecting over 100 points," Lidstrom said. "The record streak of wins at home in the middle of the season made us feel really comfortable playing at the Joe. I wasn't worried going into the playoffs that we weren't good enough."

The opening round of the 2012 Stanley Cup playoffs had Detroit facing the Nashville Predators in the Western Conference quarterfinals. The teams split the first two games in Nashville, where the Predators won the first battle 3–2, with the Red Wings tying the series after a 3–2 win in the second game. Back home in Detroit at Joe Louis Arena, the Red Wings lost both games, 3–2 and 3–1. Suddenly, they needed to win the fifth game in Nashville to survive.

That did not happen. The Predators closed out the series with a 2–1 win on April 20. David Legwand had the game-winning goal, just 13 seconds into the third period. Alexander Radulov had given Nashville the lead late in the first and Jiri Hudler tied the game in the second, assisted by Valtteri Filppula and Henrik Zetterberg. Lidstrom did not record any points in the five games.

"They were all close games, but Nashville was a little better than us," Lidstrom said. "It felt like they stepped up and scored the important goals when they needed to. Plus, their goalie, Pekka Rinne, was impossible to beat. We were only able to score nine goals on 160 shots during those five games. What I remember from the last game in Nashville was that we had some good opportunities at the end of the game to tie it. I think Zetterberg was in a good position to score on a rebound, but Rinne made another key save."

During the traditional handshake after the last game of the series, Barry Trotz, the Nashville coach, stopped Lidstrom in order to tell him how much he admired him. "Trotz shook my hand and wanted to congratulate me for a long and great career and said he hoped that I wouldn't retire," Lidstrom recalled. "That was a classy thing to do."

This was a moment filled with a variety of emotions for Lidstrom. This might be it. The end. "When I stood there on the ice after the final buzzer and had shaken hands with all the Nashville players, the thought came over me that this could have been my last NHL game," Lidstrom remembered. "I felt disappointed over both the loss and the fact that this could have been my final game. It really hit me hard and it was an uncomfortable feeling. We talked about it on the flight home, but I didn't feel like going deeper on the issue. I needed time to let everything sink in before I made my decision."

He had dwelled on the question of when to retire for a number of years. "I consulted with a number of other players that had gone through the same scenario," Lidstrom said. "I remember that I talked to Mats Sundin about it when he visited Vancouver during the 2010 Olympic Games. I just wanted to hear about his experience after he retired from the NHL. Chris Chelios was another former teammate that I spoke with. I knew him well from our time together on the Red Wings, and his advice was that I should continue playing as long as I could. He had himself been forced to quit after a long career when he wasn't offered a new contract anywhere around the league."

Lidstrom also spoke to a number of players back in Sweden but ultimately decided that nobody had the perfect answers to his questions. "Everybody has their own agenda and looks at their careers through their own eyes," Lidstrom said. "I understood that I had to leave the game on my own terms and not be pushed out, like Sundin at the end of his time in the league."

Lidstrom wrestled with the decision for the month after the loss to Nashville. He was 42 years old and had signed only one-year deals with the Red Wings the previous two seasons. He made his decision official in a press conference at Joe Louis Arena on May 31 with Annika at his side.

"It wasn't an easy decision to make," Lidstrom admitted. "I had lived with hockey for 20 years but didn't have that drive to give it my all anymore. The motivation that helped make me able to be a top player in the league wasn't there. The reason I had only signed one-year contracts the last two years was that I wanted to make sure that I still had fun going to practice and playing games. I didn't want to be one of those old guys who complained all the time.

"I convinced myself that I needed to enjoy everything that was hockey-related, both on and off the ice. And even if I didn't perform as well as I had done before, I still had fun. The early loss against Nashville made me think twice about continuing playing. I think that was the deciding factor."

Lidstrom felt he had given his all to the Red Wings, including taking a lower salary during his last two seasons with the team. "I told my parents back in Sweden 10 days before the press conference that I was done and informed Ken Holland about my decision around the same time," Lidstrom said. "A couple of days later I was paddle boarding with Chris Chelios, which we did on a regular basis, when he brought up the issue of me retiring. He thought I should play another year, at least. I had my suspicions that he was making the argument for Kenny, that Chris was lobbying for our GM, but I didn't bring it up. It was years later that Chelios confessed to me that Ken had asked him to try to get me to stay on for another year."

"Nick could easily have played a couple of more years," Holland said. "He was still one of the top 10 defensemen in the league when he retired, but Father Time comes along, and I think the off-season preparations became too much to handle for him. You have to have a burning fire in your belly that nobody sees.

"Also, remember that Nick played against the other team's best players his whole career. He had a tough matchup night after night. Nick stayed on top all those years because he was the smartest player of them all and didn't take any big licks, even if the other teams tried to hit him all the time."

"Nick could have played two or three more years," Zetterberg said. "In my mind, he is one of the greatest hockey players ever. His lowest performance level was so high. As a teammate you could always trust him. He always stepped up when needed. To be that great during so many years is extraordinary."

Lidstrom's teammates had feared the moment their captain would tell them he was leaving the game. "I did think about it off and on during his last season, that this could be it," Kronwall admitted. "At the same time, you didn't want it to happen. He meant so much for us, so when he called that press conference and told the world he was done, it was hard to digest. We all felt emptiness. From that moment, everything would be different. In the dressing room, on the ice, going on the road without him. It all changed."

White, Lidstrom's defense partner for much of the 2011–12 campaign, cherished his brief time skating alongside such greatness. "Playing with arguably the best defenseman of all time, it was quite a thrill," White said.

It was often said of Wayne Gretzky that when the Great One retired in 1999, it was because he felt that he could no longer be Gretzky, the game's most dominant player. Lidstrom opted for retirement when he felt that he could no longer be Lidstrom, the game's most dominant defenseman.

"I had lost some of my desire," Lidstrom said. "It wasn't that fun anymore to sit in a hotel room in, let's say, Edmonton, at the end of a long road trip, and prepare myself for another game. Sure, I could have played some more years, but my mindset was that if I played, I would have to be a key member on the team. I did not want to be a sixth or seventh defenseman."

His biggest mistakes on the ice haunt him a little, but not enough to cause him nightmares. "There are a couple of plays I wish I could have back, but over a long career like mine, some bad things are bound to happen," Lidstrom said.

Four Stanley Cups, seven Norris Trophies, a Conn Smythe Trophy, an Olympic gold medal, and a World Championships gold medal. So, what is there to regret?

"The biggest headache is that seventh and deciding game in the 2009 Stanley Cup Final, where I had the puck on my stick in the ending seconds and could have tied the game, 2–2, and taken us to overtime," Lidstrom said. "It bothers me that I didn't score there. And it bothers me that we were leading the series 3–2 and could have won it in Pittsburgh in Game 6 but missed that opportunity.

"Then we go home and play in front of our own fans at Joe Louis Arena and it wasn't Sidney Crosby or Evgeni Malkin that beat us, it was Max Talbot who scored both of their goals."

Nobody has a 20-year long career in the National Hockey League without some ups and downs. Not even the Perfect Human.

12

THE ULTIMATE HONOR

WHEN NICKLAS LIDSTROM DECIDED TO RETIRE AFTER THE 2011–12 season, he and Annika had a decision to make: should they stay in Detroit or move back to Sweden?

They had talked about it for years and discussed the pros and cons. They loved their house in Northville and had made many friends in the Detroit area after spending 20 years in the U.S. Their kids were in schools nearby, so it would have been easy to stay around, at least for a while. Ultimately, Nicklas and Annika felt the time was right to move the family back to Sweden.

"It was a tough decision to make, but Annika and I had always had the understanding between us that we would move back when my playing days were over," Lidstrom said. "What made it hard was that we both had lived most of our grown-up lives in Detroit and had lost touch with our old friends at home. The distance between Sweden and the U.S. makes it hard to keep up friendships, with an ocean between you. You lose touch, something we were aware of. We knew we were going to have to start all over again."

At the same time, the Lidstroms recognized that if they wanted their children to maintain and further develop a sense of their Swedish heritage and culture, it was now or never.

"It wasn't a given that we would move back, and we did talk about staying for at least one extra year, but the timing was right for our kids if they wanted to be Swedes," Lidstrom explained. "What they do later in life is totally up to them."

Their oldest son, Kevin, had already made the move back to Sweden the year before. He had applied to the local hockey high school in Vasteras and was accepted. "That was something Kevin really wanted to do, and I almost retired in 2010 to give him a chance to do that, but we were lucky to find relatives Kevin could live with for a year in Sweden," Lidstrom said. "Our other sons now wanted to do the same thing, to play hockey in Sweden. Kevin was starting his last year of high school, Adam was just beginning high school, and Samuel was entering middle school. If we were going to move back, this was the right time, we thought.

"The only one who did not like our plans and hesitated about the move was our youngest son, Lucas. He wanted to stay in Detroit and had a hard time understanding why we would leave. For him, Sweden was a place where we spent the summer, from late June until the middle of August, every year. Then we always traveled 'home' to the U.S. Our kids always said, 'back home to the U.S.' and that was understandable, as their everyday life was there.

"Lucas was struggling a little during our first year back home and was longing for his friends in Detroit. He wanted us to move back. It took a couple of years for him to adjust to a new school and feel comfortable living year-round in Vasteras.

"I think all of our children have adjusted to Sweden now. Today, we all are settled in Sweden, but we also enjoy our visits back to Detroit to see old friends and the city we loved so much over 20 years. There's something special about that city and the suburbs where we lived. It still feels like coming home in a way."

Overall, Annika believes she and Nicklas have had a harder adjustment than their children. "It has taken a little longer for us to adapt to Swedish society then I thought it would," Annika said. "We still miss our friends in the U.S. as much as we did when we left. All these happy, spontaneous, and easygoing people that you bump into over there. That process has been faster for our children and I think it is great that they have been able to be in school and get educated both in the U.S. and Sweden."

Back in Vasteras, Annika and Nicklas have chosen to live a quiet family life. They share duties, driving their younger sons to school and to hockey rinks around the city. And they do taco Fridays like everybody else. "We even have a dog now, a Golden Doodle, so you could say that we're just an ordinary family here," Lidstrom said.

Annika looks back on the 20 years they spent as a family in Detroit and sees it as nothing but a blessing and a positive life experience. "I think I still have the same values as I've always had, but of course 20 years of living in America has made me grow as a person, especially when it comes to appreciating things around me more," Annika said.

For Nicklas' parents, Gerd and Jan-Erik, and his three sisters, it was also a new way of keeping company. "Even if Nicklas had told us the whole time that they would move back after he was done playing, Gerd and I thought that maybe they would change their mind and stay in Detroit," Jan-Erik said. "Twenty-one years is a long time. But it feels good to have them back home again, even if I have to confess that we miss the trips to Detroit.

"Gerd went more than 40 times to see them and I must have been there 35 times. Nicklas and Annika were so generous, taking care of us in a great way. We have so many beautiful memories from our visits there. For me personally, the Father Trips that the Red Wings arranged were another highlight. To be able to travel with the team and experience the NHL behind the scenes with your own son was fantastic. I will never forget that."

Lidstrom's parents have happily adapted to the change in lifestyle and are enjoying being able to see Nicklas, Annika, and their grandchildren on a more regular basis. "It's been wonderful having them here after so many years in the U.S.," Jan-Erik said "We've been able to see our grandchildren grow up and celebrate holidays like Christmas together with them. We don't live that far away, so we visit Vasteras almost every week."

Jan-Erik and Gerd don't think their son has changed much after all those years of fame in the U.S. "Nicklas has always been someone who takes responsibility for everything he does," Jan-Erik said. "He left home when he was 16, and we never put any pressure or demands on him, just gave him encouragement. So, for us, he's the same person, but with a lot more life experience, of course."

Kevin Allen, the hockey columnist for *USA Today*, followed Lidstrom at close range in Detroit and had really gotten to know the Swedish star defenseman throughout the years. Allen was not surprised when he heard their decision to go back to Sweden. "I loved the rules they lived by," Allen said. "They spoke Swedish at home, except if there was a non-Swedish speaker in the house. Then they showed an unbelievable transition game and just immediately switched to English.

"I thought for maybe a minute or two that they could be the rare Swedes that maybe stayed here after becoming Americanized, but I remember after talking to them for a big feature story about how they had prepared to go back. Their kids were all very fluent in Swedish and they had made sure that they had maintained that touch by going back every year. But I remember Annika telling me that she was almost dreading the day, because they had two lives, as they had grown close to people here, too."

Back in their hometown of Vasteras, an hour by car to the west of Stockholm, the Lidstrom family built a new home by the waterside of Lake Malaren. They had bought the lot a decade earlier, and now had invested in a huge and modern house with access to the water for boating in the summer.

"We lived in another house nearby when we were home every summer but had bought that lot with an existing summer cabin 10 years earlier," Lidstrom said. "The plan was to take down the cabin and build a new home there the day we decided to move home for good. We had lived in a large and nice house in Northville for years, so I think it was important to have something similar. With four kids you need space, and we also wanted to have our visiting friends from Detroit be able to stay with us.

"It definitely was a change of scenery for all of us. I knew it would take time for everybody to feel settled in."

Without practice to go to every morning, or needing to spend time preparing for games, Lidstrom busied himself by driving the kids to school and getting more involved in their homework and activities. He took on some coaching assignments for his youngest sons, but that was something he had done already in Detroit. In Sweden, it didn't make the headlines until somebody posted a picture on Instagram in December of 2017; Lidstrom was walking across the ice during an intermission in a junior game in Vasteras with an electric drill in his hand, ready to make the holes to put the pegs in place to hold the goal nets after the Zamboni had gone by.

That picture went viral on social media. The famous NHL legend and millionaire was helping his hometown's under-18 junior team, where his son Samuel was playing. Lidstrom could be found opening the door on the bench for the players, helping out at the timekeeper's table, and also filling in as a rink rat between periods.

"What's the big deal?" Lidstrom asked. "I always said I'm just an ordinary guy. I still love being at the rink and I like helping out."

When the picture of Lidstrom walking across the ice went public, many tweeted about it. *Expressen*, one of Sweden's largest newspapers, even published some of the tweets on their website:

"It warms my heart."

"Never seen anything like it. Sick. A legend."

"You don't find many of his kind."

"Pretty overqualified janitor."

Lidstrom couldn't help but notice some funny run-ins with players or their double takes at the junior games when they noticed who it was tracking their penalty time in the sin bin. "Sometimes, when I'm the timekeeper in the penalty box, the visiting team's players seem surprised to see me opening the door for them and then sitting there beside me," Lidstrom said. "It's kind of funny."

Hockey moved quickly and frequently to honor Lidstrom for his one-of-a-kind career, and that brought him back to North America on a regular basis. The celebration of his magnificence began on March 6, 2014, when the Red Wings officially retired Lidstrom's No. 5.

It was a typically humble Lidstrom who spoke during the ceremony at Joe Louis Arena. There were few missteps in Lidstrom's brilliant career, but he let the fans in on one of them. He told the story of when he first came to Detroit in the fall of 1991 and was asked by the equipment manager what number he would like to have if he made the team. Lidstrom asked for No. 9, the same number he had worn while playing back in Sweden.

The answer he got first surprised him, and then made him a little embarrassed. "Kid, that just ain't gonna happen," Lidstrom was told by the equipment manager. No. 9 was already hanging from the rafters in the arena. It had been retired 20 years earlier in honor of the legendary Gordie Howe.

"So, I just kept my mouth shut and No. 5 was handed to me," Lidstrom told the crowd with a chuckle. That night, as No. 5 was raised to the rafters next to No. 9, many in attendance had tears in their eyes.

"It was a very emotional moment," Lidstrom said. "I had been on the bench when Steve Yzerman's jersey was retired some years earlier and I remembered how special that was. Now it was my turn, and I could feel the excitement. I don't know how many times I had been laying down on the ice stretching during game warm-ups and looked at the retired numbers in the rafters. You understood how important those players had been for the club."

Lidstrom was the first defenseman to have his jersey retired by the Red Wings. He is now in the company of legendary names like Terry Sawchuk (No. 1), Red Kelly (No. 4), Ted Lindsay (No. 7), Howe (No. 9), Alex Delvecchio (No. 10), Sid Abel (No. 12), and Yzerman (No. 19).

"It's not like winning a trophy for a successful season or playoff. It's not winning an individual trophy. This is something different. This is all about being a Detroit Red Wing," Lidstrom said from the podium on the ice.

He had been gone from the NHL for a season and a half when his jersey was retired. "No regrets, but that doesn't mean I don't miss it," Lidstrom said. "I miss playing, but I never had any urge to get back to being on the ice and playing in a game."

Attending the jersey ceremony was Christopher Ilitch, the son of Red Wings owners Mike and Marian Ilitch and at that time the team's president. He is now the CEO of parent company Ilitch Holdings, Inc. Also in attendance were senior vice president Jimmy Devellano, general manager Ken Holland, coach Mike Babcock, and former coach Scotty Bowman. Ilitch thanked Lidstrom for everything he had done for the organization and paid homage to his nickname by also anointing him "the Perfect Red Wing."

Also on hand were 16 former teammates, among them Chris Osgood, Chris Chelios, Tomas Holmstrom, Brendan Shanahan, Kris Draper, Kirk Maltby, Darren McCarty, Igor Larionov, and Vladimir Konstantinov.

Lidstrom addressed Holmstrom, his closest friend, with a special thank-you. "I don't know how many shots you blocked or how many goals I scored that were disallowed because you were in the crease," Lidstrom said. "But I do know one thing: without you standing there, I wouldn't have scored as many goals."

Babcock relayed how much he had enjoyed having Lidstrom as his captain and that the communication between them was open, honest, and free-flowing. "I had the opportunity to coach Nick for seven years," Babcock said. "Many people think he coached me.

Nick was an incredible, incredible player. As good of a player as he was, he was a better man and better teammate. Beyond humble, no maintenance, led by example, did it right every day—whether that be summer training, whether that be preparation, whether that be practice. Attention to detail is what he was. His ability to communicate with his teammates and his coaches was second to none.

"Nick Lidstrom is a true role model. He's someone for our community, for Hockeytown, to trust, to admire, to respect. Nick is going to look great up there right next to Stevie."

The Red Wings gave Lidstrom a new truck as a gift. The players, represented by new captain Henrik Zetterberg and his assistant captains Pavel Datsyuk and Niklas Kronwall, presented Lidstrom with a trip to Africa. When Nicklas thanked everybody at the end of the hour-long ceremony, the fans in the arena yelled "Don't leave us, Nick" and "We love you, Nick."

As he stood on the ice with Annika and their four sons, Lidstrom was deeply emotional as his No. 5 jersey was raised up to its place beside the other Red Wings legends. Even now, a number of years later, he still has trouble grasping the fact that his jersey was retired. "To think that nobody will ever wear No. 5 again in Detroit is hard to take in," Lidstrom said. "That the number is immortalized and is hanging next to Gordie Howe's No. 9 feels unreal for me."

Lidstrom had invited 30 family members and friends from Sweden to the ceremony. Gerd and Jan-Erik were trying to hold back the tears. "The ceremony was so powerful and gripping that I had to pinch myself to understand it was real," Jan-Erik said. "Nicklas has a unique trophy collection and is in a class by himself when it comes to Swedish defensemen that have played in the

NHL. But I think he retired at the right time, even if I'm sure he could have played one or two more years."

Over the years, Holland had often joked that he would announce his retirement the day after Lidstrom did, painfully aware of the impact his absence would have on the franchise.

"Do we miss him?" Holland asked, fully certain of the answer. "The league has been around for 100 years and Nick is on the short list of the greatest players we have ever seen. He is a generational player, one of those that comes around every 10 to 30 years. When he retired, it was a massive hole to fill, and it might take us 20 years to find a player of that stature. Or it might never happen."

Holland pointed to Lidstrom's versatility as his biggest strength. "He was a great offensive defenseman, but in my mind, he was an even better defensive defenseman, because he never got beat," Holland said. "The way he walked the blueline in the offensive zone, the way he could always pass the puck tape-to-tape, and the way he kept his head up when he shot the puck to the net was amazing. Nick was here for 20 years and we never missed the play-offs that whole time. He is definitely one of the greatest."

Other honors were about to come Lidstrom's way, and in the summer of 2015 the greatest acknowledgment that a hockey player can receive would be his—induction into the Hockey Hall of Fame.

The phone call came before lunch on a warm Monday in late June of 2015 during a visit to Detroit. It was a call that Lidstrom had hoped he would get. He was aware that the Hall's selection committee was meeting in Toronto, and that he was on the short list for being inducted that year. It had been three years since he had played his last game in the NHL, so he was now eligible.

On the other end of the line was selection committee chairman John Davidson, the former NHL goaltender and then the president of the Columbus Blue Jackets. He congratulated Nicklas for being voted into the Hall together with former teammate Sergei Fedorov and defensemen Chris Pronger and Phil Housley. The fourth inductee in the player category for 2015 was Angela Ruggiero, one of the biggest stars U.S. women's hockey has ever seen, with Olympic and World Championships gold medals among numerous other accolades. Bill Hay (former NHL player and Hockey Canada and Calgary Flames executive) and Carolina Hurricanes owner Peter Karmanos Jr. were inducted in the builders' category.

"It was a big moment and unreal when the call came through, even if people had been telling me for weeks that I would get in on the first try," Lidstrom said. "But you never know until you get the confirmation. Lanny McDonald was also on the call with John Davidson." He had already been told by his friends Mats Sundin and Peter Forsberg how special that induction weekend in Toronto would be. Lidstrom had a couple of months to prepare for the ceremony later that year on November 9.

"I have to admit that I was more nervous than usual, because I had to prepare to hold a much longer speech than what I was used to at the NHL Awards show," Lidstrom said. "Speaking from the podium in front of so many NHL legends added more pressure, but as soon as I got up there and started talking, I felt much calmer. It all went pretty smoothly, in my mind.

"The speech was the last thing on the schedule after a fun and hectic weekend, where us inductees had a chance to sit down for a Q&A session with fans, play in the Red Wings alumni game as well as the Legends Classic, and do a ceremonial puck drop before the

Toronto-Detroit game at the Air Canada Centre. That was extra fun for me, doing it with Henrik Zetterberg as the Red Wings captain and Dion Phaneuf representing the Maple Leafs."

The Legends Classic put Lidstrom back on the ice in Toronto with Borje Salming for the first time since the 1991 Canada Cup. Both were picked for Pavel Bure's World Team. "It brought back a lot of memories," Lidstrom said. "My first game in North America was in Toronto and with Borje, so it kind of made my pro career come full circle."

Twelve members of his family attended the festivities. Lidstrom had also invited Tomas Holmstrom and his wife, Annelie; Swedish friend Patrik Mellgren with his partner, Johanna; Northville neighbors Jim and Robin Cerretani; and his financial adviser from his time in Detroit, Rick Weinerman, and his wife, Linda.

"The staff at the Hockey Hall of Fame did a fabulous job in making the weekend so special for everybody," Lidstrom said. "The police escort we got from our hotel to the gala at Brookfield Place on 30 Yonge Street was the highlight for our kids. For me, that night was the conclusion of my long career and it couldn't have ended better."

The NHL Network broadcast the gala with two retired stars in the TV studio, Darren Pang and Scott Stevens. They summed up Lidstrom's career with these words: "He is the prototype for a defense machine that we will never see again."

On January 27, 2017, two days before the 2017 NHL All-Star Game in Los Angeles, the league announced a list of the 100 greatest players of all time at a gala held at the Microsoft Theater. The list was the centerpiece in commemorating 100 years of NHL hockey and the players were chosen by a panel of 58 people, consisting of NHL executives, coaches, general managers, and seasoned members of the media.

Lidstrom was one of 21 defensemen on the list. He was in good company; the list included legendary defensemen like Eddie Shore, Bobby Orr, Doug Harvey, Serge Savard, Larry Robinson, Denis Potvin, Ray Bourque, Paul Coffey, and Scott Stevens, among others. "Being on the Top 100 list was a huge honor for me," Lidstrom said. "The panel had thousands of names to choose from. We're talking about everybody that played in the NHL since the start of the league a hundred years ago."

Among the forwards on the list were names like Wayne Gretzky, Gordie Howe, Jean Beliveau, Bobby Hull, Bobby Clarke, Phil Esposito, Guy Lafleur, and Mark Messier. When asked which three forwards he had the hardest time defending against, Lidstrom picked three names that were also on the Top 100 list.

"Mario Lemieux was probably the best I ever played against," Lidstrom said. "He had such a reach and controlled the puck so well. He was really tough to get to. Pavel Bure caused me problems because of his speed and ability to handle the puck. I couldn't keep up with his speed when he came flying up the ice. My third choice would be Jaromir Jagr. When he was at the top of his career, it was so hard to stop him. With his size and power, he protected the puck extremely well."

The list did not rank the players, instead presenting them alphabetically. "I think that was a good decision by the league," Lidstrom said. "It would have been nearly impossible to rank players from 1 to 100. We're talking about different eras, different generations of players. You have to consider that."

Lidstrom was one of four Swedish players who made the list, all four of them members of the Hockey Hall of Fame. He was in the company of Salming, Sundin, and Forsberg. "Four out of a hundred, I think that is a good outcome for Swedish hockey and I'm proud of being a part of that," Lidstrom said. "Another fact that shows how tough the competition was is that only six active players made it.

"It is hard to compare or rank the three accomplishments. Getting your jersey retired to the rafters of Joe Louis Arena was a great achievement for me locally in Detroit. The 100 list and being inducted into the Hockey Hall of Fame makes it a broader thing. Both huge honors. I have to say that making the 100 list was very special, because we're talking about such a long time span."

The Red Wings were the team with the most players on the list (28), and if you ask Lidstrom, they most certainly measured up. "We had all been asked to send in our measurements so they could tailor the suits we would wear during the centennial gala," Lidstrom said. "As soon as we had checked into the hotel across the street from the Staples Center, we tried them on. Mine fit perfect. The tailors had done a great job. No changes needed to be made."

Lidstrom flew in from Sweden with Annika for the celebration in Los Angeles. It was a weekend full of appearances and parties for the nominated stars. "I had a really good time meeting all these players," Lidstrom said. "Some of them I had played against, some of them I had only read about. It was a humbling experience and put everything in perspective."

Before the All-Star Game, the league lined up the 2017 stars with the former stars on the ice. They all shook hands as a way to symbolically pass the baton. This was the moment when

Norris Trophy winner and two-time Stanley Cup champion Drew Doughty approached Lidstrom to shake his hand and to tell him how much he admired him.

"Yeah, I remember that," Lidstrom said. "It was fun to hear him say that. Doughty is one of the shining stars among today's defensemen in the NHL. I had heard that he had me as an idol when he grew up and I am a fan of his, too."

"So many of us in the league today have been trying to copy Nicklas Lidstrom's game," Doughty said. "I had never met him one-on-one before, so I thought it was the right moment to show him my admiration and respect.

"He was just the whole package, really. He brought a good game every night and good leadership every night and that is something I'm trying to kind of follow in his footsteps doing. I remember Mike Babcock made a comment that he never saw Lidstrom allow his partner to be in a two-on-one against. That is a testament of how hard he worked and how well positioned he was.

"He just didn't make mistakes. That was so cool. He made it look effortless. He never seemed to have to skate at full speed because he was in the right position all the time. That's one thing I definitely learned from him. I use my skating a lot when I have the puck and when I don't have the puck I think I'm very sound defensively. I learned a lot of that from him, honestly."

Lidstrom has a lot to teach the next generation of NHL defensemen and is happy and willing to do it—but not from the bench. "I have no plans to start coaching right now, but that could change later on when our kids get older," Lidstrom said. "We'll see. I'm not closing any doors."

When they walk away from the game, finding a new pursuit can be a somewhat daunting task for many athletes. After a couple of years of helping his family settle in following the move home from Detroit in 2012, and doing some part-time scouting for the Red Wings, Lidstrom was ready for a new challenge.

He contacted former Swedish tennis star Stefan Edberg, who was ranked No. 1 in the world in both singles and doubles in the 1980s and early 1990s. He was someone who had gone through the same transition of moving back to Sweden after a successful professional sports career abroad. Edberg, who won six individual Grand Slam titles and an additional three in doubles between 1985 and 1996, was based in London during his tennis career. Now he was living in his hometown of Vaxjo and was an investor in a boutique investment firm called Case.

Splitting his time between Vaxjo and Stockholm, Edberg was someone who had experienced the life Lidstrom was just beginning to adjust to and could relate. "I was just curious how Stefan had handled it all and asked him if we could meet," Lidstrom explained. "I think it was in 2015 and I went to his company's headquarters in Stockholm to just listen to what Stefan had to say.

"We did not know each other before. Stefan was very open and told me about his decision to leave pro tennis and a life on the road to settle down in his home country and find a new challenge. I liked what I heard. It was very similar to my journey in Detroit and the NHL; the traveling, the pressure, and the decision to stop playing and moving your family back to Sweden.

"We did not discuss any partnership during that first meeting, I just thanked him for taking his time in meeting me and telling me his story about how he had been dealing with everything after his playing days were over."

Back home in Vasteras, Lidstrom thought about what Edberg had told him and soon asked for another meeting. Lidstrom felt getting involved in the financial market could be something that would be of interest.

Edberg remembers the mutual respect these two sporting giants held for each other was instantly apparent. "I had never met Nicklas before," Edberg said. "The first contact came through one of the company's founders, Fredrik Svensson, who also lives in Vasteras. Nicklas is one of our country's most acclaimed sports stars and has a strong brand. Add to that, he is a very grounded person with excellent views on things.

"I felt we got along well from the start and that we agreed on many things that you go through after finishing your career. He also had a genuine interest for the business world and financial investments. It felt right from the start to have him be a partner in the company."

Lidstrom had been missing the competitive aspect of his life since retiring from the NHL. Signing on as a partner with Case helped him get that back. "I've never been a huge gambler who bets hard and takes big risks, so I like our company's philosophy," Lidstrom said. "I follow the same strategy when I make decisions in my other businesses; real estate, for example. I seek help from the best advisers that I can find."

Their typical clients are high-net-worth individuals, sports stars, and entrepreneurs. Wealth management for private clients is the core of the company's business. "I really enjoy the different aspects of the company," Lidstrom said. "I'm sitting in on strategic meetings we have with analytics and CEOs and I take part in conference calls when we talk about our stock portfolios.

"So, you could say that I am an active partner and I'm learning all the time. I'm not yet a voice when we discuss buying or selling a certain stock, but I'm out there taking meetings with clients, banks, stockbrokers, and others. Both Stefan and I are directly involved in customer relations."

Edberg, like Lidstrom, also sees Case as a good outlet for his competitiveness that grew from all the years on the ATP tour. "Sure, that is part of it, it pumps you up on a daily basis, but for me it is also a way to help other athletes after retiring to make the right choices when it comes to investments," Edberg said. "I like what we have accomplished so far and I see a bright future for Case.

"We have a great team in place and Nicklas is a huge asset for us in so many ways. With golfer Henrik Stenson now added to the owner group, we couldn't be happier. He is still active in his sport and a fantastic ambassador for the game of golf. We are not looking for any more partners right now. With Nicklas and Henrik, I feel we have a solid organization."

Though he grew up cheering for the Boston Bruins, Edberg admits that with all the Swedes on the Red Wings over so many years, they also became a favorite team. As much as he admired Lidstrom's work on the ice, Edberg is equally impressed with his acclimation to the world of business. "I get the feeling he really loves being involved and he definitely has made the company better with his thoughtful standing on different topics," Edberg said.

Lidstrom never saw Edberg live during the tennis star's time at the top but became a fan after watching him and Mats Wilander win Grand Slam tournaments. "Wilander's win at the French Open in 1982 got everybody's attention back in Sweden," Lidstrom said. "He became an idol for me. Then Edberg won the Australian Open in 1985 and went on to win Wimbledon in 1988. Tennis was really big in Sweden at that time."

Lidstrom is an avid tennis fan and enjoys playing on a regular basis. Since they became partners, he and Edberg have spent time on the court together. "Without counting points, thank god," Lidstrom said. "As soon as he puts some power behind his serve and starts putting his shots out of my reach, it becomes really hard for me to keep up."

The company's low-risk funds seem to mirror Lidstrom and Edberg's playing philosophies. Edberg was a serve-and-volley guy not known for taking undue risks and Lidstrom played the game with a cool and calm demeanor. To nobody's surprise, recently started funds at Case have been named Safe Play, Fair Play, Power Play, and All-Star. Case won the Best Swedish Corporate Bond Fund in 2017 for Safe Play in Morningstar's annual Fund Awards. "We are incredibly happy about winning this award, and it shows that we have chosen the right strategy, which is to give our investors a safe and stable return," Lidstrom said.

He has an hour-long commute to company headquarters in Stockholm and makes the trip once or twice a week. He and Edberg are on the phone on a regular basis and take part in company-sponsored events like the Stockholm Open, an annual tennis tournament. Stenson shares his time between the PGA Tour and the European Tour. He lives in Florida part of the year.

As for Lidstrom's other hometown, the city of Detroit had experienced both peaks and valleys during his 20 years there. He noticed the empty buildings, the abandoned storefronts, and the destruction of bungalows and Tudor homes when he'd first come to Detroit in 1991. It was something he had never seen back home in Sweden.

"The city was pretty beaten down when I arrived," Lidstrom remembered. "Then they started to rebuild downtown in the late '90s and early 2000s, but the financial crisis in 2007–08 cut it short. The real estate market fell off and the automobile industry stumbled, which brought some of the efforts that were underway in downtown Detroit to a halt. It was noticeable.

"Tearing down the old baseball arena, Tiger Stadium, and replacing it with the new Comerica Park was a starting jolt. Then, they moved the Lions football team to a new stadium in the city from the Silverdome out in Pontiac. With two state-of-the art stadiums and new restaurants around them, the foundation of a new and modern downtown was there. It made a big difference.

"They tried hard to change the area, but remember how huge the surface is and you have to understand it will take time. The owner of Quicken Loans, Dan Gilbert, who is also an owner of the Cleveland Cavaliers, has bought many buildings and restored them to create more apartments in downtown. It will take time to fix it all, but that process started already when I was living in Detroit and when I visit today, I can now see how the city is growing from the inside.

"Thanks to the Ilitch family and their investment in the new hockey temple, Little Caesars Arena, another part of downtown is coming to life. I mean, they are rebuilding 50 blocks around the new arena with apartments, restaurants, a school, and other amenities. Adding new homes for both the Red Wings and the Pistons there is a huge addition to downtown. Now you have all four pro teams playing close to each other. I think that will be a big lift for the city and I'm really happy about it."

Lidstrom's picture is hanging on the wall with all the other famous players in the Red Wings dressing room at the new Little Caesars Arena. Lidstrom never got a chance to play in the rink, which opened in the fall of 2017.

"If they could bring any of them back, it would be Nick. They would be a different team with him in the lineup," said *Detroit Free Press* hockey writer Helene St. James.

"I told Ken Holland that the new arena came 10 years too late," Lidstrom said. "It should have been built 10 years earlier. Walking in there, you get a rush wanting to play again. You see all the spacious dressing rooms, all the facilities in there with their own kitchen, a huge lounge, and a gym that is three times larger than the one we had at the Joe. Plus, the new training facility, just 50 meters away. It's all there and it's convenient for everybody, the players and the fans. I've been trying out different seats in the new arena during games there, so I know that it gives you a first-class experience anywhere in the building. It would have been fun to play my last season there."

Lidstrom tries to stay in touch with the Ilitch family by trying to see them whenever he is in Detroit. "I did meet Mrs. Ilitch on opening night at the new arena and I see Chris almost every time I'm there catching a game," Lidstrom said. "They are a successful business family with a genuine heart for Detroit and the people there. I have only good things to say of them. Mr. I, as we all called him, was somebody I looked up to and it was really sad when he passed away in 2017."

Winning four Stanley Cups between 1997 and 2008 lifted the spirit of Detroit and its hockey fans. Motown became Hockeytown and Lidstrom and his teammates could see the importance of bringing high-level sports entertainment to the city. Joe Louis Arena turned into a showroom next to the Cobo Convention Center and helped generate revenue for the surrounding hotels and restaurants. Greektown was a bright spot for tourists, walking distance from the Renaissance Center, but the rest of downtown was still seen as less than welcoming.

The victory parades had shown everybody what the city could be. With hundreds of thousands of people coming out to celebrate their hockey heroes, a vibrant atmosphere from the golden days of Detroit suddenly reappeared.

Lidstrom fondly remembers the Joe for the excitement, the roaring fans in the stands, and the goals where he purposely shot the puck at the back boards for Holmstrom to finish it off with a rebound. It was the time of his life and Lidstrom will never forget his 20 years in Detroit. The early morning drive from the suburbs into the arena, with the regular stop at a Starbucks to get his grande cappuccino with a blueberry muffin, chats over a cup of coffee in equipment manager Paul Boyer's room, and the pregame lunches at Andiamo Trattoria, eating his favorite pasta over and over.

"It gives me chills to think back at what we accomplished," Lidstrom said. "We were such a tight group of players and staff. I can hear the laughs from the dressing room in the back of my head still, the moments of camaraderie.

"Coming back to Detroit is like coming home. You get that feeling already at the airport. Then you visit friends, stop at the old Starbucks for a coffee, and go by the mall where you shopped for years. It gets a little emotional. I think I always will experience that. Just being able to find your way around everywhere you're going makes you feel at home."

The Lidstroms' home in Northville is something they also miss. "We talk about that house off and on," Lidstrom said. "It would have been fun to still have it, but you have to be realistic and know that it wouldn't have worked. Our kids remind us on a regular basis how much they loved living there. It's not that they don't like it in Sweden now. It's just one more sign that our hearts are divided between Vasteras and Detroit."

Moving back to Detroit is something the Lidstroms will consider in the future. "It's not on the agenda right now, but we'll see what happens when our kids get older," Lidstrom said. "I don't have an answer to the question if we will stay here or move back to Detroit. We'll see when the kids have decided where they want to live. I don't spend much time thinking about that right now. It will sort itself out. I can see us having a place also in Detroit or Florida. That would be nice.

"As I said, time will tell."

APPENDIX
NICK BY THE NUMBERS

NHL

Most games played by a player for one team (1,564)

Most Stanley Cup games played by a player for one team (263)

Most games played by a European-born player (1,564)

Four-time Stanley Cup champion with Detroit Red Wings (1996–97, 1997–98, 2001–02, and 2007–08)

Seven-time James Norris Memorial Trophy winner (2000–01, 2001–02, 2002–03, 2005–06, 2006–07, 2008–09, and 2010–11)

Conn Smythe Trophy winner (2001–02)

Ten-time selection to NHL First All-Star Team (1997–98, 1998–99, 1999–2000, 2000–01, 2001–02, 2002–03, 2005–06, 2006–07, 2007–08, and 2010–11)

12-time NHL All-Star (1996, 1998, 1999, 2000, 2001, 2002, 2003, 2004, 2007, 2008, 2009 (DNP), and 2011)

Inducted into Hockey Hall of Fame (2015)

Named one of NHL's 100 Greatest Players (2017)

DETROIT RED WINGS

Career

Most games played by a defenseman (1,564)

Most goals by a defenseman (264)

Most assists by a defenseman (878)

Most points by a defenseman (1,142)

Most power play goals by a defenseman (132)

Best regular season plus/minus (plus-450)

Most consecutive seasons in the postseason (20)

Most postseason games played (263)

Most postseason power play goals (30)

Most postseason assists (129)

Most postseason goals by a defenseman (54)

Most postseason points by a defenseman (183)

Best postseason plus/minus (plus-61)

Most All-Star Game appearances by a defenseman (12)

Inducted into Michigan Hall of Fame (2014)

Single Season

Most points by a defenseman (80 in 2005–06)

Most assists by a defenseman (64 in 2005–06)

Most assists by a rookie (49 in 1991–92)

Most assists by a rookie defenseman (49 in 1991–92)

Most points by a rookie defenseman (60 in 1991–92)

Most goals in postseason by a defenseman (six in 1998)

Most points in postseason by a defenseman (19 in 1998)

Single Game

Most assists in one postseason game (four, April 21, 2007)

IIHF

Won Olympic gold medal with Sweden (2006)

Named to Olympic All-Tournament Team (2006)

Won World Championships gold medal with Sweden (1991)

Won World Championships silver medal with Sweden (2004)

Won World Championships bronze medal with Sweden (1994)

Member of Triple Gold Club (Olympic gold medal, World Championships gold medal, Stanley Cup champion)

Inducted into IIHF Hall of Fame (2014)

ACKNOWLEDGMENTS

Kevin Allen, Gary Bettman, Rob Blake, Paul Boyer, Scotty Bowman, Chris Chelios, Damien Cox, Sidney Crosby, Eric Duhatschek, Drew Doughty, Kris Draper, Stefan Edberg, Oliver Ekman-Larsson, Anders Eriksson, Conny Evensson, Michael Farber, Ray Ferraro, Peter Forsberg, Jim Fox, Johan Garpenlov, Wayne Gretzky, Rikard Gronborg, Brian Hayward, Victor Hedman, Ken Holland, Tomas Holmstrom, Calle Johansson, Chris Johnston, Keith Jones, Erik Karlsson, John Klingberg, Niklas Kronwall, Lou Lamoriello, Igor Larionov, Jan Lennartsson, Carl Lindberg, Henrik Lundqvist, Iain MacIntyre, Evgeni Malkin, Par Marts, Pierre McGuire, Bob McKenzie, Don Meehan, Larry Robinson, Luc Robitaille, Christer Rockstrom, Thomas Rundqvist, Helene St. James, Borje Salming, Brendan Shanahan, Barry Smith, Kevin Weekes, Steve Yzerman, and Henrik Zetterberg.

Special thanks to:

Nicklas Lidstrom, for all the hours of talks in Vasteras, Detroit, Stockholm, Los Angeles, and an endless stream of emails and phone calls.

Annika Lidstrom, for telling your story in such an honest way.

Gerd and Jan-Erik Lidstrom, for being more than just proud parents.

Brian Wood, my agent, who put this project together.

Adam Motin and Noah Amstadter at Triumph Books in Chicago, for good guidance and patience.

Todd Beam, director of public relations, Detroit Red Wings, for your generous assistance.

Frank Brown, NHL communications vice president.

Jennifer Bullano Ridgley, senior director of communications, Pittsburgh Penguins.

Mike Kalinowski, director communications and media services, Los Angeles Kings.

Eddie Fischermann, manager communications and media services, Los Angeles Kings.

Steve Keogh, director media relations, Toronto Maple Leafs.

Brian Kennedy, literature professor at Pasadena City College and a passionate hockey writer.

Finally, and most importantly, I thank my wife, Kristen, and sons, Patrick and Marcus, for all your support and advice.

—Gunnar Nordstrom

I'm thankful that Nicklas Lidstrom trusted Gunnar and I to tell his story. I was privileged to cover Nick's entire NHL career as a Detroit Red Wings beat writer. In all my years in journalism, I've never encountered a better combination of player and person.

I'd be remiss if I didn't tip my cap to the work that Gunnar put into this book. He left no stone unturned in his tireless efforts to track down people inside and outside the game who were impacted by Nick's unparalleled career.

—Bob Duff